D0116478

Audubon's Wildlife

From the portrait in the White House Collection.

JOHN JAMES AUDUBON

Audubon's Wildlife

Edwin Way Teale

with selections from the writings of John James Audubon

Castle Books • New York

DESIGNED BY CHARLES O. HYMAN : STUDIO 35 LTD.

First published in 1964 by The Viking Press, Inc.
625 Madison Avenue, New York, N. Y. 10022

Published simultaneously in Canada by
The Macmillan Company of Canada Limited

Library of Congress catalog card number : 64-20858
Color plates and text printed in the U.S.A.
Monochrome gravure plates printed in Switzerland

This edition published by arrangement with Viking Press, Inc.

Contents

Editor's Note

The sensation produced by John James Audubon's paintings when they were first viewed by the public more than a century ago was due in large measure to the dramatic sense of action and life they presented. All nature art that had come before seemed static in comparison.

This volume provides a new look at Audubon. That look enhances this sense of life and action in his work. The reader himself provides a new dimension, moving from the over-all to the closeup. He sees details expand to full life size, arresting in a portion of a plate the intense vitality that Audubon's genius caught and stilled and preserved. For those familiar with the plates of the Elephant Folio, small identifying reproductions appear beside the text in the margins of many pages.

Some of the mammal plates from *The Viviparous Quadrupeds of North America,* such as the jaguar, the musk ox, the hooded skunk, and the mountain beaver, were produced, under Audubon's supervision, by his gifted son, John Woodhouse Audubon. This was done during the American Woodsman's last period, when his strength was failing. In a few cases in which a bird or mammal is found in more than one type of habitat, the position of the plate has been dictated by considerations of balance, variety, and impact in the sequence of the art.

Virtually all of the bird paintings have been reproduced directly from the Elephant Folio at the artist's first home in America — Mill Grove, some twenty miles northwest of Philadelphia. This was done through the courtesy of the Curator of the Audubon Shrine and Wildlife Sanctuary, J. d'Arcy Northwood. The majority of the plates from the *Quadrupeds,* also specially photographed by Henry S. Fullerton III, are from an edition made available by the New York Public Library.

Acknowledgments are also due to the Butler Art Institute, Youngstown, Ohio, for "Fox Carrying Goose" (detail) on page 18; to the American Museum of Natural History for "Spaniel and Pheasants" (detail) on page 19; to the Ferargil Gallery for the photograph of "Otter and Trout" (detail) on pages 19 and 154; to the Pierpont Morgan Library for "Eastern Cottontail Rabbit" (detail) on page 36; to the Boatmen's National Bank of St. Louis, for the "Western Fox Squirrel" on pages 86 and

87; to the New-York Historical Society for the photograph of "Snowy Owl" on pages 214 and 221.

Although Audubon kept journals of his frontier experiences and observations for many years and although he began arranging some of his material for publication as early as 1821, it was not until the fall of 1826 that he put down the first words of his five-volume *Ornithological Biography.* Sitting at a small table in a room in Edinburgh, Scotland, before dawn on November 20, 1826, he began recording his memories of the wild turkey. He left his breakfast untouched, for in imagination he was back in America, following its trails and rivers. He wrote on and on until the biography was finished.

Much of Audubon's writing was produced under pressure. He turned out about a quarter of Volume III of his biographies of the birds in a single month. Often he composed in headlong haste, pouring out his recollections in long sentences, replete with commas. His paragraphs sometimes ran to a page or more. In the interests of appearance and readability, I have broken into smaller units some of the longest paragraphs in the selected material. Either to conform to modern usage or to make the meaning clear, the spelling of a few words has been changed; for example, *Allabama* has been changed to *Alabama, shewed* to *showed, minxes* to *minks, marratees* to *manatees.*

Where the modern scientific names of birds are indicated, the Fifth Edition of *The A.O.U. Check-List of North American Birds* (1957) has been used as the source.

In Audubon's biography of the whooping crane, it is often difficult to be sure whether he is referring to this bird or to the sandhill crane, inasmuch as he confused the latter with the young of the former. Only the adult birds, unquestionably whooping cranes, are dealt with in the selections that have been made. In the case of the *Quadrupeds,* only one of the three volumes of text appeared in Audubon's lifetime. All the material contained in the three volumes was prepared for the press by John Bachman. However, certain portions are unmistakably formed from notes supplied by Audubon. In the material taken from this source, I have chosen only that which springs from his personal experiences or is otherwise linked to him.

—Edwin Way Teale

Trail Wood
Hampton, Connecticut

Audubon and Wildlife

In 1803, the year of the Louisiana Purchase, the seventeenth state had just been admitted to the Union. Thomas Jefferson occupied the White House. The valley of the Ohio represented the American frontier. New England and states adjacent to the Atlantic then held almost eight-tenths of the population. The land from the Eastern seaboard to the Great Plains was largely covered by forest. Beyond the Mississippi stretched Indian country, a land virtually unknown. In 1803, the start of the Lewis and Clark Expedition was still a year away. Rivers were the arteries of transportation, and a quarter of a century would pass before the first steam locomotive rolled on American rails. The center of population of the United States, in 1803, lay only eighteen miles west of Baltimore, Maryland.

In that year John James Audubon, eighteen years old, sailed westward across the Atlantic from his home in France.

Once before, briefly, he had seen the land. Then he was four and George Washington was President. His father, Jean Audubon, a sea captain turned planter, had taken him to France by way of the United States from his birthplace on the island of Haiti. Now he was returning to live in the New World, a continent only partially explored, a young country where wilderness and wildlife abounded.

When Christopher Columbus made his report to Ferdinand and Isabella, he described the new land he had discovered as a place where there were "birds of a thousand sorts." In all Europe, east of the Urals, scientists have listed, down to the present, slightly more than four hundred breeding species of birds. In North America, the total is well over seven hundred. James Fisher, a modern authority on the ornithology of Great Britain, has estimated that the present population of land birds in the British Isles numbers in the region of 200,000,000 individuals. Even years after Audubon came to America, ten times that number of birds sometimes formed a single flock, as when passenger pigeons moved south in autumn in a vast living river of migrants, miles wide.

The westward voyage of Columbus had opened up not only a new world of land but a new world of wildlife. It was 311 years later that the youthful Audubon—his destiny as one of the great explorers of America's wildlife unsuspected—landed in

New York City. That destiny was to lead him on foot, on horseback, by flatboat and stagecoach and river steamer, back and forth across the frontiers of America. It was to bestow on him a life rich with forest experiences and show him the wilderness as few men saw it. Although Audubon never realized his dream of crossing the Rockies, he traveled through wild country from Maine to Texas and from Florida to Montana.

Audubon knew the American wilderness at a time when its great forests were almost untouched, when its streams were unpolluted, when the age-old balance of nature was virtually undisturbed by man. He knew it at a time when the red man was just giving way before the white man. He knew it when forms of wildlife, now extinct, lived in incredible abundance. This was the world the young and impressionable Audubon entered. The time was right. Against the backdrop of primitive woods and rivers and prairies, he carried on his great work. With brush and pen, he preserved for posterity its most vivid glimpses of this wilderness era.

For more than 130 years, a maze of contradictions, legends, and misinformation surrounded Audubon's earliest days. It is to Francis Hobart Herrick—whose two-volume biography, *Audubon the Naturalist,* appeared in 1917—that the world is indebted for separating fact from fiction. Years of painstaking research, through old letters, account books, and legal documents in America, France, and Haiti enabled him to sort and straighten the tangled skeins of Audubon's life. The date of Audubon's birth was April 26, 1785. He was the natural son of Jean Audubon and a Creole woman known only as Mlle. Rabin. His birthplace was Les Cayes, on the island of Haiti, then known as Santo Domingo. It appears that his mother died when he was less than one year old.

In matters concerning the facts of his life, it must be admitted that Audubon himself has proved a most unreliable witness. His vivid imagination and sanguine nature tended to distort the facts in his favor. In memory he added nearly six inches to his father's height. He reported erroneously that his mother had once lived in Pennsylvania and that his father had met George Washington at Valley Forge. Concerning his early years, he gave varied and conflicting reports. At one time he maintained he was born in Louisiana, where his father had married a woman "as wealthy as she was beautiful." At other times he hinted that he was of royal blood, one "who should command all." That veiled statement was, for years, the slender thread that supported the romantic legend that the lost Dauphin, son of Louis XVI and Marie Antoinette, was in reality Audubon. In truth, the facts of his life are sufficient. No fictional embroidery is needed to reveal him as a romantic, adventurous figure of the first order.

After his initial glimpse of America—between the ages of four and eighteen—Audubon lived at his father's home near the mouth of the Loire in France. The childless wife of Jean Audubon proved a kind, indulgent mother. When he was eight, he was legally adopted. Here, in the country near Nantes, the boy spent the years of the French Revolution wandering along the river, collecting nests for his home museum, and producing his first sketches of birds. "My pencil," he wrote later, "gave birth to a family of cripples." On each birthday, for years, he made a bonfire of the drawings he considered unsatisfactory. For a short period before his departure for America, Audubon studied in the Paris studio of Jacques Louis David, court painter under Napoleon. This was the only formal art instruction he ever received.

On reaching America in 1803, young Audubon led a carefree existence of riding, hunting, and sketching at Mill Grove, a large country place owned by his father on Perkiomen Creek, in eastern Pennsylvania. He lived the life of a rich man's son, riding afield on the finest horses and going shooting in satin breeches and silk stockings. But already the intensity of his attachment to nature had become clear. As he wrote later, in words that now appear on the bronze plaque below his bust in the Hall of Fame: "The productions of nature . . . soon became my playmates. . . . I felt that an intimacy with them, not consisting of friendship merely, but bordering on phrenzy, must accompany my steps through life."

An important event of this period occurred in a cave on the banks of the Perkiomen. There Audubon made his first serious study of the habits of birds, watching day after day the progress of a nest of phoebes. Around the legs of the fledglings he placed silver threads. These were to prove that the birds returned to the same area the following spring. Thus, at the age of nineteen, Audubon conducted the first bird-banding experiments in the New World.

Soon after he reached Mill Grove, the adjoining farm, Fatland Ford, was purchased by William Bakewell, a well-to-do commission merchant who had emigrated with his family from England. Before the year was out, Audubon and Bakewell's eldest daughter, Lucy, had become engaged. Francis Dacosta, Audubon's guardian, objected. A quarrel ensued. In midwinter, young Audubon set out on foot for New York and sailed for home. A year later, in the spring of 1806, he landed again on American shores, this time ostensibly as a businessman. With him came a companion, Ferdinand Rozier, a young man from Nantes. They were partners, commissioned to look for commercial oportunities.

Their first employment was as clerks in the importing house of William Bakewell, in New York City. There, among the linens, laces, and gloves in which the company dealt, Audubon soon demonstrated his incapacity for business, once mailing out eight thousand dollars in an unsealed envelope. Every spare moment he had was spent observing and collecting waterfowl on Long Island. He sketched ducks at the rate of two a day. It was at this period that a constable appeared, responding to complaints of neighbors about the odor of dead birds emanating from his rooms.

By the following summer the business partners were ready to try their luck in the West. With a supply of merchandise, they rode a flatboat down the Ohio and established a pioneer store in Louisville, Kentucky. In 1807, Louisville was a frontier town of a thousand inhabitants. The forests around represented to Audubon a wild paradise. He hunted and sketched while Rozier, who later became one of the leading merchants of the frontier, with trade that extended over most of the upper Louisiana Territory, remained behind the counter. Hardly had the partners opened their doors when the Embargo Act paralyzed trade. It made it impossible for them to sell produce sent to New York for export.

Under the cloud of this business depression, Audubon, always sanguine and optimistic, returned to Pennsylvania and married Lucy Bakewell on April 8, 1808. Together, by stagecoach and flatboat, they returned to Louisville. This was the beginning of one of the most remarkable of marriages. Lucy's stability provided a balance wheel for Audubon's emotional nature. Later on, she supported herself and her family for a dozen years, leaving her artist-husband free to wander through the wilderness sketching and observing birds. Twenty years of vicissitude, of failure, of debt, even of Audubon's imprisonment, failed to shake Lucy's faith in his genius. In his darkest days, Audubon was wont to speak of "my ornithology, in which my Lucy and myself alone have faith."

By 1810, Audubon's portfolios held paintings of nearly two hundred American birds, life-size, in true colors, drawn from nature. They were produced without a plan, without, apparently, any thought of their ever being published, merely as the outgrowth of his passionate avocation. Then on March 19, 1810, there occurred what represents an initial step toward the dramatic future that—for drawings and for artist—lay ahead.

On that Monday in March, Audubon happened to be behind the counter when a sandy-haired man of forty-four entered the store. He had traveled a thousand miles down the Ohio River in winter in an open skiff. His clothes were coarse. Under his arm he carried two red-backed books. That "hunter of bird's nests and sparrows," the self-taught ornithologist Alexander Wilson, former schoolmaster on the Schuylkill, hardly more than twenty miles from Mill Grove, was making his last exhausting travels in search of new subscribers for his *American Ornithology.*

As he opened his books on the counter of the frontier store while the two men talked—one with a Scottish burr, the other with a French accent—Wilson obviously never had heard of Audubon. He had no inkling of his work. How great, then, must have been his inner amazement when in this unlikely place he was, in turn, shown sketches vibrant with life, dramatic in composition, the product of Audubon's genius!

NOTES ON THE PLATES

5. MANGROVE CUCKOO *(Coccyzus minor).* In the United States, this bird is confined to the mangrove swamps of the coast and keys of lower Florida. A summer resident, absent in winter.

6–7. RACCOON *(Procyon lotor).* Clever and curious, able to swim and climb, omnivorous in its feeding habits, this ring-tailed mammal can survive under widely varying conditions.

8. CLAPPER RAIL *(Rallus longirostris).* The coastal marshes from New England to Texas provide a home for this chicken-like bird.

9. PINE WARBLER *(Dendroica pinus).* Like the clapper rail, it is associated with a special habitat, in this instance the open pine woods.

10. EASTERN WOOD RAT *(Neotoma floridana).* The members of one family are shown here. These rats inhabit caves, swamps, plains.

11. EASTERN CHIPMUNK *(Tamias striatus).* A small, active, burrowing squirrel, the chipmunk prefers areas where there are deciduous woodlands, fallen logs, and old stone walls.

12. COLLIE'S MAGPIE-JAY *(Calocitta colliei).* Audubon, who never saw a living specimen of this bird, mistakenly placed it in the forests of the Columbia River region. It is a native of western Mexico, not found in the United States.

13. ESKIMO DOG *(Canis familiaris).* In the far north, Eskimos and Indians have long made use of this dog to pull their sleds in winter.

14. (Top) ANNA'S HUMMINGBIRD *(Calypte anna).* Breeds west of Sierras in California. (Bottom) BALD EAGLE *(Haliaeetus leucocephalus).* The national emblem of the United States.

15. (Top and center) SCARLET IBIS *(Eudocimus ruber).* A tropical species accidental in the United States. (Bottom) HARRIS'S HAWK *(Parabuteo unicinctus).* A bird of the southwestern mesquite and chaparral.

16–17. BLUE JAY *(Cyanocitta cristata).* This noisy, colorful bird is conspicuous throughout its range. Originally a bird of the woodland, it has become common around towns in the East.

18. (Top) GRAY WOLF *(Canis lupus).* The timber wolf of the north. (Bottom) Fox carrying goose.

19. (Top) SPANIEL AND PHEASANTS. A painting by Audubon with an English setting. (Center) OTTER AND TROUT. One of Audubon's few wildlife paintings done in oil. (Bottom) BLACK RAT *(Rattus rattus).* Introduced from the Old World.

20. TUFTED TITMOUSE *(Parus bicolor).* The loud, clear, whistled song of this relative of the chickadee is given throughout the year.

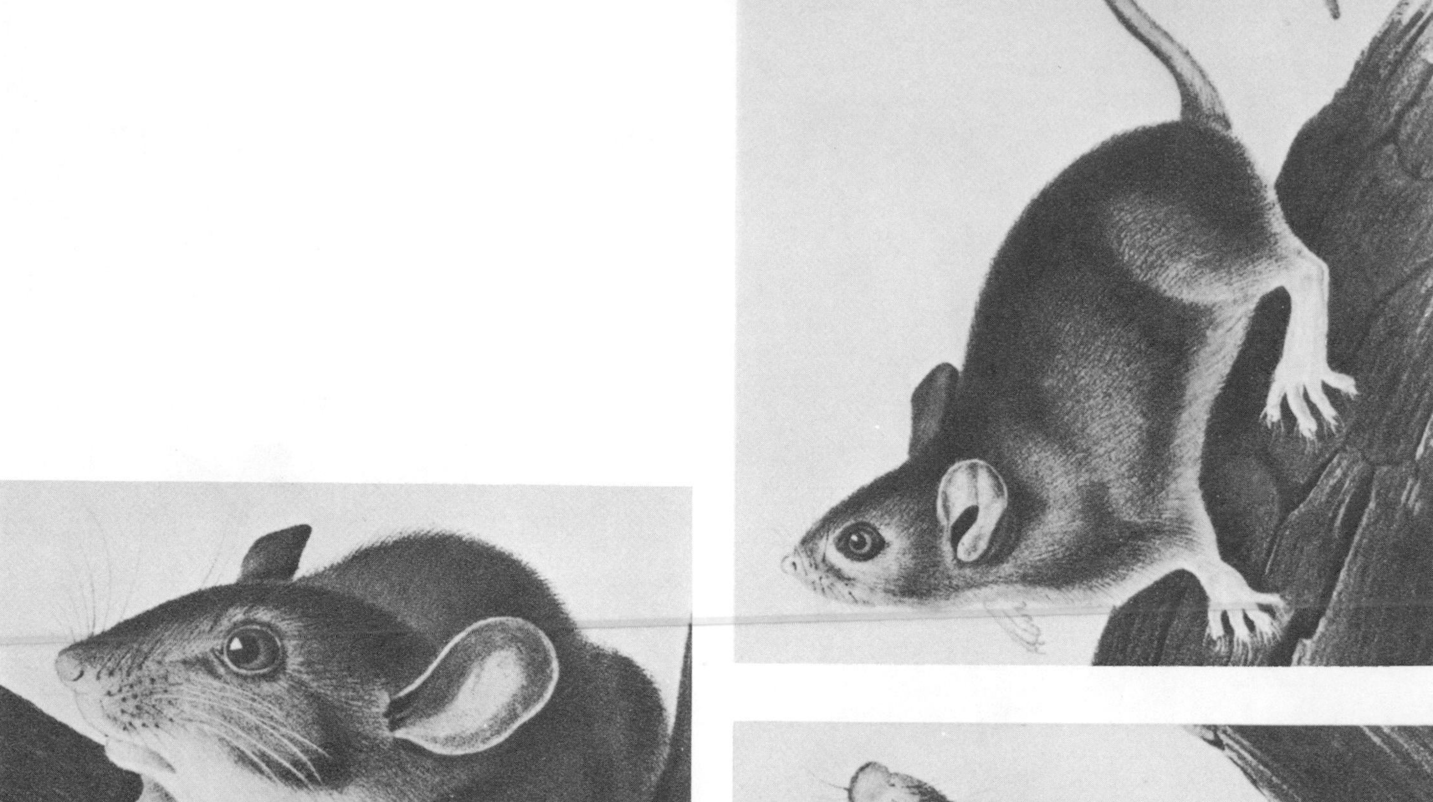

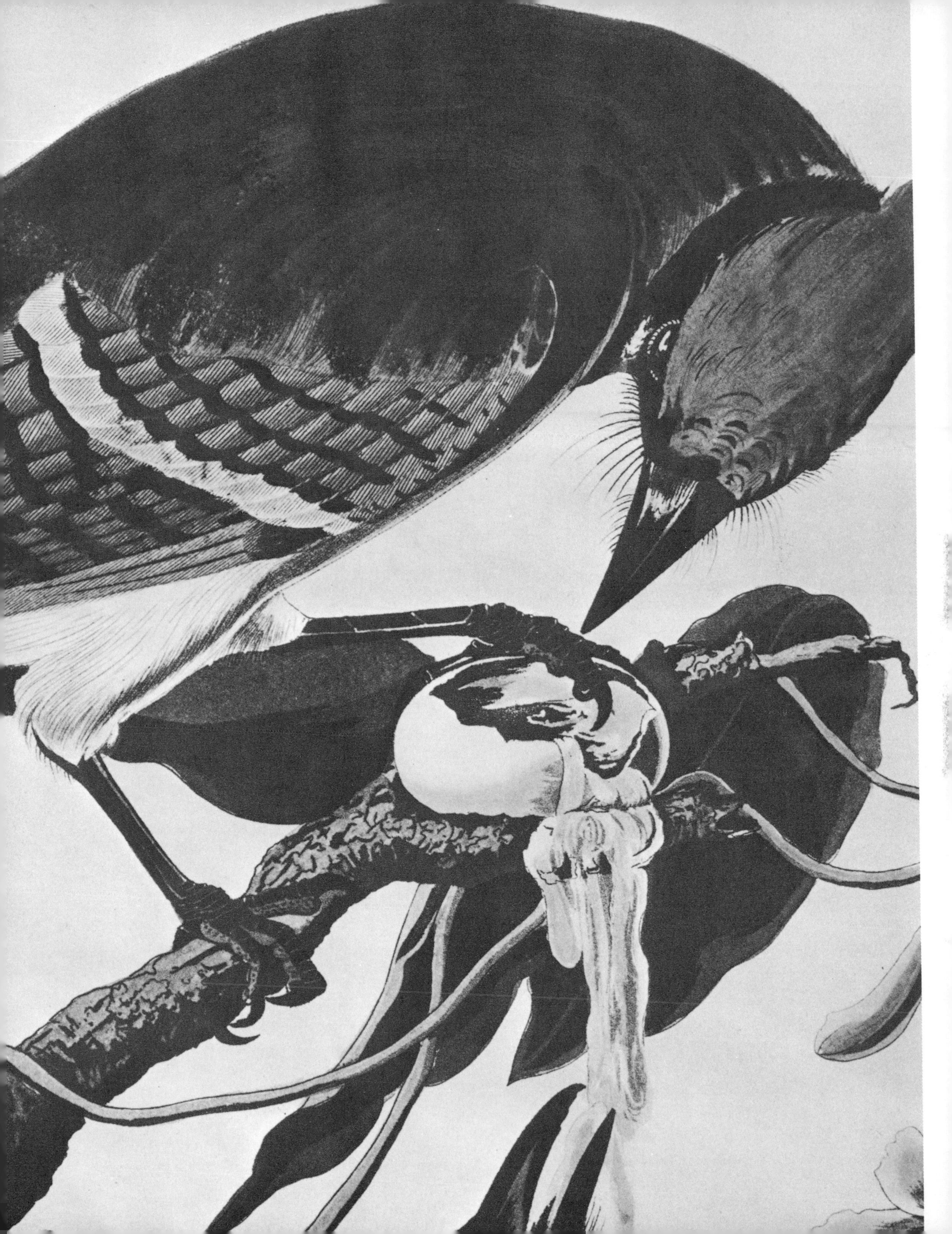

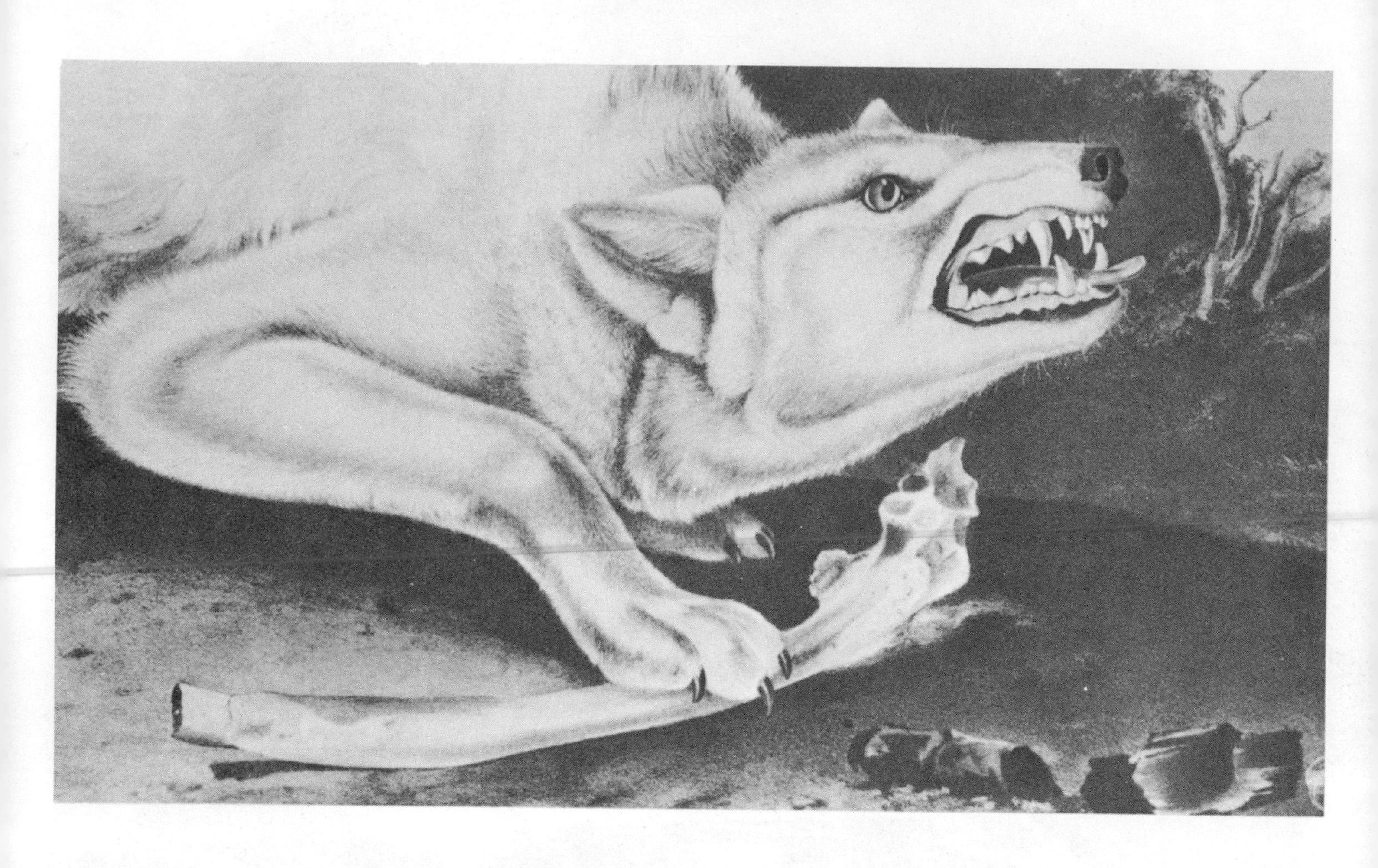

Wilson moved on, obtaining no subscriptions in Louisville, and three years later his ill-starred life came to an end. He was never aware of the bitter wrangling between partisans of Audubon and Wilson that continued for decades. Without doubt, the lower figure in Audubon's plate of the Mississippi kite is a reversed copy of Wilson's drawing. It may, as some have suggested, have been inserted by the engraver. On the other hand, Audubon's accusation that Wilson copied his small-headed flycatcher seems less valid. The drawings are dissimilar. Curiously, although each figures such a flycatcher, apparently none ever existed. Both seem to have sketched the young of another species, possibly the immature hooded warbler. At least it is comforting for the baffled modern bird watcher to learn that, in their time, the two great pioneers of American ornithology were also bewildered by the "confusing fall warblers."

In the spring of Wilson's visit, the business affairs of the two partners were close to foundering. They decided to move 125 miles downstream to Henderson, Kentucky, then called Red Banks. Instead of the thriving community they expected, they found themselves in a frontier village of 159 inhabitants. The main demand was for whisky, coarse woolens, and gunpowder. But if business was bad, hunting was good. Game abounded in the canebrakes, fish in the river. A clerk, hired to help with the store, spent most of his time hunting with Audubon. At the end of six months, the partners were on the move again. In a December snowstorm they floated away down the river with all their remaining merchandise loaded on a flatboat, leaving Lucy and Audubon's infant son, Victor, at the home of friends.

Nine weeks were consumed reaching the mouth of the Ohio and ascending a hundred miles up the Mississippi. Again and again the men were locked in ice. They camped in the wilderness, using breast of wild turkey for bread and bear's grease for butter. Audubon took advantage of every delay, hunting by day with Indians and sketching by night beside the campfire. At last their flatboat tied up at the French community of Ste. Genevieve, in what is now Missouri. Here, on April 6, 1811, the partnership of these two dissimilar friends was dissolved. Audubon walked back to Henderson through 165 miles of forest and swamp.

The long succession of vicissitudes that marked the darkest period of Audubon's life was now beginning. He started a commission house to deal in pork and lard with his brother-in-law, Thomas W. Bakewell. It opened just in time to be ruined by the War of 1812. He built a small river steamer and sold it to a purchaser for what turned out to be a worthless piece of paper. Although a second son, John Woodhouse Audubon, survived, his two daughters died in infancy. For a time, a retail store Audubon started, in a one-story, hewn-log building in what is now the center of Henderson, seemed to prosper. Then, again with his brother-in-law, he constructed a huge steam-operated lumber and grist mill on the riverbank at Henderson. "Audubon's Mill" was a landmark on the Ohio for ninety-five years, until it burned down in 1913. When the venture failed in 1819, Audubon reached his lowest point. Jailed for debt, then released as a bankrupt, allowed to keep only his gun, his drawings, and the clothes he wore, he again left his family with friends and walked alone, without a dollar in his pocket, to Louisville.

Looking back on his life in later years, he wrote: "Poverty, too, at times walked hand in hand with me and on more than one occasion urged me to throw away my pencils." But only once in his life, only on this walk to Louisville, he said, did the birds seem like his enemies and make him wish they had never existed.

During these disastrous years, one of Audubon's greatest assets was his buoyant nature. Dragged down to the depths, he bobbed to the surface again. On one occasion, while he was away from home for several weeks, he left two hundred of his original drawings in a wooden box. On his return, he discovered that Norway rats had nested there, destroying all his pictures. "The burning heat which instantly rushed through my brain was too great to be endured . . ." he wrote years afterward. "I slept not for several nights and the days passed like days of oblivion." Then, his spirits recovered, almost blithely he went afield in search of new specimens and began the three years of labor required to replace the drawings, consoling himself that now he could do them better.

In the five years that followed that saddest journey of his life, the walk from Henderson to Louisville, the story of Audubon's days reads like some work of fiction in which the hero wanders over the face of the earth from adventure to adventure. While Lucy supported her family by teaching and acting as governess, he lived a hand-to-mouth existence. He earned his way by painting portraits, panel scenes on riverboats, and even street signs. To obtain passage on the rivers, he sketched the likenesses of captains and their wives. Once he drew the portrait of a shoemaker for a pair of boots. For a time, in company with another itinerant painter, he roamed through the South with a horse and wagon. When his fortunes were at a low point, a woman in Natchez promised him three hundred dollars for a painting of the city. Before he could finish the picture, she died and her heirs refused to honor the bill. On another occasion when his purse was empty, a friend raffled off one of his paintings at ten dollars a ticket. Not only did the proceeds temporarily refill the artist's pockets but his own ticket won the picture. More than once in his travels, what little money he had was stolen, and for a period of several months he was unable to continue the journal of his observations because he could not afford a blank book in which to write.

These years of strain and poverty were also part of Audubon's most productive period. He was sketching continually, painting not only birds but varied forms of wildlife that ranged from reptiles to insects. Now in possession of Mrs. Kirby Chambers, of New Castle, Kentucky, is the sketchbook that traveled with him during the years from 1821 to 1824. It contains painstaking delineations of such diverse creatures as butterflies, grasshoppers, sowbugs, snakes, moths, wasps, lizards, caterpillars, dragonflies, spiders, crickets, toads, and praying mantises. The appearance, in 1952, of Alice Ford's *Audubon's Butterflies, Moths, and Other Studies* made available to the public these products of the artist's fieldwork, done more than 125 years ago.

But wherever he went during this time, at each plantation landing where the river steamers stopped, he searched for new birds to reproduce for his ever-growing portfolio of drawings. By now his plan had crystallized. His great design was clear. Characteristically, at the very time his future seemed bleakest, when all his business ventures had failed, when he was entirely without funds or prospects, he had set himself to see to completion the most ambitious and costly project ever attempted by a student of nature.

This was the publication of life-size, full-color paintings of every known species of American bird together with characteristic plants and flowers. On this lavish scale he would introduce to the Old World the flora and avifauna of the New. Moreover, in accompanying volumes of text, he would present his biographies of the birds he pictured. This vast publishing venture he would finance, like Alexander Wilson, by means of subscriptions. But where Wilson's subscriptions had been $120, Audubon's would be $1000.

As his plan eventually developed, the plates—double elephant folio size—were issued in eighty-seven parts, each comprising five plates. Subscribers signed for the complete work, paying at the rate of two pounds, two shillings apiece as the parts appeared. From the artist's original paintings, now housed at the New-York Historical Society in New York City, engravings were made, the plates were printed, and then, in a day before color presses were invented, hand colorists painstakingly tinted the engravings, duplicating the colors Audubon had used. Each plate was then carefully examined. If any proved inferior, the colors were washed off and the work redone. Providing text to accompany the paintings, the *Ornithological Biography* was sold separately. Subscribers to the plates received the five volumes at a reduced rate. This was the grand scheme that began taking shape in Audubon's mind while he roamed the frontier in search of new wild subjects to paint.

Up to this time in his life, Audubon had been rather self-indulgent. Now he had a goal, and all of his tremendous enthusiasm and vitality was channeled, flowing in one direction. His strength of character, his fortitude and courage, his capacity for work, and his relentless drive all came to the fore in the paramount undertaking of his life.

When, in the fall of 1820, Audubon started down the Ohio by flatboat, accompanied by his dog, Dash, and the remarkable Joseph R. Mason, his eighteen-year-old pupil-assistant, his goal for his travels was a hundred new species of birds. In what he called his "method," he arranged freshly killed specimens on wires before a background ruled off in small squares. Sketching on paper of the same size and similarly marked, he was able to reproduce all features of his subjects exactly to size. Because he worked on the frontier and in the wilderness, because he went directly to nature, unlike the closet-naturalists of his time who studied merely the dried skins of birds, his problems were multiplied.

Once while on a river boat, he opened his chest to find that gunpowder from a broken bottle had stained and ruined paintings which had taken him months to produce. On another occasion, all his drawings were lost for several months. On the Great Lakes, when a gale drove his steamer toward shore, he and his pictures had to be carried to safety in a small boat. Throughout his wanderings, his work was achieved in spite of innumerable handicaps. Sometimes he worked by candlelight or by the illumination of campfires. Sometimes he sketched on river boats that continually shook and vibrated with the laboring of the engines. In Labrador, later on, as his vessel tossed on foggy seas, he produced his pictures below a skylight from which water dripped onto his sheet of drawing paper.

By the spring of 1824, Audubon was working his way toward Philadelphia, seeking a sponsor for his projected "ornithology." He found no patron. To obtain the best engravings, he was advised to go to Europe. So, as he started back down the Ohio, having had to borrow fifteen dollars for boat fare, he was planning a voyage to England. When he reached Louisiana, where Lucy's private school in the parish of West Feliciana had prospered, she placed all her savings at his disposal. Intent on increasing this capital, Audubon taught French, music, drawing, and dancing for more than a year. Early in 1826, the trip to Europe materialized.

On May 17, 1826, the cotton steamer *Delos* bore him away from New Orleans. At the age of forty-one, he was embarking on one of the great dramatic journeys into fame. He landed at Liverpool, knowing not a single soul in England. A week later, he was invited to exhibit his paintings at the Royal Institution. At Liverpool, Edinburgh, and London, the pictures he had produced on the American frontier attracted immense attention. The tide of fortune turned with a rush. The American Woodsman was acclaimed in the press, invited to dine at the homes of the aristocracy, received at Cambridge at a time when Charles Darwin was an undergraduate. He was elected to learned societies. Against the dark years of struggle and poverty, this skyrocketing European success appeared all the more dazzling.

The sensation he produced abroad was based solidly but not exclusively on the superiority of his art. Audubon was a showman. His wolfskin coat and his shoulder-length hair, which he announced was oiled only with bear's grease, became the talk of Edinburgh. He attracted wide attention as a colorful frontiersman, an original, a Rousseau-type hero, a representative of the great American wilderness. With a striking appearance, handsome features, and winning manners, he made friends easily. But those who considered him a simple, guileless backwoodsman ignored the complexity of his mind and character. The woodsman was adept at flattery. He made full use of the slightest connection with those of rank or royalty. He sought out and cultivated the rich and powerful, those who could aid him best. In his campaign to advance his grand scheme, Audubon combined many of the traits of the French courtier and the American salesman.

The whole immense project for the publication of *The Birds of America*—an undertaking that consumed twelve years; that entailed the engraving of 435 plates,

NOTES ON THE PLATES

25. PASSENGER PIGEON *(Ectopistes migratorius)*. Once flew in flocks numbering millions. Now it is extinct. The last survivor died in 1914.

26–27. REDHEADED WOODPECKER *(Melanerpes erythrocephalus)*. Brilliant of plumage and loud of voice, this conspicuous woodpecker is associated with open woods and farmland.

28. GREEN HERON *(Butorides virescens)* and LUNA MOTH *(Actias luna)*. The green heron is the most widely distributed of our herons.

29. (Top) JACK RABBIT *(Lepus californicus)*. The famed long-eared, long-legged hare of the western dry country. (Bottom) SILVER FOX *(Vulpes fulva)*. This is a color phase of the red fox.

30–31. WOOD DUCK *(Aix sponsa)*. One of the most beautiful of American waterfowl. Mostly vegetarian. Generally nests in holes in trees.

32. (Top) POLAR BEAR *(Thalarctos maritimus)*. A bear of the Arctic coast. Found on ice far from land. (Bottom) OREGON WHITE-TAILED DEER *(Odocoileus leucurus)*. A western white-tail.

33. (Top) WHITE-TAILED JACK RABBIT *(Lepus townsendii)*. Swiftness of foot enables these animals to escape predators. (Bottom) GRAY FOX *(Urocyon cinereoargenteus)*. Less crafty, more nocturnal than red fox. It may climb trees.

34–35. PAINTED BUNTING *(Passerina ciris)*. No other bird in North America is more gaudily colored than this bunting of southern states.

36. (Top) YELLOW-THROATED VIREO *(Vireo flavifrons)*. An orchard, woodland, and shade-tree bird. (Bottom) EASTERN COTTONTAIL RABBIT *(Sylvilagus floridanus)*. From the Atlantic to the Rockies, one of the most familiar mammals.

37. (Top) WHITE-TAILED DEER *(Odocoileus virginianus)*. This animal, which provided venison for pioneers, is found throughout much of the United States. (Bottom) EASTERN BLUEBIRD *(Sialia sialis)*. A favorite eastern songbird. Often attracted to orchards.

38–39. CAROLINA PARAKEET *(Conuropsis carolinensis)*. In vast numbers, this brilliantly colored parrot once flew through river-bottom woods in the eastern states. It is now extinct.

40. BLACK-BILLED MAGPIE *(Pica pica)*. Open western country forms the home of the striking, carnivorous black-and-white magpie.

2

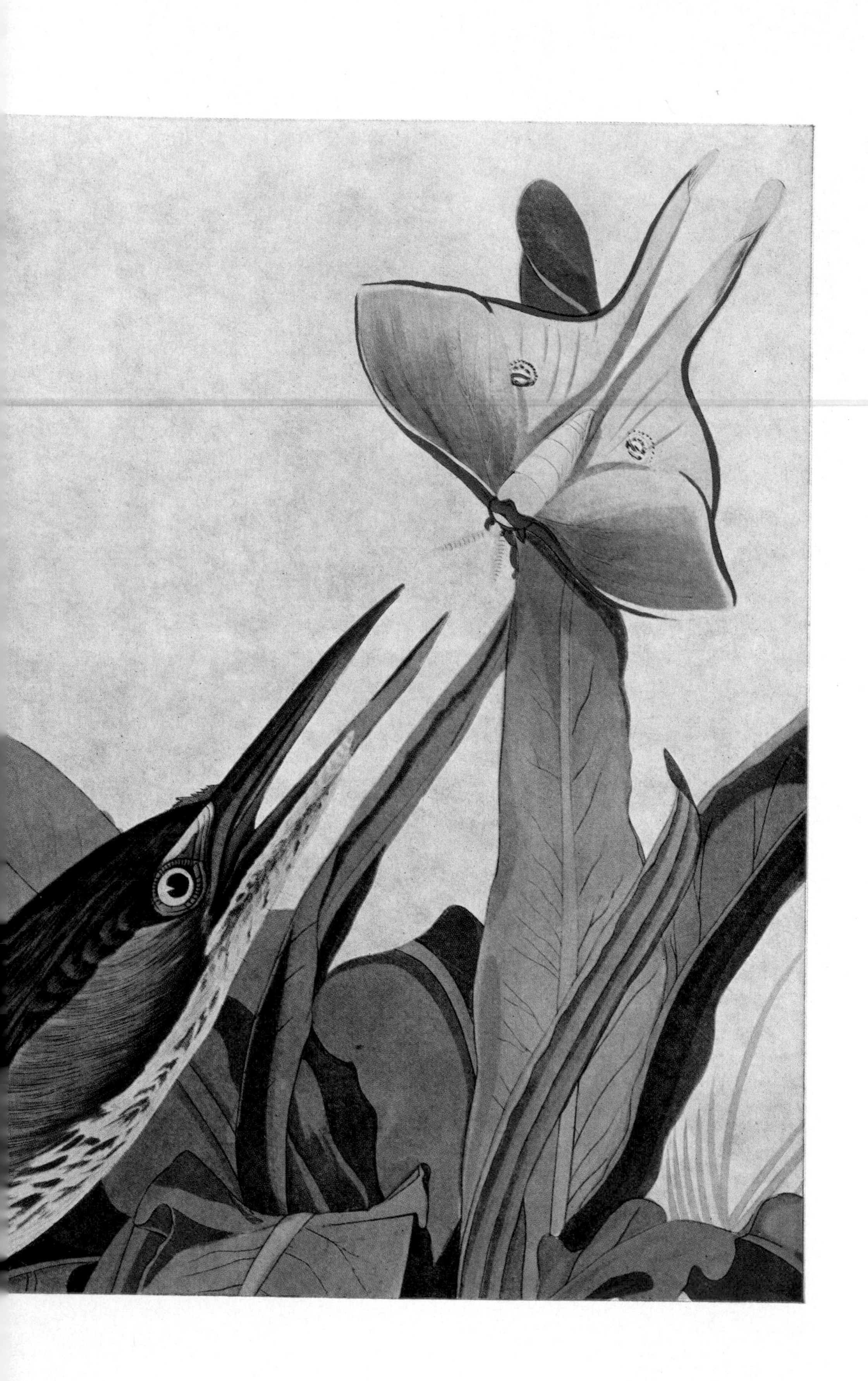

3
2
1

4

3

2
2
1

each with an area of not less than five square feet, altogether comprising more than a thousand individual birds together with additional thousands of plants, flowers, fruits, insects, reptiles, and mammals; that kept as many as fifty colorists working by hand to duplicate the tints of the artist's original paintings on a total of upward of 100,000 plates—all this was carried out at Audubon's expense. It was done without grants or aids or patronage funds of any kind. The total cost of publishing *The Birds of America* came to more than $100,000. To make it possible, Audubon had to interrupt his painting and study of birds to engage in long and exhausting selling trips, traveling in England, France, Canada, and the United States in search of new subscribers. At the same time he had the additional expense of expeditions to Texas, the Florida keys, even to Labrador to add to his knowledge of unfamiliar species.

When Audubon delivered his first drawings to the engraver, he had not a single subscriber. His total was only thirty subscribers even after fifty plates had been engraved. When he finished the first volume of his *Ornithological Biography,* in 1831, he could find no publisher in Edinburgh who would take it. Again at his own expense he issued the five volumes, comprising more than three thousand pages.

"I know," he wrote in the midst of his labors, "I am engaged in an arduous undertaking, but if I live to complete it, I will offer to my country a beautiful monument to the varied splendor of American nature." It is this varied splendor, the inclusion of so many diverse forms of plant and animal life—trees, shrubs, wildflowers, beetles, wasps, snakes, snails, frogs, berries, bees, spiders—that enhances the value of his work. While he is thought of primarily as a bird artist, while birds hold the center of the stage in his most famous pictures—birds often so amazingly lifelike they seem ready to leap into flight—the beauty of moth and flower, leaf and butterfly, is more than mere embellishment of the background. At best they put the bird in its setting, they show it in relationship to its environment. And always they reveal to the beholder the infinite variety of American nature. It is this universal appreciation of the out-of-doors that makes Audubon's wildlife, as recorded both in text and plates, fall so naturally into such ecological groupings as the creatures of wood and forest, marsh and swamp, lake and river, prairie and open land, sea and shore.

One of the most memorable days in Audubon's life came on June 20, 1838. It was then that he saw the last plate of *The Birds of America* come from the press. A little less than a year later, in May 1839, the fifth and last volume of his *Ornithological Biography* appeared. He could then write: "I find my journeys all finished, my anxieties vanished, my mission accomplished." Once, going down the Ohio in later life, he noted that he had passed the old mill at Henderson "poor no longer."

But hardly had he accomplished his original mission than Audubon plunged into another formidable enterprise, one he did not live to see completed—an attempt to present on the same grand scale the mammals of his adopted country. It was in connection with this work, *The Viviparous Quadrupeds of North America,* that he made his last visit to the wilderness, "the great western journey" as he called it, up the Missouri River to the Yellowstone. It occupied eight months of the year 1843. Audubon was then fifty-eight. Newspaper accounts of the time describe him as an old man with white hair falling to his shoulders. Three years later, in 1846, his eyes began to fail and his mind to sink into the gradual twilight that deepened until, at the age of sixty-six, on January 27, 1851, at Minnie's Land, his home on the Hudson just north of New York City, his adventure-filled life came to an end. Lucy Audubon outlived her husband by nearly a quarter of a century, dying at eighty-six, on June 13, 1874.

The vast accomplishments of Audubon, the immense amount of work he achieved, never could have been produced single-handed. He was indebted to many persons for help. Foremost was Robert Havell, Jr., the English engraver of all the plates of the Elephant Folio. A painter of distinction himself, he sometimes, at the artist's direction, inserted material that aided the composition or enriched the background. Joseph R. Mason, the gifted boy who for a year and a half was Audubon's companion in his wanderings, supplied some of the finest of the botanical "accessories." Maria Martin, sister-in-law of Audubon's friend and collaborator, John Bachman, painted numerous flowers, plants, and insects that formed background material for the bird studies. Both the artist's sons—John particularly in painting, Victor in painting and in business matters—contributed substantially to the success of his projects.

Three and a half years before Henry Thoreau built his hut at the edge of Walden Pond, he set down these words in his *Journal:* "Books of natural history make the most cheerful winter reading. I read in Audubon with a thrill of delight, when the snow covers the ground, of the magnolia, and the Florida keys, with their warm sea-breezes; of the fence rail, and the cotton-tree, and the migration of the rice-bird; of the breaking up of winter in Labrador, and the melting of the snow on the forks of the Missouri; and we owe an accession of health to these reminiscences of luxuriant nature."

Just as in his painting, Audubon in his writing—his Journals, his Episodes, and his classic bird biographies—stresses action rather than repose. Vividness and vitality, color and flavor are in his pages. He sometimes writes with French flourishes but never with a leaden pen. He becomes excited. He tends to run rather than walk. An exhilarating current flows through many of his avian biographies and many of the pages of his voluminous Journals. They present in another medium the animation he infused into his pictures. One complements the other. Always, whether his hand held a pen or a brush, he sought to show the living creature, its activity arrested in the midst of some interesting and often dramatic moment.

If he writes with emotion, if his paragraphs are often highly colored, he crams his biographies of the birds with the details of their lives, usually gleaned from firsthand observation. Audubon wrote less from other books than from the out-of-doors. He had *been there.* And sometimes ornithologically he had been there *first.* Like his fellow Frenchman, Hector St. John de Crèvecœur, Audubon in his writings tended to present an idealized picture of the American frontier and of the pleasures of the pioneer life. Both, in so doing, reflected the exuberance and optimism of the new country in which they lived.

There is about Audubon's writings a wonderful intimacy, sustained from beginning to end, as though he were talking to the reader directly, relating his adventures beside a campfire. This is only partly due to his insertion of "Dear Reader" and "Kind Reader," a literary device that has since gone out of fashion. When William MacGillivray, the young Scottish ornithologist, corrected Audubon's manuscript—changing such French spellings as *compagnons* to *companions*—he had the good sense to retain this quality of intimacy. Thus, in the last volume of the *Ornithological Biography,* when the author writes: "Now, Reader, farewell! . . . may the study of the admirable productions of nature ever prove as agreeable to you as it has been to me," those who have followed him through the three thousand and more pages of the five volumes feel that they are parting from a companion they have come to know well.

Audubon's lifework occurred not only on the frontiers of the nation but on the frontiers of American ornithology. He had both the advantages and the handicaps of the pioneer. He lived in a time before bird guides and high-powered binoculars. He had no stroboscopic pictures or full-color movies to help him. The modern bird painter has advantages Audubon never knew. So it is fair enough that, both in his painting and in his writing, he should be accorded a latitude of error that a modern worker would not receive.

The mistakes that Audubon or his helpers made are there to see. In some instances the very fidelity that characterizes his plates reveals the error. His painting of the red-eyed vireo, for example, shows a spider constructing a web. Its carefully depicted form and the distinctive markings on its back enable us to identify it as *Phidippus audax.* This is a species of jumping spider. It never builds a web.

For decades a storm raged around Audubon's head. On one side were the rabid Audubon-haters who overlooked all his excellences and saw only his errors—his mistaking the sandhill crane for the young of the whooping crane; his describing a bird song as running down the scale when it actually goes up; his reporting a new species, the bird of Washington, that nobody else has ever seen and that is now believed to have been a young bald eagle. Opposed were extremists of the other side. For them, Audubon was Audubon and the case was closed. They gave the impression at times of being willing to believe wrong was right if Audubon had done it. Somewhere between the two lay the truth. As Francis Hobart Herrick puts it, in a wonderful understatement: "If Audubon possessed faults, he was not lacking in merits."

By temperament Audubon was impulsive. His eye was for the dramatic. Moreover, most of his adult life was spent on the frontier where the tall story was the tradition, where the precise and literal truth was often considered merely something that got in the way of a good story. So neither his temperament nor his environment aided him in becoming a careful, cautious, exact observer. At first he was more frontiersman than scientist. But he kept growing in many ways. As his character became more disciplined and reliable, he increased in stature as an accurate observer. His output was staggering; viewed against its magnitude, his errors take on a reduced importance.

Just as Audubon began more frontiersman than scientist, so he began more hunter than naturalist, more gunner than conservationist. His pages contain reports of slaughter unthinkable today. He tells of firing as fast as two double-barreled guns could be reloaded for one hour by his watch in the midst of a colony of nesting puffins and leaving with two boatloads of dead birds. Among the Florida keys, he engaged in "rare sport"—killing pelicans on their roosts. "You must be aware," he wrote to a friend, "that I call birds few when I shoot less than one hundred per day." For a considerable period in his life, probably the most terrifying sight a bird could see was the approach of John James Audubon. Even after allowances are made for the fact that he had no binoculars and needed specimens in the hand to study, and that he paid part of his expenses by supplying bird skins to collectors, his gunner's delight in killing game is unmistakable. In this, of course, he reflected the outlook of his time. His pages present one of the clearest pictures we have of the attitude that prevailed in a period of age-old abundance, when wildlife seemed inexhaustible.

As Audubon grew older, his viewpoint on wildlife evolved. He observed the mounting destruction of the country's living resources, the great waste of its natural heritage. He noted the reduction in numbers of various species of wild birds. He spoke out against the senseless slaughter of the bison. He became more humane, sparing the lives of individual birds, begging hunters to kill wounded bison dying in slow agony on the prairie, expressing a growing dislike for the wanton destruction of bird life. His concern increased for the future of the American wildlife he had so great a part in making known to the world.

Thus Audubon became the patron saint not only of the Audubon gun clubs that flourished in the last decades of the nineteenth century, but of the later Audubon societies devoted to the protection not only of birds but of all of America's wild heritage. Such organizations as the National Audubon Society have proved to be—aside from the body of work he himself produced—the American Woodsman's finest monument.

Long before Audubon's death, the product of his brush and pen was recognized as an outstanding cultural heritage of his century. His was one of the initial busts placed in the Hall of Fame for Great Americans, in New York City. There are Audubon Parks in Louisville and New Orleans. An Audubon Memorial Bridge spans the Ohio. On the outskirts of Henderson, there is an Audubon Museum and an Audubon State Park. Communities widely scattered across the country—in New Jersey, Minnesota, Iowa, Pennsylvania, Florida, and Texas—have been named in his honor. And Mill Grove, his youthful home on the Perkiomen, is now maintained as a shrine and wildlife sanctuary.

The lifetime of Audubon spanned great changes in America. In 1803, when he arrived, the seventeenth state, Ohio, was only a few months old. In 1851, when he died, the thirty-first state, California, had been admitted to the Union. The population of the United States had climbed from about 6,000,000 to more than 23,000,000. The center of population had shifted from near Baltimore almost to the Ohio line in West Virginia. The Mexican War had been fought and won. The frontier was advancing toward the Rockies. The Gold Rush had carried the Forty-Niners to California.

Hardly had Audubon died when the great auk became extinct to be followed by the Labrador duck, the Carolina parakeet, and the passenger pigeon. Within a few decades, the bison had been shot almost to extinction. In his pages of text, as well as in his plates of illustrations, Audubon had captured a living wilderness that was slipping away even as he portrayed it. He worked in a period when wildlife was at its prime, when the natural richness of the country was as the white man found it, as nature prepared it. It was the world's good fortune that so great a master of his art could know it all and appreciate it all and depict it all in a time before the swift change of later years accelerated its pace.

1. Woods, Fields, and Brushland

Introduction

At the time the Pilgrim Fathers stepped ashore at Plymouth Bay, it has been estimated, over nine hundred million acres of virgin forest extended westward before them. Of that original woodland, hardly more than 5 per cent remains today. This lies almost entirely within state and nationally owned parks, forests, and wilderness areas.

The Colonial period saw the gradual pushing back of the forests around settlements in the East. By the time Audubon reached America, concern was already being expressed for the lack of firewood near the larger cities. In the eastern forests it was the great stands of white and red pine that were the first to disappear. By the early 1890s, this exploitation of timberlands had reached a peak. As many as four billion board feet of lumber were cut in a single year. Widespread forest fires added to the devastation. As the forests went down, the number of hunters increased. Profound changes in wildlife were inevitable.

Even as early as the latter part of the seventeenth century, in 1672, John Josselyn was writing of parts of New England near the larger settlements: " 'Tis very rare to meet a wild turkie in the woods." This famous game bird, so important in early days, first decreased, then disappeared over much of its former range. The last wild turkey in Massachusetts was shot near Mount Tom in 1851, the year that Audubon died. As the hardwood forests fell, the seemingly inexhaustible supply of food—acorns and beechnuts and chestnuts—went with them. Where Audubon knew the wild turkey best, in the lower Ohio Valley, it disappeared entirely. By the early decades of the present century, the comparatively few birds that remained were confined mainly to the wilder, wooded mountain regions of the Middle Atlantic States and to areas of the South. From this stock, with the help of conservationists, the species is slowly being re-established.

But the story of the passenger pigeon, whose incredible numbers Audubon so vividly describes, has ended without the possibility of a note of hope. It is the classic example of a living creature, existing in uncounted millions, that has been destroyed completely. Audubon, misjudging the destructiveness of man, thought it would survive all shooting. However, less than twenty years after his death, the slaughter had reached the point where one small community, Hartford, Michigan, sent to market three carloads of pigeons a day for a period of forty days, a total of 11,880,000 birds. The tragic end of the story came on September 1, 1914. On that date, the last passenger pigeon on earth died in the zoo at Cincinnati, Ohio, hardly more than a hundred miles from the spot where, 101 years before, Audubon had watched the flocks stream by in numbers so vast that "the light of noonday was obscured as by an eclipse."

The name "republican swallow" for the cliff swallow, *Petrochelidon pyrrhonota,* at one time had wide currency among earlier ornithologists although it has now fallen into discuse. It originated with Audubon. In Volume I of the *Ornithological Biography,* he records how he first found a colony of these birds, with their globular nests of mud, on the banks of the Ohio, near Henderson, Kentucky. "I drew up a description at the time," he writes, "naming the species *Hirundo republicana,* the republican swallow, in allusion to the mode in which the individuals belonging to it associate, for the purpose of forming their nests and rearing their young."

Audubon's "cotton-tree" is the cottonwood, or necklace poplar, *Populus deltoides.* Its range extends from Quebec to Florida and westward to the Rockies. In speaking of the "pewee flycatcher" and the "pewee," he refers to the Eastern phoebe, *Sayornis phoebe;* not, as has sometimes been assumed, to the Eastern wood pewee, *Contropus virens.* Cambridge College is a former name for Harvard University.

Of all the mammals of Audubon's woodland world, curiously enough, one that has survived the best is that slow-moving, stupid-appearing creature, the most primitive of all North American quadrupeds, the lowly opossum. In recent times, the opossum has been slowly expanding its range and extending it northward.

The following extracts from Audubon's own writings begin with a selection from the first bird biography he wrote.

The Wild Turkey (*Meleagris gallopavo*)

While at Henderson, on the Ohio, I had, among many other wild birds, a fine male turkey, which had been reared from its earliest youth under my care, it having been caught by me when probably not more than two or three days old. It became so tame that it would follow any person who called it, and was the favorite of the little village. Yet it would never roost with the tame turkeys, but regularly betook itself at night to the roof of the house, where it remained until dawn. When two years old, it began to fly to the woods, where it remained for a considerable part of the day, to return to the enclosure as night approached. It continued this practice until the following spring, when I saw it several times fly from its roosting place to the top of a high cotton-tree, on the bank of the Ohio, from which, after resting a little, it would sail to the opposite shore, the river being there nearly half a mile wide, and return toward night.

One morning I saw it fly off, at a very early hour, to the woods, in another direction, and took no particular notice of the circumstance. Several days elapsed, but the bird did not return. I was going toward some lakes near Green River to shoot, when, having walked about five miles, I saw a fine large gobler cross the path before me, moving leisurely along. Turkeys being then in prime condition for the table, I ordered my dog to chase it, and put it up. The animal went off with great rapidity, and as it approached the turkey, I saw, with great surprise, that the latter paid little attention. Juno was on the point of seizing it, when she suddenly stopped, and turned her head toward me. I hastened to them, but you may easily conceive my surprise when I saw my own favorite bird, and discovered that it had recognized the dog, and would not fly from it; although the sight of a strange dog would have caused it to run off at once. A friend of mine happening to be in search of a wounded deer, took the bird on his saddle before him, and carried it home for me.

The following spring it was accidentally shot, having been taken for a wild bird, and brought to me on being recognized by the red ribbon which it had around its neck. Pray, Reader, by what word will you designate the recognition made by my favorite turkey of a dog which had been long associated with it in the yard and grounds? Was it the result of instinct, or of reason—an unconsciously revived impression, or the act of an intelligent mind?

At the time when I removed to Kentucky, rather more than a fourth of a century ago, turkeys were so abundant that the price of one in the market was not equal to that of a common barn fowl now. I have seen them offered for the sum of threepence each, the birds weighing from ten to twelve pounds. A first-rate turkey, weighing from twenty-five to thirty pounds avoirdupois, was considered well sold when it brought a quarter of a dollar.

Ornithological Biography, Volume I

The Passenger Pigeon *(Ectopistes migratorius)*

The passenger pigeon, or, as it is usually named in America, the wild pigeon, moves with extreme rapidity, propelling itself by quicky repeated flaps of the wings, which it brings more or less near to the body, according to the degree of velocity which is required. Like the domestic pigeon, it often flies, during the love season, in a circling manner, supporting itself with both wings angularly elevated, in which position it keeps them until it is about to alight. Now and then, during these circular flights, the tips of the primary quills of each wing are made to strike against each other, producing a smart rap, which may be heard at a distance of thirty or forty yards. Before alighting, the wild pigeon, like the Carolina parrot and a few other species of birds, breaks the force of its flight by repeated flappings, as if apprehensive of receiving injury from coming too suddenly into contact with the branch or the spot of ground on which it intends to settle.

I have commenced my description of this species with the above account of its flight because the most important facts connected with its habits relate it its migrations. These are entirely owing to the necessity of procuring food, and are not performed with the view of escaping the severity of a northern latitude, or of seeking a southern one for the purpose of breeding. They consequently do not take place at any fixed period or season of the year. Indeed, it sometimes happens that a continuance of a sufficient supply of food in one district will keep these birds absent from another for years. I know, at least, to a certainty, that in Kentucky they remained for several years constantly, and were nowhere else to be found. They all suddenly disappeared one season when the mast was exhausted, and did not return for a long period. Similar facts have been observed in other States.

Their great power of flight enables them to survey and pass over an astonishing extent of country in a very short time. This is proved by facts well known in America. Thus, pigeons have been killed in the neighborhood of New York, with their crops full of rice, which they must have collected in the fields of Georgia and Carolina, these districts being the nearest in which they could possibly have procured a supply of that kind of food. As their power of digestion is so great that they will decompose food entirely in twelve hours, they must in this case have traveled between three hundred and four hundred miles in six hours, which shows their speed to be at an average about one mile in a minute. A velocity such as this would enable one of these birds, were it so inclined, to visit the European continent in less than three days.

This great power of flight is seconded by as great a power of vision, which enables them, as they travel at that swift rate, to inspect the country below, discover their food with facility, and thus attain the object for which their journey has been undertaken. This I have also proved to be the case, by having observed them, when passing over a sterile part of the country, or one scantily furnished with food suited to them, keep high in the air, flying with an extended front, so as to enable them to survey hundreds of acres at once. On the contrary, when the land is richly covered with food, or the trees abundantly hung with mast, they fly low, in order to discover the part most plentifully supplied.

Their body is of an elongated oval form, steered by a long well-plumed tail, and propelled by well-set wings, the muscles of which are very large and powerful for the size of the bird. When an individual is seen gliding through the woods and close to the observer, it passes like a thought, and on trying to see it again, the eye searches in vain; the bird is gone.

The multitudes of wild pigeons in our woods are astonishing. Indeed, after having viewed them so often, and under so many circumstances, I even now feel inclined to pause, and assure myself that what I am going to relate is fact. Yet I have seen it all, and that too in the company of persons who, like myself, were struck with amazement.

In the autumn of 1813, I left my house at Henderson, on the banks of the Ohio, on my way to Louisville. In passing over the Barrens a few miles beyond Hardensburg, I observed the pigeons flying from northeast to southwest, in greater numbers than I thought I had ever seen them before, and feeling an inclination to count the flocks that might pass within the reach of my eye in one hour, I dismounted, seated myself on an eminence, and began to mark with my pencil, making a dot for every flock that passed. In a short time, finding the task which I had undertaken impracticable, as the birds poured in in countless multitudes, I rose, and counting the dots then put down, found that 163 had been made in twenty-one minutes. I traveled on, and still met more the farther I proceeded. The air was literally filled with pigeons; the light of noonday was obscured as by an eclipse; the dung fell in spots, not unlike melting flakes of snow; and the continued buzz of wings had a tendency to lull my senses to repose.

Whilst waiting for dinner at Young's Inn, at the confluence of Salt River with the Ohio, I saw, at my leisure, immense legions still going by, with a front reaching far beyond the Ohio on the west, and the beechwood forests directly on the east of me. Not a single bird alighted; for not a nut or acorn was that year to be seen in the neighborhood. They, consequently, flew so high that different trials to reach them with a capital rifle proved ineffectual; nor did the reports disturb them in the least.

I cannot describe to you the extreme beauty of their aerial evolutions when a hawk chanced to press upon the rear of a flock. At once, like a torrent, and with a noise like thunder, they rushed into a compact mass, pressing upon each other toward the center. In these almost solid masses, they darted forward in undulating and angular lines, descended and swept close over the earth with inconceivable velocity, mounted perpendicularly so as to resemble a vast column, and, when high, were seen wheeling and twisting within their continued lines, which then resembled the coils of a gigantic serpent.

Before sunset I reached Louisville, distant from Hardensburg fifty-five miles. The pigeons were still passing in undiminished numbers, and continued to do so for three days in succession. The people were all in arms. The banks of the Ohio were crowded with men and boys, incessantly shooting at the pilgrims, which there flew lower as they passed the river. Multitudes were thus destroyed. For a week or more, the population fed on no other flesh than that of pigeons, and talked of nothing but pigeons. The atmosphere, during this time, was strongly impregnated with the peculiar odor which emanates from the species.

It is extremely interesting to see flock after flock performing exactly the same evolutions which had been traced as it were in the air by a preceding flock. Thus, should a hawk have charged on a group at a certain spot, the angles, curves, and undulations that have been described by the birds, in their efforts to escape from the dreaded talons of the plunderer, are undeviatingly followed by the next group that comes up. Should the bystander happen to witness one of these affrays, and, struck with the rapidity and elegance of the motions exhibited, feel desirous of seeing them repeated, his wishes will be gratified if he only remain in the place until the next group comes up.

It may not, perhaps, be out of place to attempt an estimate of the number of pigeons contained in one of those mighty flocks and of the quantity of food daily consumed by its members. The inquiry will tend to show the astonishing bounty of the great Author of Nature in providing for the wants of His creatures. Let us take a column of one mile in breadth, which is far below the average size, and suppose it passing over us without interruption for three hours, at the rate mentioned above of one mile in the minute. This will give us a parallelogram of 180 miles by 1, covering 180 square miles. Allowing two pigeons to the square yard, we have one billion, one hundred and fifteen million, one hundred and thirty-six thousand pigeons in one flock. As every pigeon daily consumes fully half a pint of food, the quantity necessary for supplying this vast multitude must be eight million, seven hundred and twelve thousand bushels per day.

As soon as the pigeons discover a sufficiency of food to entice them to alight, they fly round in circles, reviewing the country below. During their evolutions, on such occasions, the dense mass which they form exhibits a beautiful appearance, as it changes its direction, now displaying a glistening sheet of azure, when the backs of the birds come simultaneously into view, and anon, suddenly presenting a mass of rich deep purple. They then pass lower, over the woods, and for a moment are lost among the foilage, but again emerge, and are seen gliding aloft. They now alight, but the next moment, as if suddenly alarmed, they take to wing, producing by the flappings of their wings a noise like the roar of distant thunder, and sweep through the forests to see if danger is near. Hunger, however, soon brings them to the ground.

When alighted, they are seen industriously throwing up the withered leaves in quest of the fallen mast. The rear ranks are continually rising, passing over the main body, and alighting in front, in such rapid succession, that the whole flock seems still on wing. The quantity of ground thus swept is astonishing, and so completely has it been cleared, that the gleaner who might follow in their rear would find his labor completely lost. Whilst feeding, their avidity is at times so great that in attempting to swallow a large acorn or nut, they are seen gasping for a long while, as if in the agonies of suffocation.

On such occasions, when the woods are filled with these pigeons, they are killed in immense numbers, although no apparent diminution ensues. About the middle of the day, after their repast is finished, they settle on the trees, to enjoy rest and digest their food. On the ground they walk with ease, as well as on the branches, frequently jerking their beautiful tail, and moving the neck backward and forward in the most graceful manner. As the sun begins to sink beneath the horizon, they depart *en masse* for the roosting place, which not unfrequently is hundreds of miles distant, as has been ascertained by persons who have kept an account of their arrivals and departures.

Let us now, Kind Reader, inspect their place of nightly rendezvous. One of these curious roosting places, on the banks of the Green River in Kentucky, I repeatedly visited. It was, as is always the case, in a portion of the forest where the trees were of great magnitude, and where there was little underwood. I rode through it upward of forty miles, and, crossing it in different parts, found its average breadth to be rather more than three miles. My first view of it was about a fortnight subsequent to the period when they had made choice of it, and I arrived there nearly two hours before sunset. Few pigeons were then to be seen, but a greater number of persons, with horses and wagons, guns and ammunition, had already established encampments on the borders.

Two farmers from the vicinity of Russelsville, distant more than a hundred miles, had driven upward of three hundred hogs to be fattened on the pigeons which were to be slaughtered. Here and there, the people employed in plucking and salting what had already been procured were seen sitting in the midst of large piles of these birds. The dung lay several inches deep, covering the whole extent of the roosting place, like a bed of snow. Many trees two feet in diameter, I observed, were broken off at no great distance from the ground; and the branches of many of the largest and tallest had given way, as if the forest had been swept by a tornado. Everything proved to me that the number of birds resorting to this part of the forest must be immense beyond conception.

As the period of their arrival approached, their foes anxiously prepared to receive them. Some were furnished with iron pots containing sulphur, others with torches of pine knots, many with poles, and the rest with guns. The sun was lost to our view, yet not a pigeon had arrived. Everything was ready, and all eyes were gazing on the clear sky, which appeared in glimpses amidst the tall trees. Suddenly there burst forth a general cry of "Here they come!" The noise which they made, though yet distant, reminded me of a hard gale at sea, passing through the rigging of a close-reefed vessel. As the birds arrived and passed over me, I felt a current of air that surprised me.

Thousands were soon knocked down by the polemen. The birds continued to pour in. The fires were lighted, and a magnificent, as well as wonderful and almost terrifying, sight presented itself. The pigeons, arriving by thousands, alighted everywhere, one above another, until solid masses as large as hogsheads were formed on the branches all round. Here and there the perches gave way under the weight with a crash, and, falling to the ground, destroyed hundreds of the birds beneath, forcing down the dense groups with which every stick was loaded. It was a scene of uproar and confusion. I found it quite useless to speak, or even to shout to those persons who were nearest to me. Even the reports of the guns were seldom heard, and I was made aware of the firing only by seeing the shooters reloading.

No one dared venture within the line of devastation. The hogs had been penned up in due time, the picking up of the dead and wounded being left for the next morning's employment. The pigeons were constantly coming, and it was past midnight before I perceived a decrease in the number of those that arrived. The uproar continued the whole night; and as I was anxious to know to what distance the sound reached, I sent off a man, accustomed to perambulate the forest, who, returning two hours afterward, informed me he had heard it distinctly when three miles distant from the spot. Toward the approach of day, the noise in some measure subsided, long before objects were distinguishable, the pigeons began to move off in a direction quite different from that in which they had arrived the evening before, and at sunrise all that were able to fly had disappeared. The howlings of the wolves now reached our ears, and the foxes, lynxes, cougars, bears, raccoons, opossums, and polecats were seen sneaking off, whilst eagles and hawks of different species, accompanied by a crowd of vultures, came to supplant them, and enjoy their share of the spoil.

It was then that the authors of all this devastation began their entry amongst the dead, the dying, and the mangled. The pigeons were picked up and piled in heaps, until each had as many as he could possibly dispose of, when the hogs were let loose to feed on the remainder.

Persons unacquainted with these birds might naturally conclude that such dreadful havoc would soon put an end to the species. But I have satisfied myself, by long observation, that nothing but the gradual diminution of our forest can accomplish their decrease, as they not unfrequently quadruple their numbers yearly, and always at least double it. In 1805 I saw schooners loaded in bulk with pigeons caught up the Hudson River, coming into the wharf at New York, when the birds sold for a cent apiece. I knew a man in Pennsylvania, who caught and killed upward of five hundred dozens in a clapnet in one day, sweeping sometimes twenty dozens or more at a single haul. In the month of March, 1830, they were so abundant in the markets of New York that piles of them met the eye in every direction. I have seen the Negroes at the United States' Salines or saltworks of Shawanee Town, wearied with killing pigeons, as they alighted to drink the water issuing from the leading pipes, for weeks at a time; and yet in 1826, in Louisiana, I saw congregated flocks of these birds as numerous as ever I had seen them before, during a residence of nearly thirty years in the United States.

The breeding of the wild pigeons, and the places chosen for that purpose, are points of great interest. The time is not much influenced by season, and the place selected is where food is most plentiful and most attainable, and always at a convenient distance from water. Forest trees of great height are those in which the pigeons form their nests. Thither the countless myriads resort, and prepare to fulfill one of the great laws of nature. At this period the note of the pigeon is a soft *coo-coo-coo-coo,* much shorter than that of the domestic species. The common notes resemble the monosyllables *kee-kee-kee-kee,* the first being the loudest, the others gradually diminishing in power. The male assumes a pompous demeanor, and follows the female whether on the ground or on the branches, with spread tail and drooping wings, which it rubs against the part over which it is moving. The body is elevated, the throat swells, the eyes sparkle. He continues his notes, and now and then rises on the wing, and flies a few yards to approach the fugitive and timorous female.

Like the domestic pigeon and other species, they caress each other by billing, in which action, the bill of the one is introduced transversely into that of the other, and both parties alternately disgorge the contents of their crop by repeated efforts. These preliminary affairs are soon settled, and the pigeons commence their nests in general peace and harmony. They are composed of a few dry twigs, crossing each other, and are supported by forks of the branches. On the same tree from fifty to a hundred nests may frequently be seen—I might say a much greater number, were I not anxious, Kind Reader, that however wonderful my account of the wild pigeon is, you may not feel disposed to refer it to the marvelous. The eggs are two in number, of a broadly elliptical form, and pure white. During incubation, the male supplies the female with food. Indeed, the tenderness and affection displayed by these birds toward their mates are in the highest degree striking. It is a remarkable fact that each brood generally consists of a male and female.

Here again, the tyrant of the creation, man, interferes, disturbing the harmony of this peaceful scene. As the young birds grow up, their enemies, armed with axes, reach the spot, to seize and destroy all they can. The trees are felled, and made to fall in such a way that the cutting of one causes the overthrow of another, or shakes the neighboring trees so much that the young pigeons, or *squabs,* as they are named, are violently hurried to the ground. In this manner, also, immense quantities are destroyed.

The young are fed by the parents in the manner described above; in other words, the old bird introduces its bill into the mouth of the young one in a transverse manner, or with the back of each mandible opposite the separations of the mandibles of the young bird, and disgorges the contents of its crop. As soon as the young birds are able to shift for themselves, they leave their parents, and continue separate until they attain maturity. By the end of six months they are capable of reproducing their species.

The flesh of the wild pigeon is of a dark color, but affords tolerable eating. That of young birds from the nest is much esteemed. The skin is covered with small white filmy scales. The feathers fall off at the least touch, as has been remarked to be the case in the Carolina turtle. I have only to add that this species, like others of the same genus, immerses its head up to the eyes while drinking.

In March 1830, I bought about 350 of these birds in the market of New York, at four cents apiece. Most of these I carried alive to England, and distributed amongst several noblemen, presenting some at the same time to the Zoological Society.

Ornithological Biography, Volume I

The Black-Capped Chickadee (*Parus atricapillus*)

Hardy, smart, restless, industrious, and frugal, the black-cap titmouse ranges through the forest during the summer, and retiring to its more secluded parts, as if to ensure a greater degree of quiet, it usually breeds there. Numerous eggs produce numerous progeny, and as soon as the first brood has been reared, the young range hither and thither in a body, searching for food, while their parents, intent on forming another family, remain concealed and almost silent, laying their eggs in the hole deserted by some small woodpecker, or forming one for themselves.

As it has been my fortune to witness a pair at this work, I will here state what occurred, notwithstanding the opinion of those who inform us that the bill of the titmouse is "not shaped for digging." While seated one morning under a crab-apple tree (very hard wood, Reader), I saw two black-cap titmice fluttering about in great concern, as if anxious to see me depart. By their manners indeed I was induced to believe that their nest was near, and, anxious to observe their proceedings, I removed to the distance of about twenty paces. The birds now became silent, alighted on the apple tree, gradually moved toward the base of one of its large branches, and one of them disappeared in what I then supposed to be the hole of some small woodpecker; but I saw it presently on the edge, with a small chip in its bill, and again cautiously approached the tree. When three or four yards off I distinctly heard the peckings or taps of the industrious worker within, and saw it come to the mouth of the hole and return many times in succession in the course of half an hour, after which I got up and examined the mansion. The hole was about three inches deep, and dug obliquely downward from the aperture, which was just large enough to admit the bird. I had observed both sexes at this labor, and left the spot perfectly satisfied as to their power of boring a nest for themselves.

The black-cap titmouse, or chickadee, as it is generally named in our Eastern States, though exceedingly shy in summer or during the breeding season, becomes quite familiar in winter, although it never ventures to enter the habitations of man; but in the most boisterous weather, requiring neither food nor shelter there, it may be seen amidst the snow in the rugged paths of the cheerless woods, where it welcomes the traveler or the woodcutter with a confidence and cheerfulness far surpassing the well-known familiarity of the robin redbreast of Europe. Often, on such occasions, should you offer it no matter how small a portion of your fare, it alights without hesitation, and devours it without manifesting any apprehension. The sound of an ax in the woods is sufficient to bring forth several of these busy creatures, and having discovered the woodman, they seem to find pleasure in his company. If, as is usually the case, he is provided with a dinner, the chickadee at once evinces its anxiety to partake of it, and loses no opportunity of accomplishing its object, although it sets about it with much circumspection, as if it were afraid of being detected, and brought to punishment.

A woodcutter in Maine assured me that one day he happened to be at work, and had scarcely hung up his basket of provisions, when he was observed by a flock of these birds, which, having gathered into it at once, attacked a piece of cold beef; but after each peck, he saw their heads raised above the edge, as if to guard against the least appearance of danger. After picking until they were tired or satisfied, they left the basket and perched directly over his fire, but out of the direction of the smoke. There they sat enjoying themselves and ruffling their feathers to allow the warmth more easy access to their skin, until he began his dinner, when they immediately alighted near him, and in the most plaintive tones seemed to solicit a portion.

Ornithological Biography, Volume IV

The Phoebe *"The Pewee Flycatcher" (Sayornis phoebe)*

Connected with the biography of this bird are so many incidents relative to my own that could I with propriety deviate from my proposed method, the present volume would contain less of the habits of birds than of those of the youthful days of an American woodsman. While young, I had a plantation that lay on the sloping declivities of a creek, the name of which I have already given, but as it will ever be dear to my recollection, you will, I hope, allow me to repeat it—the Perkioming. I was extremely fond of rambling along its rocky banks, for it would have been difficult to do so either without meeting with a sweet flower, spreading open its beauties to the sun, or observing the watchful king's-fisher perched on some projecting stone over the clear water of the stream. Nay, now and then, the fish hawk itself, followed by a white-headed eagle, would make his appearance, and by his graceful aerial motions, raise my thoughts far above them into the heavens, silently leading me to the admiration of the sublime Creator of all. These impressive, and always delightful, reveries often accompanied my steps to the entrance of a small cave scooped out of the solid rock by the hand of nature. It was, I then thought, quite large enough for my study. My paper and pencils, with now and then a volume of Edgeworth's natural and fascinating *Tales* or Lafontaine's *Fables,* afforded me ample pleasures. It was in that place, Kind Reader, that I first saw with advantage the force of parental affection in birds. There it was that I studied the habits of the pewee; and there I was taught most forcibly that to destroy the nest of a bird, or to deprive it of its eggs or young, is an act of great cruelty.

I had observed the nest of this plain-colored flycatcher fastened, as it were, to the rock immediately over the arched entrance of this calm retreat. I had peeped into it: although empty, it was yet clean, as if the absent owner intended to revisit it with the return of spring. The buds were already much swelled, and some of the trees were ornamented with blossoms, yet the ground was still partially covered with snow, and the air retained the piercing chill of winter.

I chanced one morning early to go to my retreat. The sun's glowing rays gave a rich coloring to every object around. As I entered the cave, a rustling sound over my head attracted my attention, and, on turning, I saw two birds fly off and alight on a tree close by—the pewees had arrived! I felt delighted, and fearing that my sudden appearance might disturb the gentle pair, I walked off, not, however, without frequently looking at them. I concluded that they must have just come, for they seemed fatigued—their plaintive note was not heard, their crests were not erected, and the vibration of the tail, so very conspicuous in this species, appeared to be wanting in power. Insects were yet few, and the return of the birds looked to me as prompted more by their affection to the place than by any other motive. No sooner had I gone a few steps than the pewees, with one accord glided down from their perches and entered the cave. I did not return to it any more that day, and as I saw none about it, or in the neighborhood, I supposed that they must have spent the day within it. I concluded also that these birds must have reached this haven, either during the night, or at the very dawn of that morn. Hundreds of observations have since proved to me that this species always migrates by night.

Filled with the thoughts of the little pilgrims, I went early next morning to their retreat, yet not early enough to surprise them in it. Long before I reached the spot, my ears were agreeably saluted by their well-known note, and I saw them darting about through the air, giving chase to some insects close over the water. They were full of gaiety, frequently flew into and out of the cave, and while alighted on a favorite tree near it, seemed engaged in the most interesting converse. The light fluttering or tremulous motions of their wings, the jetting of their tails, the erection of their crests, and the neatness of their attitudes, all indicated that they were no longer fatigued, but on the contrary refreshed and happy. On my going into the cave, the male flew violently toward the entrance, snapped his bill sharply and repeatedly, accompanying this action with a tremulous rolling note, the import of which I soon guessed. Presently he flew into the cave and out of it again, with a swiftness scarcely credible: it was like the passing of a shadow.

Several days in succession I went to the spot, and saw with pleasure that as my visits increased in frequency, the birds became more familiarized to me, and, before a week had elapsed, the pewees and myself were quite on terms of intimacy. It was now the tenth of April; the spring was forward that season, no more snow was to be seen, redwings and grackles were to be found here and there. The pewees, I observed, began working at their old nest. Desirous of judging for myself, and anxious to enjoy the company of this friendly pair, I determined to spend the greater part of each day in the cave. My presence no longer alarmed either of them. They brought a few fresh materials, lined the nest anew, and rendered it warm by adding a few large soft feathers of the common goose, which they found strewn along the edge of the water in the creek. There was a remarkable and curious twittering in their note while both sat on the edge of the nest at those meetings, and which is never heard on any other occasion. It was the soft, tender expression, I thought, of the pleasure they both appeared to anticipate of the future. Their mutual caresses, simple as they might have seemed to another, and the delicate manner used by the male to please his mate, riveted my eyes on these birds, and excited sensations which I can never forget.

The female one day spent the greater part of the time in her nest; she frequently changed her position; her mate exhibited much uneasiness, he would alight by her sometimes, sit by her side for a moment, and suddenly flying out, would return with an insect, which she took from his bill with apparent gratification. About three o'clock in the afternoon, I saw the uneasiness of the female increase; the male showed an unusual appearance of despondence, when, of a sudden, the female rose on her feet, looked sidewise under her, and flying out, followed by her attentive consort, left the cave, rose high in the air, performing evolutions more curious to me than any I had seen before. They flew about over the water, the female leading her mate, as it were, through her own meanderings. Leaving the pewees to their avocations, I peeped into their nest, and saw there their first egg, so white and so transparent—for I believe that eggs soon lose this peculiar transparency after being laid—that to me the sight was more pleasant than if I had met with a diamond of the same size. The knowledge that in an enclosure so frail, life already existed, and that ere many weeks would elapse, a weak, delicate, and helpless creature, but perfect in all its parts, would burst the shell, and immediately call for the most tender care and attention of its anxious parents, filled my mind with as much wonder as when, looking toward the heavens, I searched, alas in vain, for the true import of all that I saw.

In six days, six eggs were deposited; but I observed that as they increased in number, the bird remained a shorter time in the nest. The last she deposited a few minutes after alighting. Perhaps, thought I, this is a law of nature, intended for keeping the eggs fresh to the last. Kind Reader, what are your thoughts on the subject? About an hour after laying the last egg, the female pewee returned, settled in her nest, and, after arranging the eggs, as I thought, several times under her body, expanded her wings a little, and fairly commenced the arduous task of incubation.

Day after day passed by. I gave strict orders that no one should go near the cave, much less enter it, or indeed destroy any bird's nest on the plantation. Whenever I visited the pewees, one or other of them was on the nest, while its mate was either searching for food, or perched in the vicinity, filling the air with its loudest notes. I not unfrequently reached out my hand near the sitting bird; and so gentle had they both become, or rather so well acquainted were we, that neither moved on such occasions, even when my hand was quite close to it. Now and then the female would shrink back into the nest, but the male frequently snapped at my fingers, and once left the nest as if in great anger, flew round the cave a few times, emitting his querulous whining notes, and alighted again to resume his labors.

At this very time, a pewee's nest was attached to one of the rafters of my mill, and there was another under a shed in the cattle yard. Each pair, anyone would have felt assured, had laid out the limits of its own domain, and it was seldom that one trespassed on the grounds of its neighbor. The pewee of the cave generally fed or spent its time so far above the mill on the creek that he of the mill never came in contact with it. The pewee of the cattle yard confined himself to the orchard, and never disturbed the rest. Yet I sometimes could hear distinctly the notes of the three at the same moment. I had at that period an idea that the whole of these birds were descended from the same stock. If not correct in this supposition, I had ample proof afterward

57. CANADA LYNX *(Lynx canadensis)*. With its bob-tail, ear-tufts, neck-ruff, and oversized feet, the Canada lynx is a distinctive animal. Its range extends through the coniferous forests of the far north beyond treeline onto the tundra. It is oftenest found in the dense thickets, forests, and swamps that are inhabited by its favored prey, the varying hare. The lynx is nocturnal and largely silent. It usually hunts alone, using both sight and smell to find its prey. It climbs well and, when necessary, can swim for considerable distances. Its large, padded feet aid the lynx in running over the snow.

58. OPOSSUM *(Didelphis marsupialis)*. The most primitive of American mammals, the opossum carries its young in a fur-lined pouch. Most often abroad at night, it is omnivorous in its feeding. The opossum is famed for feigning death when attacked. Usually thought of as a southern animal, it lives as far north as Vermont and New Hampshire.

59. HOODED WARBLER *(Wilsonia citrina)*. Moist woodlands with thick undergrowth form the main habitat of this active warbler.

60. MAGNOLIA WARBLER *(Dendroica magnolia)*. From Newfoundland south to the mountains of Virginia, this colorful warbler makes its nest in coniferous trees, spruce, fir, and hemlock.

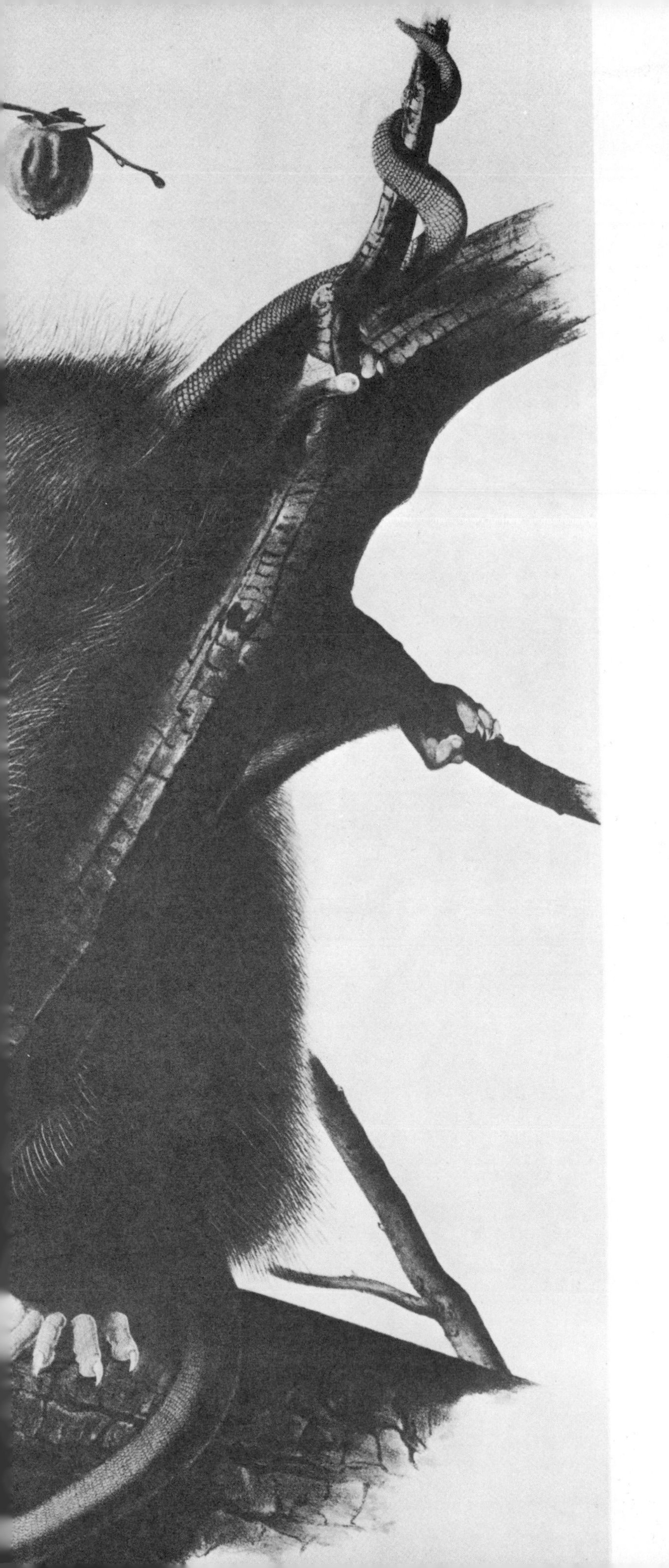

that the brood of young pewees raised in the cave returned the following spring, and established themselves farther up on the creek, and among the outhouses in the neighborhood.

On some other occasion, I will give you such instances of the return of birds, accompanied by their progeny, to the place of their nativity, that perhaps you will become convinced, as I am at this moment, that to this propensity every country owes the augmentation of new species, whether of birds or of quadrupeds, attracted by the many benefits met with, as countries become more open and better cultivated: but now I will, with your leave, return to the pewees of the cave.

On the thirteenth day, the little ones were hatched. One egg was unproductive, and the female, on the second day after the birth of her brood, very deliberately pushed it out of the nest. On examining this egg, I found it containing the embryo of a bird partly dried up, with its vertebra quite fast to the shell, which had probably occasioned its death. Never have I since so closely witnessed the attention of birds to their young. Their entrance with insects was so frequently repeated that I thought I saw the little ones grow as I gazed upon them. The old birds no longer looked upon me as an enemy, and would often come in close by me, as if I had been a post. I now took upon me to handle the young frequently; nay, several times I took the whole family out, and blew off the exuviae of the feathers from the nest. I attached light threads to their legs: these they invariably removed, either with their bills, or with the assistance of their parents. I renewed them, however, until I found the little fellows habituated to them; and at last, when they were about to leave the nest, I fixed a light silver thread to the leg of each, loose enough not to hurt the part, but so fastened that no exertions of theirs could remove it.

Sixteen days had passed when the brood took to wing; and the old birds, dividing the time with caution, began to arrange the nest anew. A second set of eggs were laid, and in the beginning of August a new brood made its appearance.

The young birds took much to the woods, as if feeling themselves more secure there than in the open fields; but before they departed, they all appeared strong, and minded not making long sorties into the open air, over the whole creek, and the fields around it. On the eighth of October, not a pewee could I find on the plantation: my little companions had all set off on their travels. For weeks afterward, however, I saw pewees arriving from the north, and lingering a short time, as if to rest, when they also moved southward.

At the season when the pewee returns to Pennsylvania, I had the satisfaction to observe those of the cave in and about it. There again, in the very same nest, two broods were raised. I found several pewees' nests at some distance up the creek, particularly under a bridge, and several others in the adjoining meadows, attached to the inner part of sheds erected for the protection of hay and grain. Having caught several of these birds on the nest, I had the pleasure of finding that two of them had the little ring on the leg.

I was now obliged to go to France, where I remained two years. On my return, which happened early in August, I had the satisfaction of finding three young pewees in the nest of the cave; but it was not the nest which I had left in it. The old one had been torn off from the roof, and the one which I found there was placed above where it stood. I observed at once that one of the parent birds was as shy as possible, while the other allowed me to approach within a few yards. This was the male bird, and I felt confident that the old female had paid the debt of nature. Having inquired of the miller's son, I found that he had killed the old pewee and four young ones, to make bait for the purpose of catching fish. Then the male pewee had brought another female to the cave! As long as the plantation of Mill Grove belonged to me, there continued to be a pewee's nest in my favorite retreat; but after I had sold it, the cave was destroyed, as were nearly all the beautiful rocks along the shores of the creek, to build a new dam across the Perkioming.

This species is so peculiarly fond of attaching its nest to rocky caves that, were it called the rock flycatcher, it would be appropriately named. Indeed I seldom have passed near such a place, particularly during the breeding season, without seeing the pewee, or hearing its notes. I recollect that, while traveling in Virginia with a friend, he desired that I would go somewhat out of our intended route to visit the renowned Rock Bridge of that State. My companion, who had passed over this natural bridge before, proposed a wager that he could lead me across it before I should be aware of its existence. It was early in April; and, from the descriptions of this place which I had read, I felt confident that the pewee flycatcher must be about it. I accepted the proposal of my friend and trotted on, intent on proving to myself that, by constantly attending to one subject, a person must sooner or later become acquainted with it. I listened to the notes of the different birds, which at intervals came to my ear, and at last had the satisfaction to distinguish those of the pewee. I stopped my horse, to judge of the distance at which the bird might be, and a moment after told my friend that the bridge was short of a hundred yards from us, although it was impossible for us to see the spot itself. The surprise of my companion was great. "How do you know this?" he asked, "for," continued he, "you are correct." "Simply," answered I, "because I hear the notes of the pewee, and know that a cave, or a deep rocky creek, is at hand." We moved on; the pewees rose from under the bridge in numbers; I pointed to the spot and won the wager.

This rule of observation I have almost always found to work, as arithmeticians say, both ways. Thus the nature of the woods or place in which the observer may be, whether high or low, moist or dry, sloping north or south, with whatever kind of vegetation, tall trees or low shrubs, will generally disclose the nature of their inhabitants.

The flight of the pewee flycatcher is performed by a fluttering light motion, frequently interrupted by sailings. It is slow when the bird is proceeding to some distance, rather rapid when in pursuit of prey. It often mounts perpendicularly from its perch after an insect, and returns to some dry twig, from which it can see around to a considerable distance. It then swallows the insect whole, unless it happens to be large. It will at times pursue an insect to a considerable distance, and seldom without success. It alights with great firmness, immediately erects itself in the manner of hawks, glances all around, shakes its wings with a tremulous motion, and vibrates its tail upward as if by a spring. Its tufty crest is generally erected, and its whole appearance is neat, if not elegant. The pewee has its particular stands, from which it seldom rambles far. The top of a fence stake near the road is often selected by it, from which it sweeps off in all directions, returning at intervals, and thus remaining the greater part of the morning and evening. The corner of the roof of the barn suits it equally well, and if the weather requires it, it may be seen perched on the highest dead twig of a tall tree. During the heat of the day it reposes in the shade of the woods. In the autumn it will choose the stalk of the mullein for its stand, and sometimes the projecting angle of a rock jutting over a stream. It now and then alights on the ground for an instant, but this happens principally during winter, or while engaged during spring in collecting the materials of which its nest is composed, in our Southern States, where many spend their time at this season.

I have found this species abundant in the Floridas in winter, in full song and as lively as ever, also in Louisiana and the Carolinas, particularly in the cotton fields. None, however, to my knowledge, breed south of Charleston in South Carolina, and very few in the lower parts of that State. They leave Louisiana in February, and return to it in October. Occasionally during winter they feed on berries of different kinds, and are quite expert at discovering the insects impaled on thorns by the loggerhead shrike, and which they devour with avidity. I met with a few of these birds on the Magdalen Islands, on the coast of Labrador, and in Newfoundland.

The nest of this species bears some resemblance to that of the barn swallow, the outside consisting of mud with which are firmly impacted grasses or mosses of various kinds deposited in regular strata. It is lined with delicate fibrous roots, or shreds of vine bark, wool, horsehair, and sometimes a few feathers. The greatest diameter across the open mouth is from five to six inches, and the depth from four to five. Both birds work alternately, bringing pellets of mud or damp earth, mixed with moss, the latter of which is mostly disposed on the outer parts, and in some instances the whole exterior looks as if entirely formed of it. The fabric is firmly attached to a rock, or a wall, the rafter of a house, &c. In the barrens of Kentucky I have found the nests fixed to the side of those curious places called *sinkholes,* and as much as twenty feet below the surface of the ground. I have observed that when the pewees return in spring they strengthen their tenement by adding to the external parts attached to the rock, as if to prevent it from falling, which after all it sometimes does when several years old. Instances of their taking possession of the nest of the republican swallow *(Hirundo fulva)* have been observed in the State of Maine. The eggs are from four to six, rather elongated, pure white, generally with a few reddish spots near the larger end.

In Virginia, and probably as far as New York, they not unfrequently raise two broods, sometimes three, in a season. My learned friend, Professor Nuttall, of Cambridge College, Massachusetts, thinks that the pewee seldom raises more than one brood in the year in that State.

This species ejects the hard particles of the wings, legs, abdomens, and other parts of insects, in small pellets, in the manner of owls, goatsuckers, and swallows.

Ornithological Biography, Volume II

The Rose-Breasted Grosbeak (Pheucticus ludovicianus)

One year, in the month of August, I was trudging along the shores of the Mohawk River when night overtook me. Being little acquainted with that part of the country, I resolved to camp where I was, the evening was calm and beautiful, the sky sparkled with stars, which were reflected by the smooth waters, and the deep shade of the rocks and trees of the opposite shore fell on the bosom of the stream, while gently from afar came on the ear the muttering sound of a cataract. My little fire was soon lighted under a rock, and, spreading out my scanty stock of provisions, I reclined on my grassy couch. As I looked around on the fading features of the beautiful landscape, my heart turned toward my distant home, where my friends were doubtless wishing me, as I wished them, a happy night and peaceful slumbers. Then were heard the barkings of the watchdog, and I tapped my faithful companion to prevent him answering them. The thoughts of my worldly mission then came over my mind, and having thanked the Creator of all for His never-failing mercy, I closed my eyes, and was passing away into the world of dreaming existence, when suddenly there burst on my soul the serenade of the rose-breasted bird, so rich, so mellow, so loud in the stillness of the night, that sleep fled from my eyelids. Never did I enjoy music more: it thrilled through my heart and surrounded me with an atmosphere of bliss. One might easily have imagined that even the owl, charmed by such delightful music, remained reverently silent. Long after the sounds ceased did I enjoy them, and when all had again become still, I stretched out my wearied limbs, and gave myself up to the luxury of repose. In the morning I awoke vigorous as ever, and prepared to continue my journey.

Ornithological Biography, Volume II

The Pine Grosbeak *(Pinicola enucleator)*

The pine grosbeak is a charming songster. Well do I remember how delighted I felt, while lying on the moss-clad rocks of Newfoundland near St. George's Bay, as I listened to its continuous lay, so late as the middle of August, particularly about sunset. I was reminded of the pleasure I had formerly enjoyed on the banks of the clear Mohawk, under nearly similar circumstances, when lending an attentive ear to the mellow notes of another grosbeak. But, Reader, at Newfoundland I was still farther removed from my beloved family; the scenery around was thrice wilder and more magnificent. The stupendous dark granite rocks fronting the north, as if bidding defiance to the wintry tempests, brought a chillness to my heart, as I thought of the hardships endured by those intrepid travelers who, for the advancement of science, had braved the horrors of the polar winter. The glowing tints of the western sky, and the brightening stars twinkling over the waters of the great Gulf, riveted me to the spot, and the longer I gazed, the more I wished to remain; but darkness was suddenly produced by the advance of a mass of damp fog, the bird ceased its song, and all around seemed transformed into chaos. Silently I groped my way to the beach, and soon reached the *Ripley.*

Ornithological Biography, Volume IV

The Opossum *(Didelphis marsupialis)*

This singular animal is found more or less abundant in most parts of the Southern, Western, and Middle States of the Union. It is the *Didelphis virginiana* of Pennant, Harlan, and other authors who have given some accounts of its habits; but as none of them, so far as I know, have illustrated its propensity to dissimulate, and as I have had opportunities of observing its manners, I trust that a few particulars of its biography will prove amusing.

The opossum is fond of secluding itself during the day, although it by no means confines its predatory rangings to the night. Like many other quadrupeds which feed principally on flesh, it is also both frugivorous and herbivorous, and when very hard pressed by hunger, it seizes various kinds of insects and reptiles. Its gait, while traveling, and at a time when it supposes itself unobserved, is altogether ambling; in other words, it, like a young foal, moves the two legs of one side forward at once. The Newfoundland dog manifests a similar propensity. Having a constitution as hardy as that of the most northern animals, it stands the coldest weather, and does not hibernate, although its covering of fur and hair may be said to be comparatively scanty even during winter. The defect, however, seems to be compensated by a skin of considerable thickness, and a general subcutaneous layer of fat. Its movements are usually rather slow, and as it walks or ambles along, its curious prehensile tail is carried just above the ground, its rounded ears are directed forward, and at almost every step its pointed nose is applied to the objects beneath it, in order to discover what sort of creatures may have crossed its path.

Methinks I see one at this moment slowly and cautiously trudging over the melting snows by the side of an unfrequented pond, nosing as it goes for the fare its ravenous appetite prefers. Now it has come upon the fresh track of a grouse or hare, and it raises its snout and snuffs the keen air. At length it has decided on its course, and it speeds onward at the rate of a man's ordinary walk. It stops and seems at a loss in what direction to go, for the object of its pursuit has either taken a considerable leap or has cut backward before the opossum entered its track. It raises itself up, stands for a while on its hind feet, looks around, snuffs the air again, and then proceeds; but now, at the foot of a noble tree, it comes to a full stand. It walks round the base of the huge trunk, over the snow-covered roots, and among them finds an aperture which it at once enters. Several minutes elapse, when it reappears, dragging along a squirrel already deprived of life, with which in its mouth it begins to ascend the tree. Slowly it climbs. The first fork does not seem to suit it, for perhaps it thinks it might there be too openly exposed to the view of some wily foe; and so it proceeds, until it gains a cluster of branches intertwined with grapevines, and there composing itself, it twists its tail round one of the twigs, and with its sharp teeth demolishes the unlucky squirrel, which it holds all the while with its forepaws.

The pleasant days of spring have arrived, and the trees vigorously shoot forth their buds; but the opossum is almost bare, and seems nearly exhausted by hunger. It visits the margins of creeks, and is pleased to see the young frogs, which afford it a tolerable repast. Gradually the pokeberry and the nettle shoot up, and on their tender and juicy stems it gladly feeds. The mating calls of the wild turkey cock delight the ear of the cunning creature, for it well knows that it will soon hear the female and trace her to her nest, when it will suck the eggs with delight. Traveling through the woods, perhaps on the ground, perhaps aloft, from tree to tree, it hears a cock crow, and its heart swells as it remembers the savory food on which it regaled itself last summer in the neighboring farmyard. With great care, however, it advances, and at last conceals itself in the very henhouse.

Honest farmer! why did you kill so many crows last winter? ay and ravens too? Well, you have had your own way of it; but now hie to the village and procure a store of ammunition, clean your rusty gun, set your traps, and teach your lazy curs to watch the opossum. There it comes. The sun is scarcely down, but the appetite of the prowler is keen; hear the screams of one of your best chickens that has been seized by him! The cunning beast is off with it, and nothing can be done, unless you stand there to watch the fox or the owl, now exulting in the thought that you have killed their enemy and your own friend, the poor crow. That precious hen under which you last week placed a dozen eggs or so is now deprived of them. The opossum, notwithstanding her angry outcries and rufflings of feathers, has removed them one by one, and now look at the poor bird as she moves across your yard; if not mad, she is at least stupid, for she scratches here and there, calling to her chickens all the while. All this comes from your shooting crows. Had you been more merciful or more prudent, the opossum might have been kept within the woods, where it would have been satisfied with a squirrel, a young hare, the eggs of a turkey, or the grapes that so profusely adorn the boughs of our forest trees. But I talk to you in vain.

There cannot be a better exemplification of maternal tenderness than the female opossum. Just peep into that curious sack in which the young are concealed, each attached to a teat. The kind mother not only nourishes them with care, but preserves them from their enemies; she moves with them as the shark does with its progeny, and now, aloft on the tulip tree, she hides among the thick foliage. By the end of two months they begin to shift for themselves; each has been taught its particular lesson, and must now practice it.

But suppose the farmer has surprised an opossum in the act of killing one of his best fowls. His angry feelings urge him to kick the poor beast, which, conscious of its inability to resist, rolls off like a ball. The more the farmer rages, the more reluctant is the animal to manifest resentment; at last there it lies, not dead, but exhausted, its jaws open, its tongue extended, its eye dimmed; and there it would lie until the bottle fly should come to deposit its eggs, did not its tormentor at length walk off. "Surely," says he to himself, "the beast must be dead." But no, it is only "possuming," and no sooner has its enemy withdrawn than it gradually gets on its legs, and once more makes for the woods.

Once, while descending the Mississippi, in a sluggish flat-bottomed boat, expressly for the purpose of studying those objects of nature more nearly connected with my favorite pursuits, I chanced to meet with two well-grown opossums, and brought them alive to the "ark." The poor things were placed on the roof or deck, and were immediately assailed by the crew, when, following their natural instinct, they lay as if quite dead. An experiment was suggested, and both were thrown overboard. On striking the water, and for a few moments after, neither evinced the least disposition to move; but finding their situation desperate, they began to swim toward our uncouth rudder, which was formed of a long slender tree, extending from the middle of the boat thirty feet beyond its stern. They both got upon it, were taken up, and afterward let loose in their native woods.

In the year 1829, I was in a portion of lower Louisiana, where the opossum abounds at all seasons, and having been asked by the President and the Secretary of the Zoological Society of London, to forward live animals of this species to them, I offered a price a little above the common, and soon found myself plentifully supplied, twenty-five having been brought to me. I found them excessively voracious, and not less cowardly. They were put into a large box, with a great quantity of food, and conveyed to a steamer bound for New Orleans. Two days afterward, I went to that city, to see about sending them off to Europe; but, to my surprise, I found that the old males had destroyed the younger ones, and eaten off their heads, and that only sixteen remained alive. A separate box was purchased for each, and some time after they reached my friends, the Rathbones of Liverpool, who, with their usual attention, sent them off to London, where, on my return, I saw a good number of them in the Zoological Gardens.

This animal is fond of grapes, of which a species now bears its name. Persimmons are greedily eaten by it, and in severe weather I have observed it eating lichens. Fowls of every kind, and quadrupeds less powerful than itself, are also its habitual prey.

The flesh of the opossum resembles that of a young pig, and would perhaps be as highly prized, were it not for the prejudice generally entertained against it. Some "very particular" persons, to my knowledge, have pronounced it excellent eating. After cleaning its body, suspend it for a whole week in the frosty air, for it is not eaten in summer; then place it on a heap of hot wood embers; sprinkle it when cooked with gunpowder; and now tell me, Good Reader, does it not equal the famed canvasback duck? Should you visit any of our markets, you may see it there in company with the best game.

Ornithological Biography, Volume III

The Winter Wren (*Troglodytes troglodytes*)

The extent of the migratory movements of this diminutive bird is certainly the most remarkable fact connected with its history. At the approach of winter it leaves its northern retreats, perhaps in Labrador or Newfoundland, crosses the inlets of the Gulf of St. Lawrence on tiny concave wings, and betakes itself to warmer regions, where it remains until the beginning of spring. Playfully and with alacrity it performs the task, hopping from one stump or fallen log to another, flitting from twig to twig, from bush to bush, here and there flying a few yards; feeding, singing, and bustling on, as if quite careless as to time or distance. It has reached the shore of some broad stream, and here a person ignorant of its habits might suppose it would be stopped; but no, it spreads its wings, and glides over like a meteor.

I have found the winter wren in the lower parts of Louisiana, and in the Floridas, in December and January, but never saw one there after the end of the latter month. Their stay in those parts rarely exceeds three months; two more are employed in forming a nest and rearing their broods; and as they leave Labrador by the middle of August at the latest, they probably spend more than half of the year in traveling. It would be interesting to know whether those which breed along the Columbia River, near the Pacific Ocean, visit the shores of our Atlantic States. My friend Thomas Nuttall informs me that he occasionally saw the winter wren feeding its young in the woods along the northwest coast.

At Eastport, in Maine, when on my way to Labrador, I found this species in full song, and extremely abundant, although the air was chill and icicles hung from every rock, it being then the ninth of May. On the eleventh of June, I found it equally plentiful in the Magdalen Islands, and wondered how it could have made its way there, but was assured by the inhabitants that none were ever seen in winter. On the twentieth of July, I met with it at Labrador, and again asked myself, how it could possibly have reached those remote and rugged shores? Was it by following the course of the St. Lawrence, or by flying from one island to another across the Gulf? I have seen it in almost every State of the Union, but only twice found it breeding there, once near the Mohawk River in New York, and again in the Great Pine Swamp in Pennsylvania. It breeds abundantly in Maine, and probably in Massachusetts, but few spend the winter even in the latter State.

The song of the winter wren excels that of any other bird of its size with which I am acquainted. It is truly musical, full of cadence, energetic, and melodious; its very continuance is surprising, and dull indeed must be the ear that thrills not on hearing it. When emitted, as it often is, from the dark depths of the unwholesome swamp, it operates so powerfully on the mind that it by contrast inspires a feeling of wonder and delight, and on such occasions has usually impressed me with a sense of the goodness of the Almighty Creator, who has rendered every spot of earth in some way subservient to the welfare of His creatures.

Once when traveling through a portion of the most gloomy part of a thick and tangled wood in the Great Pine Forest, not far from Maunchunk in Pennsylvania, at a time when I was intent on guarding myself against the venomous reptiles which I expected to encounter, the sweet song of this wren came suddenly on my ear, and with so cheering an effect that I instantly lost all apprehension of danger and pressed forward through the rank briars and stiff laurels in pursuit of the bird, which I hoped was not far from its nest. But he, as if bent on puzzling me, rambled here and there

69. BROAD-WINGED HAWK *(Buteo platypterus).* The broad-wing is a hawk of the woods, where it hunts frogs, toads, rodents, small snakes, and insects. Its distinctive call is a long-drawn-out whistle that decreases in volume. It breeds from New Brunswick to Florida and west to Texas. In the autumn, broad-winged hawks gather in flocks and begin their flight to their winter home, many of them traveling as much as 4000 or 5000 miles to South America.

70–71. VARYING HARE *(Lepus americanus).* Brown in summer and white in winter, the pelt of the varying hare provides camouflage in both seasons of the year. Here Audubon has shown it in its summer pelage. The fleetest animal of the forest, it can leap as much as twelve feet at a bound and attain a speed of thirty miles an hour or more. It feeds on buds, bark, leaves, grass, and twigs in the swamps and forests of the north. It sometimes obtains moisture from dew in summer and snow in winter. In western mountains, the varying hare has been found living at elevations as great as 10,000 feet above sea level.

72–73. VARYING HARE *(Lepus americanus).* In its winter coat, in which Audubon depicts it here, the varying hare blends with its snowy surroundings. It is active mainly at night, spending its days resting motionless in its form. Usually these forest animals remain close to home. Rarely does one travel a mile from the place where it is born. The huge feet of the varying hare enable it to run over the surface of the snow. This ability has given it the common name of "snowshoe rabbit."

74. SONG SPARROW *(Melospiza melodia).* The loud and cheerful song of this sparrow is familiar throughout much of the United States. During breeding season, it is repeated on an average of half a dozen times a minute. The song sparrow prefers brushy cover such as is found in cut-over land and abandoned fields.

75. CHESTNUT-BACKED CHICKADEE *(Parus rufescens).* The dense evergreen forests of the West form the home of this chickadee. In western Washington and Oregon, and in the moist coniferous forests of the northern California coast, it is one of the commonest birds. Usually it hunts for its food, wandering about among the trees, in loose flocks.

76. PORCUPINE *(Erethizon dorsatum).* As many as 30,000 needle-sharp quills protect one of these arboreal animals. Its main food is bark but in spring it also eats tender new leaves and tree flowers. It is active the year around. When necessary, it swims well, the hollow quills giving it added buoyancy. Slow of movement, the porcupine is sure-footed when aloft in trees.

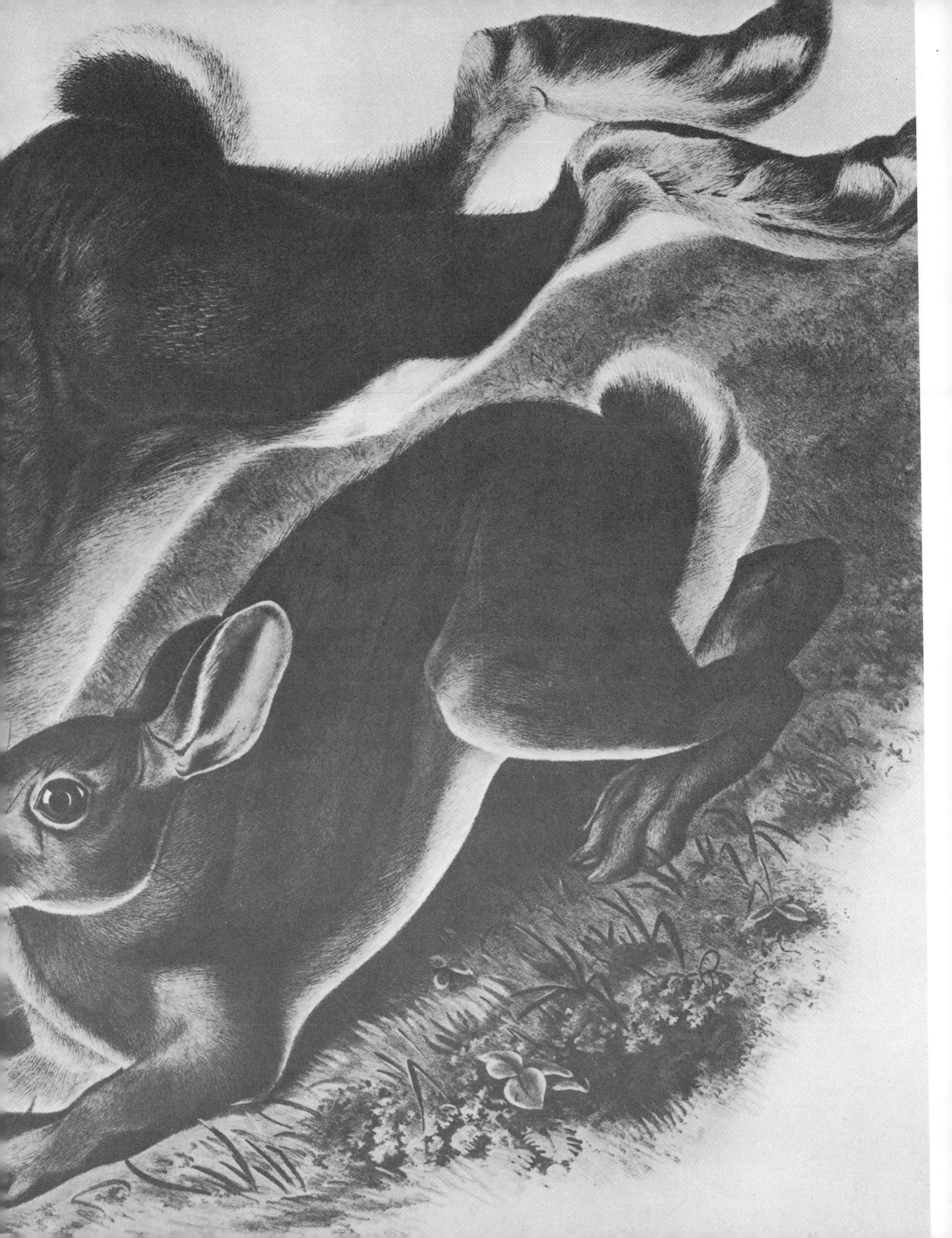

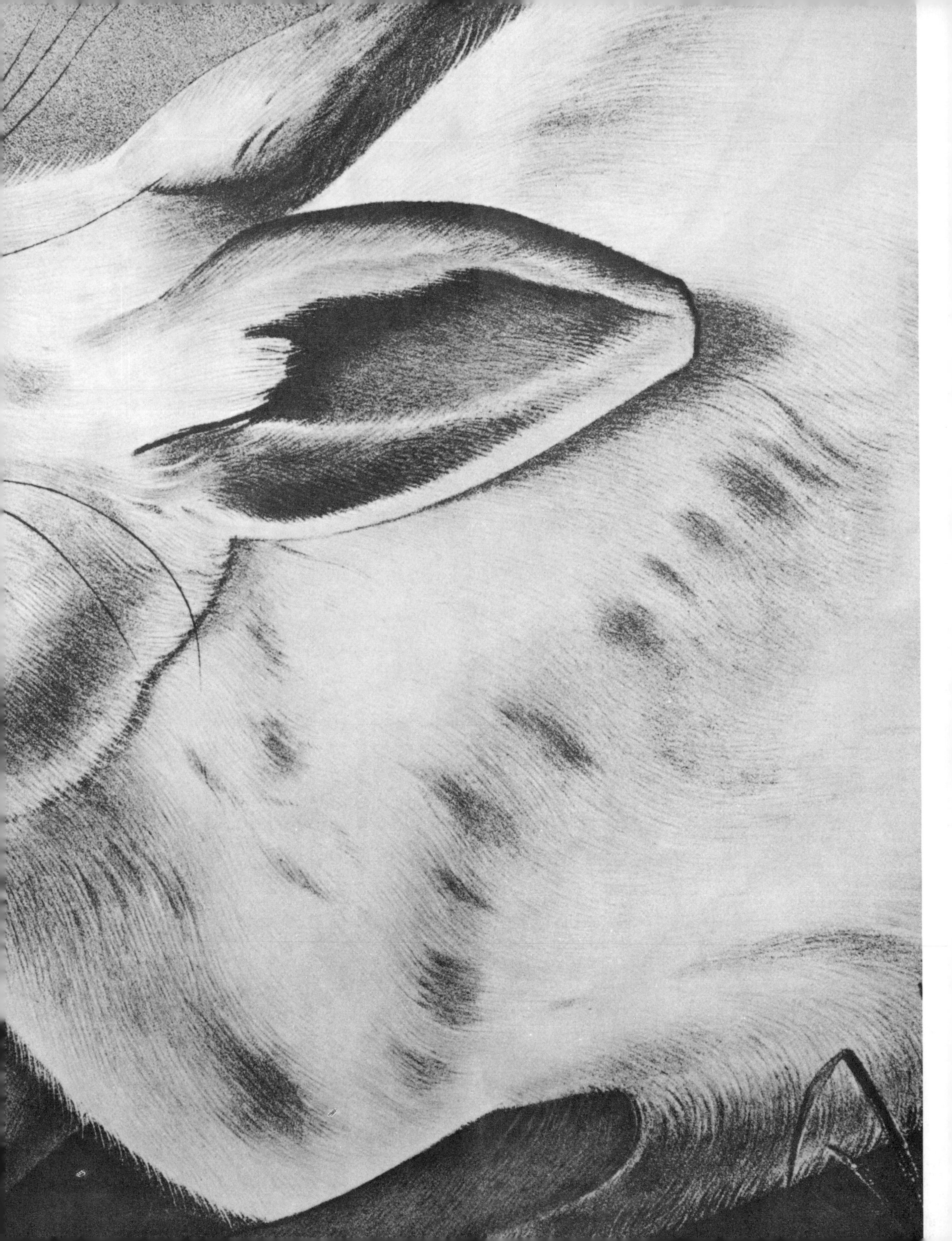

among the thickest bushes with uncommon cunning, now singing in one spot not far distant, and presently in another in a different direction. After much exertion and considerable fatigue, I at last saw it alight on the side of a large tree, close to the roots, and heard it warble a few notes, which I thought exceeded any it had previously uttered.

Suddenly another wren appeared by its side, but darted off in a moment, and the bird itself which I had followed disappeared. I soon reached the spot, without having for an instant removed my eyes from it, and observed a protuberance covered with moss and lichens, resembling those excrescences which are often seen in our forest trees, with this difference, that the aperture was perfectly rounded, clean, and quite smooth. I put a finger into it, and felt the pecking of a bird's bill, while a querulous cry was emitted. In a word, I had, the first time in my life, found the nest of our winter wren.

Having gently forced the tenant from his premises, I drew out the eggs with a sort of scoop which I formed. I expected to find them numerous, but there were not more than six, and the same number I afterward found in the only other nest of this species ever discovered by me. The little bird called upon its mate, and their united clamor induced me to determine upon leaving their treasures with them; but just as I was about going off, it struck me that I ought to take a description of the nest, as I might not again have such an opportunity. I hope, Reader, you will believe that when I resolved to sacrifice this nest, it was quite as much on your account as my own. Externally it measured seven inches in length, four and a half in breadth; the thickness of its walls, composed of moss and lichen, was nearly two inches; and thus it presented internally the appearance of a narrow bag, the wall, however, being reduced to a few lines where it was in contact with the bark of the tree. The lower half of the cavity was compactly lined with the fur of the American hare, and in the bottom or bed of the nest there lay over this about half a dozen of the large downy abdominal feathers of our common grouse, *Tetrao umbellus*. The eggs were of a delicate blush color, somewhat resembling the paler leaves of a partially decayed rose, and marked with dots of reddish brown, more numerous toward the larger end.

The nest which I found near the Mohawk was discovered by mere accident. One day in the beginning of June, and about noon, feeling fatigued, I sat down on a rock overhanging the water, where, while resting, I might have the pleasure of watching the motions of some fishes in sight. The damp of the place produced a sudden chillness, and caused me to sneeze aloud, when from beneath my feet there flew off a winter wren. The nest, which I soon found, was attached to the lower parts of the rock, and presented the same form and structure as that already described; but it was smaller, the eggs, six in number, contained young far advanced.

The motions of this interesting bird are performed with great rapidity and decision. While searching for food it hops, creeps, and leaps about from one spot to another, as if it derived pleasure from exercise. At each movement it bends its breast downward, so as almost to touch the object on which it stands, and by a sudden extension of its strong feet, aided by the action of its half-drooping concave wings, jerks itself forward, keeping its tail elevated all the while. Now through a hollow log it passes like a mouse, now it clings to the surface in various attitudes, suddenly disappears, but presently shows itself by your side; at times it chirrups in a querulous rolling tone, then emits single clear sharp chirps resembling the syllables *tshick, tshick,* and again remains silent for a time. It will now and then reach the upper branches of a small tree or a bush by hopping and leaping from twig to twig; in the course of this transit it will present its opposite sides to you a score of times; and when at length it has gained the summit, it will salute you with its delicate melody, and then dash headlong and be out of sight in a moment. This is almost constantly observed during the spring season, when more than ever its alertness is displayed. On all such occasions however, whilst in the act of singing, its tail is seen to be depressed. In winter, when it takes possession of the woodpile, close to the husbandman's dwelling, it will challenge the cat in querulous tones, and peeping out here and there, as it frisks in security, wear out Grimalkin's patience.

The food of the winter wren consists chiefly of spiders, caterpillars, and small moths, as well as larvae. Toward autumn it eats small juicy berries.

Ornithological Biography, Volume IV

The Crow (*Corvus brachyrhynchos*)

The crow is an extremely shy bird, having found familiarity with man no way to his advantage. He is also cunning—at least he is so called, because he takes care of himself and his brood. The state of anxiety, I may say of terror, in which he is constantly kept, would be enough to spoil the temper of any creature. Almost every person has an antipathy to him, and scarcely one of his race would be left in the land did he not employ all his ingenuity, and take advantage of all his experience, in counteracting the evil machinations of his enemies. I think I see him perched on the highest branch of a tree, watching every object around. He observes a man on horseback traveling toward him; he marks his movements in silence. No gun does the rider carry—no, that is clear; but perhaps he has pistols in the holsters of his saddle! —of that the crow is not quite sure, as he cannot either see them or "smell powder." He beats the points of his wings, jerks his tail once or twice, bows his head, and merrily sounds the joy which he feels at the moment. Another man he spies walking across the field toward his stand, but he has only a stick. Yonder comes a boy shouldering a musket loaded with large shot for the express purpose of killing crows! The bird immediately sounds an alarm; he repeats his cries, increasing their vehemence the nearer his enemy advances. All the crows within half a mile round are seen flying off, each repeating the well-known notes of the trusty watchman, who, just as the young gunner is about to take aim, betakes himself to flight. But alas, he chances unwittingly to pass over a sportsman whose dexterity is greater; the mischievous prowler aims his piece, fires—down toward the earth, broken-winged, falls the luckless bird in an instant. "It is nothing but a crow," quoth the sportsman, who proceeds in search of game, and leaves the poor creature to die in the most excruciating of agonies.

Wherever within the Union the laws encourage the destruction of this species, it is shot in great numbers for the sake of the premium offered for each crow's head. You will perhaps be surprised, Reader, when I tell you that in one single State, in the course of a season, forty thousand were shot, besides the multitudes of young birds killed in their nests. Must I add to this slaughter other thousands destroyed by the base artifice of laying poisoned grain along the fields to tempt these poor birds? Yes, I will tell you of all this too. The natural feelings of everyone who admires the bounty of nature in providing abundantly for the subsistence of all her creatures prompts me to do so. Like yourself, I admire all her wonderful works, and respect her wise intentions, even when her laws are beyond our limited comprehension.

The crow devours myriads of grubs every day of the year, that might lay waste to the farmer's fields; it destroyed quadrupeds innumerable, every one of which is an enemy to his poultry and his flocks. Why then should the farmer be so ungrateful, when he sees such services rendered to him by a providential friend, as to persecute that friend even to the death? Unless he plead ignorance, surely he ought to be found guilty at the bar of common sense. Were the soil of the United States, like that of some other countries, nearly exhausted by long continued cultivation, human selfishness in such a matter might be excused, and our people might look on our crows as other people look on theirs; but every individual in the land is aware of the superabundance of food that exists among us, and of which a portion may well be spared for the feathered beings that tend to enhance our pleasures by the sweetness of their song, the innocence of their lives, or their curious habits. Did not every American open his door and his heart to the wearied traveler, and afford him food, comfort, and rest, I would at once give up the argument; but when I know by experience the generosity of the people, I cannot but wish that they would reflect a little, and become more indulgent toward our poor, humble, harmless, and even most serviceable bird, the crow.

Ornithological Biography, Volume II

The Wood Thrush *(Hylocichla mustelina)*

Kind Reader, you now see before you my greatest favorite of the feathered tribes of our woods. To it I owe much. How often has it revived my drooping spirits, when I have listened to its wild notes in the forest, after passing a restless night in my slender shed, so feebly secured against the violence of the storm as to show me the futility of my best efforts to rekindle my little fire, whose uncertain and vacillating light had gradually died away under the destructive weight of the dense torrents of rain that seemed to involve the heavens and the earth in one mass of fearful murkiness, save when the red streaks of the flashing thunderbolt burst on the dazzled eye, and, glancing along the huge trunk of the stateliest and noblest tree in my immediate neighborhood, were instantly followed by an uproar of crackling, crashing, and deafening sounds, rolling their volumes in tumultuous eddies far and near, as if to silence the very breathings of the unformed thought!

How often, after such a night, when far from my dear home, and deprived of the presence of those nearest to my heart, wearied, hungry, drenched, and so lonely and desolate as almost to question myself why I was thus situated, when I have seen the fruits of my labors on the eve of being destroyed, as the water, collected into a stream, rushed through my little camp, and forced me to stand erect, shivering in a cold fit like that of a severe ague, when I have been obliged to wait with the patience of a martyr for the return of day, trying in vain to destroy the tormenting mosquitoes, silently counting over the years of my youth, doubting perhaps if ever again I should return to my home, and embrace my family!—how often, as the first glimpses of morning gleamed doubtfully amongst the dusky masses of the forest trees, has there come upon my ear, thrilling along the sensitive cords which connect that organ with the heart, the delightful music of this harbinger of day!—and how fervently, on such occasions, have I blessed the Being who formed the wood thrush, and placed it in those solitary forests, as if to console me amidst my privations, to cheer my depressed mind, and to make me feel, as I did, that never ought man to despair, whatever may be his situation, as he can never be certain that aid and deliverance are not at hand.

The wood thrush seldom commits a mistake after such a storm as I have attempted

81. WESTERN GRAY SQUIRREL *(Sciurus griseus).* The western and eastern gray squirrels have similar habits. The western is somewhat larger.

82–83. WOLVERINE *(Gulo luscus).* So fierce it may drive a bear or mountain lion from its kill, the wolverine is solitary and irritable. It ranges north to the Arctic ocean; is rarely encountered in the United States.

84. COMMON CROW *(Corvus brachyrhynchos).* Wary and curious, intelligent and mischievous, the crow is one of our best known birds.

85. RED-SHOULDERED HAWK *(Buteo lineatus).* For nesting and feeding, this hawk usually chooses swamps, river bottoms, wet woodlands.

86–87. FOX SQUIRREL *(Sciurus niger).* This handsome animal is the largest of our tree squirrels. Nuts comprise its staple food.

88–89. RED FOX *(Vulpes fulva).* Areas where there is a mixture of wood lots and farm lands are to the liking of the red fox. Its resourcefulness in eluding dogs and hunters is famous. Unlike the gray fox, which uses a winter den, the red fox sleeps in the open. Its food ranges from rabbits and mice to birds and berries.

90. SCARLET TANAGER *(Piranga olivacea).* Foraging mainly high in treetops, this brilliant songbird feeds on leaf-eating insects.

91. BALTIMORE ORIOLE *(Icterus galbula).* Along country roads and in villages and towns, this is a bird of elms and other shade trees. Its woven nest is hung from the tip of a limb.

92–93. BLUE-GRAY GNATCATCHER *(Polioptila caerulea).* Smaller than a house wren, lively and restless, the gnatcatcher searches leaves and twigs for insect fare. Its nest, like that of the hummingbird, is a small cup formed of plant down, spider silk, and lichens.

94. FIELD SPARROW *(Spizella pusilla).* The edges of woodland, as well as abandoned farms and old pastures, provide this sparrow with its habitat. Its singing perch is usually a bush top.

95. INDIGO BUNTING *(Passerina cyanea).* The food of the indigo bunting is chiefly insects in summer, weed seeds in autumn. Its singing perch oftenest is a telephone wire or treetop.

96–97. SCRUB JAY *(Aphelocoma coerulescens).* Dense scrub or brush is the favored home of this noisy jay. Mainly a western species, it is also found in scrub oak regions of Florida, where it is at least 1000 miles east of the range of its nearest relative in the West.

98. WHITE-BREASTED NUTHATCH *(Sitta carolinensis).* In searching for insects, their eggs, and pupae, these birds characteristically creep head first down treetrunks and limbs.

99. FOX SQUIRREL *(Sciurus niger).* In this view of the fox squirrel, Audubon depicts one of the animals with a nut. Each autumn, such food is harvested and hoarded by the squirrels.

100. MARTEN *(Martes americana).* With agile speed and grace, the weasel-like marten pursues and captures red squirrels in the treetops. In winter, it often tunnels in the snow.

1

2
3
1

2

to describe; for no sooner are its sweet notes heard than the heavens gradually clear, and the bright refracted light rises in gladdening rays from beneath the distant horizon, the effulgent beams increase in their intensity, and the great orb of day at length bursts on the sight. The gray vapor that floats along the ground is quickly dissipated, the world smiles at the happy change, and the woods are soon heard to echo the joyous thanks of their many songsters. At that moment, all fears vanish, giving place to an inspiring hope. The hunter prepares to leave his camp. He listens to the wood thrush, while he thinks of the course which he ought to pursue, and as the bird approaches to peep at him, and learn somewhat of his intentions, he raises his mind toward the Supreme Disposer of events. Seldom, indeed, have I heard the song of this thrush without feeling all that tranquillity of mind to which the secluded situation in which it delights is so favorable. The thickest and darkest woods always appear to please it best. The borders of murmuring streamlets, overshadowed by the dense foliage of the lofty trees growing on the gentle declivities, amidst which the sunbeams seldom penetrate, are its favorite resorts. There it is that the musical powers of this hermit of the woods must be heard to be fully appreciated and enjoyed.

The song of the wood thrush, although composed of but few notes, is so powerful, distinct, clear, and mellow, that it is impossible for any person to hear it without being struck by the effect which it produces on the mind. I do not know to what instrumental sounds I can compare these notes, for I really know none so melodious and harmonical. They gradually rise in strength, and then fall in gentle cadences, becoming at length so low as to be scarcely audible; like the emotions of the lover, who at one moment exults in the hope of possessing the object of his affections, and the next pauses in suspense, doubtful of the result of all his efforts to please.

Several of these birds seem to challenge each other from different portions of the forest, particularly toward evening, and at that time nearly all the other songsters being about to retire to rest, the notes of the wood thrush are doubly pleasing. One would think that each individual is anxious to excel his distant rival, and I have frequently thought that on such occasions their music is more than ordinarily effective, as it then exhibits a degree of skillful modulation quite beyond my power to describe. These concerts are continued for some time after sunset, and take place in the month of June, when the females are sitting.

Ornithological Biography, Volume I

2. *Marsh and Swamp*

Introduction

During the century in which Audubon lived in America, the marshes and swamps were reduced by almost 100,000,000 acres, by more than 150,000 square miles, by more than twice the area of all the New England states combined. Ditching and draining followed in the wake of cutting the forests. In that one century, the area of wetlands which disappeared totaled more than that of all the marshes and swamps remaining in the country today.

When, in the latter part of the nineteenth century, a maze of canals and ditches drained away the water from such areas as the great Kankakee Marsh of northern Illinois and Indiana, a realm of wildlife that had been famous from Indian times for its multitudinous waterfowl and its vast number of aquatic furbearers became only a memory. Each wetland that has been drained has wiped out the habitat of many creatures. Such birds as rails and bitterns and gallinules can live nowhere else.

Only in comparatively recent decades has there been a swing toward a more widespread understanding of the value and beauty of undrained wetlands. The marsh and the swamp have been among the last features of the landscape to be appreciated. But more and more the teeming life they embrace has attracted attention; more and more they have been recognized as a feature of prime importance in the conservation movement. The restoration of such marshlands as those at the Lower Souris refuge, in North Dakota, the Bear River refuge, in Utah, and the Lower Klamath refuge, of the California-Oregon border, have been large-scale attempts to restore conditions of the past. Down the Mississippi, and along other river flyways, chains of swampland sanctuaries now offer refuge for hard-pressed migrants, while marshy tracts along the coasts have been set aside to provide food and protection for the moving or overwintering waterfowl.

The most extensive areas of wetlands remaining today are found in the South. They are the marshes and swamps Audubon knew in Florida and Louisiana. Even today, the wetlands of Florida cover something like 40 per cent of the state, those of Louisiana about 30 per cent. How vast were the number of ducks and geese that overwintered in Louisiana, near the mouth of the Mississippi, in Audubon's time can be gauged by the fact that during one season, three-quarters of a century later—the winter of 1909–1910—5,719,214 waterfowl were killed in the state.

West Feliciana, so often mentioned in the *Ornithological Biography,* the scene of Lucy's private school and many of Audubon's studies of birds, is the parish in Louisiana that lies farthest north on the eastern bank of the Mississippi River. The boundary of the two states, Louisiana and Mississippi, forms its northern edge.

The Carolina parakeet—so numerous Audubon used their bodies in his experiments with the sense of smell of turkey vultures—is gone forever from America's swampy bottomlands. So, presumably, is the largest of our woodpeckers, the spectacular ivory-bill. The parakeet became extinct early; the ivory-billed woodpecker lingered, becoming fewer and fewer down into recent years. Audubon's detailed accounts of these two birds take on added value, picturing them, as they do, in the time of their abundance.

As the Carolina parakeet was America's only representative of the parrot family, so the wood ibis is our only representative of the stork family. This bird, too, has become reduced in numbers, causing some concern in recent times. The swallow-tailed kite that ranged widely a century ago, nesting as far north as Minnesota, is now confined largely to lower Florida and a few swamps along the Gulf Coast. Incidentally, the "mosquito hawks," that Audubon tells of swallow-tailed kites capturing in the air, were dragonflies. The "hagberry" tree was the hackberry or sugarberry, *Celtis occidentalis.* In the rich bottomlands of the Ohio River basin this tree sometimes reaches a height of more than one hundred feet and a diameter of four or five feet. Its fruit is a source of food for more than thirty species of birds.

The Ivory-Billed Woodpecker (*Campephilus principalis*)

I have always imagined that in the plumage of the beautiful ivory-billed woodpecker there is something very closely allied to the style of coloring of the great Vandyke. The broad extent of its dark glossy body and tail, the large and well-defined white markings of its wings, neck, and bill, relieved by the rich carmine of the pendent crest of the male, and the brilliant yellow of its eye, have never failed to remind me of some of the boldest and noblest productions of that inimitable artist's pencil. So strongly indeed have these thoughts become engrafted in my mind, as I gradually obtained a more intimate acquaintance with the ivory-billed woodpecker, that whenever I have observed one of these birds flying from one tree to another, I have mentally exclaimed, "There goes a Vandyke!" This notion may seem strange, perhaps ludicrous, to you, Good Reader, but I relate it as a fact and whether or not it may be found in accordance with your own ideas, after you have inspected the plate in which is represented this great chieftain of the woodpecker tribe, is perhaps of little consequence.

The ivory-billed woodpecker confines its rambles to a comparatively very small portion of the United States, it never having been observed in the Middle States within the memory of any person now living there. In fact, in no portion of these districts does the nature of the woods appear suitable to its remarkable habits.

Descending the Ohio, we meet with this splendid bird for the first time near the confluence of that beautiful river and the Mississippi; after which, following the windings of the latter, either downward toward the sea, or upward in the direction of the Missouri, we frequently observe it. On the Atlantic Coast, North Carolina may be taken as the limit of its distribution, although now and then an individual of the species may be accidentally seen in Maryland. To the westward of the Mississippi, it is found in all the dense forests bordering the streams which empty their waters into that majestic river, from the very declivities of the Rocky Mountains. The lower parts of the Carolinas, Georgia, Alabama, Louisiana, and Mississippi are, however, the most favorite resorts of this bird, and in those States it constantly resides, breeds, and passes a life of peaceful enjoyment, finding a profusion of food in all the deep, dark and gloomy swamps dispersed throughout them.

I wish it were in my power to present to your mind's eye the favorite resort of the ivory-billed woodpecker. Would that I could describe the extent of those deep morasses, overshadowed by millions of gigantic dark cypresses, spreading their sturdy moss-covered branches, as if to admonish intruding man to pause and reflect on the many difficulties which he must encounter, should he persist in venturing farther into their almost inaccessible recesses, extending for miles before him, where he should be interrupted by huge projecting branches, here and there the massy trunk of a fallen and decaying tree, and thousands of creeping and twining plants of numberless species! Would that I could represent to you the dangerous nature of the ground, its oozing, spongy, and miry disposition, although covered with a beautiful but treacherous carpeting, composed of the richest mosses, flags, and water lilies, no sooner receiving the pressure of the foot than it yields and endangers the very life of the adventurer, whilst here and there, as he approaches an opening that proves merely a lake of black muddy water, his ear is assailed by the dismal croaking of frogs, the hissing of serpents, or the bellowing of alligators! Would that I could give you an idea of the sultry pestiferous atmosphere that nearly suffocates the intruder during the meridian heat of our dog days, in those gloomy and horrible swamps! But the attempt to picture these scenes would be vain. Nothing short of ocular demonstration can impress any adequate idea of them.

How often have I thought of the difference of the tasks imposed on different minds when, traveling in countries far distant from those where birds of this species and others as difficult to be procured are now and then offered for sale in the form of dried skins, I have heard the amateur or closet-naturalist express his astonishment that half a crown was asked by the person who had perhaps followed the bird when alive over miles of such swamps, and after procuring it, had prepared its skin in the best manner, and carried it to a market thousands of miles distant from the spot where he had obtained it. I must say that it has at least grieved me as much as when I have heard some idle fop complain of the poverty of the Gallery of the Louvre, where he had paid nothing, or when I have listened to the same infatuated idler lamenting the loss of his shilling, as he sauntered through the Exhibition Rooms of the Royal Academy of London, or any equally valuable repository of art. But let us return to the biography of the famed ivory-billed woodpecker.

The flight of this bird is graceful in the extreme, although seldom prolonged to more than a few hundred yards at a time, unless when it has to cross a large river, which it does in deep undulations, opening its wings at first to their full extent, and nearly closing them to renew the propelling impulse. The transit from one tree to another, even should the distance be as much as a hundred yards, is performed in a single sweep, and the bird appears as if merely swinging itself from the top of the one tree to that of the other, forming an elegantly curved line. At this moment all the beauty of the plumage is exhibited and strikes the beholder with pleasure.

It never utters any sound whilst on the wing, unless during the love season; but at all other times, no sooner has this bird alighted than its remarkable voice is heard, at almost every leap which it makes, whilst ascending against the upper parts of the trunk of a tree, or its highest branches. Its notes are clear, loud, and yet rather plaintive. They are heard at a considerable distance, perhaps half a mile, and resemble the false high note of a clarionet. They are usually repeated three times in succession, and may be represented by the monosyllable *pait, pait, pait.* These are heard so frequently as to induce me to say that the bird spends few minutes of the day without uttering them, and this circumstance leads to its destruction, which is aimed at, not because (as is supposed by some) this species is a destroyer of trees, but more because it is a beautiful bird, and its rich scalp attached to the upper mandible forms an ornament for the war dress of most of our Indians, or for the shot pouch of our squatters and hunters, by all of whom the bird is shot merely for that decorative purpose.

Travelers of all nations are also fond of possessing the upper part of the head and the bill of the male, and I have frequently remarked that on a steamboat's reaching what we call a ''wooding place,'' the *strangers* were very apt to pay a quarter of a dollar for two or three heads of this woodpecker. I have seen entire belts of Indian chiefs closely ornamented with the tufts and bills of this species, and have observed that a great value is frequently put upon them.

The ivory-billed woodpecker nests earlier in spring than any other species of its tribe. I have observed it boring a hole for that purpose in the beginning of March. The hole is, I believe, always made in the trunk of a live tree, generally an ash or a hagberry, and is at a great height. The birds pay great regard to the particular situation of the tree, and the inclination of its trunk; first, because they prefer retirement, and again, because they are anxious to secure the aperture against the access of water during beating rains. To prevent such a calamity, the hole is generally dug immediately under the junction of a large branch with the trunk. It is first bored horizontally for a few inches, then directly downward, and not in a spiral manner, as some people have imagined.

According to circumstances, this cavity is more or less deep, being sometimes not more than ten inches whilst at other times it reaches nearly three feet downward into the core of the tree. I have been led to think that these differences result from the more or less immediate necessity under which the female may be of depositing her eggs, and again have thought that the older the woodpecker is, the deeper does it make its hole. The average diameter of the different nests which I have examined was about seven inches within, although the entrance, which is perfectly round, is only just large enough to admit the bird.

Both birds work most assiduously at this excavation, one waiting outside to encourage the other, whilst it is engaged in digging, and when the latter is fatigued, taking its place. I have approached trees whilst these woodpeckers were thus busily employed in forming their nest, and by resting my head against the bark, could easily distinguish every blow given by the bird. I observed that in two instances, when the woodpeckers saw me thus at the foot of the tree in which they were digging their nest, they abandoned it forever. For the first brood there are generally six eggs. They are deposited on a few chips at the bottom of the hole and are of a pure white color. The young are seen creeping out of the hole about a fortnight before they venture to fly to any other tree. The second brood makes its appearance about the fifteenth of August.

In Kentucky and Indiana, the ivory-bills seldom raise more than one brood in the season. The young are at first of the color of the female, only that they want the crest, which, however, grows rapidly, and toward autumn, particularly in birds of the first brood, is nearly equal to that of the mother. The males have then a slight line of red on the head and do not attain their richness of plumage until spring, or their full size until the second year. Indeed, even then, a difference is easily observed between them and individuals which are much older.

The food of this species consists principally of beetles, larvae, and large grubs. No sooner, however, are the grapes of our forests ripe than they are eaten by the ivory-billed woodpecker with great avidity. I have seen this bird hang by its claws to the vines, in the position so often assumed by a titmouse, and, reaching downward, help itself to a bunch of grapes with much apparent pleasure. Persimmons are also sought for by them as soon as the fruit becomes quite mellow, as are hagberries.

The ivory-bill is never seen attacking the corn, or the fruit of the orchards, although it is sometimes observed working upon and chipping off the bark from the belted trees of the newly cleared plantations. It seldom comes near the ground, but prefers at all times the tops of the tallest trees. Should it, however, discover the half-standing broken shaft of a large dead and rotten tree, it attacks it in such a manner as nearly to demolish it in the course of a few days. I have seen the remains of some of these ancient monarchs of our forest so excavated, and that so singularly, that the tottering fragments of the trunk appeared to be merely supported by the great pile of chips by which its base was surrounded.

The strength of this woodpecker is such that I have seen it detach pieces of bark seven or eight inches in length at a single blow of its powerful bill, and by beginning at the top branch of a dead tree, tear off the bark, to an extent of twenty or thirty feet, in the course of a few hours, leaping downward with its body in an upward position, tossing its head to the right and left, or leaning it against the bark to ascertain the precise spot where the grubs were concealed, and immediately after renewing its blows with fresh vigor, all the while sounding its loud notes, as if highly delighted.

This species generally moves in pairs after the young have left their parents. The female is always the most clamorous and the least shy. Their mutual attachment is, I believe, continued through life. Excepting when digging a hole for the reception of their eggs, these birds seldom, if ever, attack living trees, for any other purpose than that of procuring food, in doing which they destroy the insects that would otherwise prove injurious to the trees.

I have frequently observed the male and female retire to rest for the night into the same hole in which they had long before reared their young. This generally happens a short time after sunset.

When wounded and brought to the ground, the ivory-bill immediately makes for the nearest tree and ascends it with great rapidity and perseverance until it reaches the top branches, when it squats and hides, generally with great effect. Whilst ascending, it moves spirally round the tree, utters its loud *pait, pait, pait* at almost every hop, but becomes silent the moment it reaches a place where it conceives itself secure. They sometimes cling to the bark with their claws so firmly as to remain clamped to the spot for several hours after death. When taken by the hand, which is rather a hazardous undertaking, they strike with great violence and inflict very severe wounds with their bills as well as claws, which are extremely sharp and strong. On such occasions, this bird utters a mournful and very piteous cry.

Ornithological Biography, Volume I

The Cougar *(Felis concolor)*

There is an extensive swamp in the section of the State of Mississippi which lies

partly in the Choctaw Territory. It commences at the borders of the Mississippi, at no great distance from a Chickasaw village situated near the mouth of a creek known by the name of Vanconnah, and partly inundated by the swellings of several large bayous, the principal of which, crossing the swamp in its whole extent, discharges its waters not far from the mouth of the Yazoo River. This famous bayou is called False River. The swamp of which I am speaking follows the windings of the Yazoo until the latter branches off to the northeast, and at this point forms the stream named Cold Water River, below which the Yazoo receives the draining of another bayou inclining toward the northwest and intersecting that known by the name of False River at a short distance from the place where the latter receives the waters of the Mississippi. This tedious account of the situation of the swamp is given with the view of pointing it out to all students of nature who may happen to go that way, and whom I would earnestly urge to visit its interior, as it abounds in rare and interesting productions—birds, quadrupeds, and reptiles, as well as molluscous animals, many of which, I am persuaded, have never been described.

In the course of one of my rambles, I chanced to meet with a squatter's cabin on the banks of the Cold Water River. In the owner of this hut, like most of those adventurous settlers in the uncultivated tracts of our frontier districts, I found a person well versed in the chase, and acquainted with the habits of some of the larger species of quadrupeds and birds. As he who is desirous of instruction ought not to disdain listening to anyone who has knowledge to communicate, however humble may be his lot, or however limited his talents, I entered the squatter's cabin, and immediately opened a conversation with him respecting the situation of the swamp and its natural productions. He told me he thought it the very place I ought to visit, spoke of the game which it contained, and pointed to some bear and deer skins, adding that the individuals to which they had belonged formed but a small portion of the number of those animals which he had shot within it. My heart swelled with delight, and on asking if he would accompany me through the great morass and allow me to become an inmate of his humble but hospitable mansion, I was gratified to find that he cordially assented to all my proposals. So I immediately unstrapped my drawing materials, laid up my gun, and sat down to partake of the homely but wholesome fare intended for the supper of the squatter, his wife, and his two sons.

The quietness of the evening seemed in perfect accordance with the gentle demeanor of the family. The wife and children, I more than once thought, seemed to look upon me as a strange sort of person, going about, as I told them I was, in search of birds and plants; and were I here to relate the many questions which they put to me in return for those I addressed to them, the catalogue would occupy several pages. The husband, a native of Connecticut, had heard of the existence of such men as myself, both in our own country and abroad, and seemed greatly pleased to have me under his roof. Supper over, I asked my kind host what had induced him to remove to this wild and solitary spot. "The people are growing too numerous now to thrive in New England," was his answer. I thought of the state of some parts of Europe, and calculating the denseness of their population compared with that of New England, exclaimed to myself, "How much more difficult must it be for men to thrive in those populous countries!" The conversation then changed, and the squatter, his sons, and myself, spoke of hunting and fishing until at length, tired, we laid ourselves down on pallets of bearskins, and reposed in peace on the floor of the only apartment of which the hut consisted.

Day dawned, and the squatter's call to his hogs, which, being almost in a wild state, were suffered to seek the greater portion of their food in the woods, awakened me. Being ready dressed I was not long in joining him. The hogs and their young came grunting at the well-known call of their owner, who threw them a few ears of corn, and counted them, but told me that for some weeks their number had been greatly diminished by the ravages committed upon them by a large panther, by which name the cougar is designated in America, and that the ravenous animal did not content himself with the flesh of his pigs, but now and then carried off one of his calves, notwithstanding the many attempts he had made to shoot it. The "painter," as he sometimes called it, had on several occasions robbed him of a dead deer; and to these exploits the squatter added several remarkable feats of audacity which it had performed, to give me an idea of the formidable character of the beast. Delighted by his description, I offered to assist him in destroying the enemy, at which he was highly pleased, but assured me that unless some of his neighbors should join us with their

NOTES ON THE PLATES

109. HORNED GREBE *(Podiceps auritus)*. The large feet of this water bird drive it forward during its long dives in search of food. After spending the summer at inland lakes, ponds, or sloughs, it usually moves to salt water along the coast when winter approaches. It consumes some vegetable matter in addition to insects, shrimp, tadpoles, and fish. Like other grebes, it has the curious habit of eating its feathers.

110–111. BOAT-TAILED GRACKLE *(Cassidix mexicanus)*. From New Jersey to Texas, this grackle, with its disproportionately huge tail, is found associated with tidal pools, mudflats, coastal swamps, and marshes. Breeding is done in colonies. In addition to feeding on crabs, shrimp, and other aquatic animals, it eats grain and follows plows for grubs.

112. BARRED OWL *(Strix varia)*. Mice form the bulk of the barred owl's diet. In addition, it eats other mammals, birds, frogs, fish, and insects. Deep woods and swamps are the chosen home of this owl, although much of its hunting is done over adjacent open country. Its call consists of a series of eight hoots.

dogs and his own, the attempt would prove fruitless. Soon after, mounting a horse, he went off to his neighbors, several of whom lived at a distance of some miles, and appointed a day of meeting.

The hunters, accordingly, made their appearance one fine morning at the door of the cabin, just as the sun was emerging from beneath the horizon. They were five in number, and fully equipped for the chase, being mounted on horses which in some parts of Europe might appear sorry nags, but which in strength, speed, and bottom are better fitted for pursuing a cougar or a bear through woods and morasses than any in that country. A pack of large, ugly curs were already engaged in making acquaintance with those of the squatter. He and myself mounted his two best horses, whilst his sons were bestriding others of inferior quality.

Few words were uttered by the party until we had reached the edge of the swamp, where it was agreed that all should disperse and seek for the fresh track of the painter, it being previously settled that the discoverer should blow his horn, and remain on the spot, until the rest should join him. In less than an hour, the sound of the horn was clearly heard, and, sticking close to the squatter, off we went through the thick woods, guided only by the now and then repeated call of the distant huntsmen. We soon reached the spot, and in a short time the rest of the party came up. The best dog was sent forward to track the cougar, and in a few moments the whole pack were observed diligently trailing, and bearing in their course for the interior of the swamp. The rifles were immediately put in trim, and the party followed the dogs, at separate distances, but in sight of each other, determined to shoot at no other game than the panther.

The dogs soon began to mouth, and suddenly quickened their pace. My companion concluded that the beast was on the ground, and putting our horses to a gentle gallop, we followed the curs, guided by their voices. The noise of the dogs increased, when all of a sudden their mode of barking became altered, and the squatter, urging me to push on, told me that the beast was *treed,* by which he meant that it had got upon some low branch of a large tree to rest for a few moments, and that should we not succeed in shooting him when thus situated, we might expect a long chase of it. As we approached the spot, we all by degrees united into a body, but on seeing the dogs at the foot of a large tree, separated again, and galloped off to surround it.

Each hunter now moved with caution, holding his gun ready, and allowing the bridle to dangle on the neck of his horse, as it advanced slowly toward the dogs. A shot from one of the party was heard, on which the cougar was seen to leap to the ground, and bound off with such velocity as to show that he was very unwilling to stand our fire longer. The dogs set off in pursuit with great eagerness and a deafening cry. The hunter who had fired came up and said that his ball had hit the monster, and had probably broken one of his forelegs near the shoulder, the only place at which he could aim. A slight trail of blood was discovered on the ground, but the curs proceeded at such a rate that we merely noticed this, and put spurs to our horses, which galloped on toward the center of the swamp. One bayou was crossed, then another still larger and more muddy; but the dogs were brushing forward, and as the horses began to pant at a furious rate, we judged it expedient to leave them and advance on foot. These determined hunters knew that the cougar, being wounded, would shortly ascend another tree, where in all probability he would remain for a considerable time, and that it would be easy to follow the track of the dogs. We dismounted, took off the saddles and bridles, set the bells attached to the horses' necks at liberty to jingle, hoppled the animals, and left them to shift for themselves.

Now, Kind Reader, follow the group marching through the swamp, crossing muddy pools, and making the best of their way over fallen trees and amongst the tangled rushes that now and then covered acres of ground. If you are a hunter yourself, all this will appear nothing to you; but if crowded assemblies of "beauty and fashion," or the quiet enjoyment of your "pleasure grounds" alone delight you, I must mend my pen before I attempt to give you an idea of the pleasure felt on such an expedition.

After marching for a couple of hours, we again heard the dogs. Each of us pressed forward, elated at the thought of terminating the career of the cougar. Some of the dogs were heard whining, although the greater number barked vehemently. We felt assured that the cougar was treed, and that he would rest for some time to recover from his fatigue. As we came up to the dogs, we discovered the ferocious animal lying across a large branch, close to trunk of a cottonwood tree. His broad breast lay toward us; his eyes were at one time bent on us and again on the dogs beneath and around him; one of his forelegs hung loosely by his side, and he lay crouched, with his ears lowered close to his head, as if he thought he might remain undiscovered. Three balls were fired at him, at a given signal, on which he sprang a few feet from the branch, and tumbled headlong to the ground. Attacked on all sides by the enraged curs, the infuriated cougar fought with desperate valor; but the squatter, advancing in front of the party, and almost in the midst of the dogs, shot him immediately behind and beneath the left shoulder. The cougar writhed for a moment in agony, and in another lay dead.

The sun was now sinking in the west. Two of the hunters separated from the rest to procure venison, whilst the squatter's sons were ordered to make the best of their way home, to be ready to feed the hogs in the morning. The rest of the party agreed to camp on the spot. The cougar was despoiled of its skin, and its carcass left to the hungry dogs. Whilst engaged in preparing our camp, we heard the report of a gun, and soon after one of our hunters returned with a small deer. A fire was lighted, and each hunter displayed his pone of bread, along with a flask of whisky. The deer was skinned in a trice, and slices placed on sticks before the fire. These materials afforded us an excellent meal, and as the night grew darker, stories and songs went round, until my companions, fatigued, laid themselves down, close under the smoke of the fire, and soon fell asleep.

I walked for some minutes round the camp to contemplate the beauties of that nature from which I have certainly derived my greatest pleasures. I thought of the occurrences of the day, and glancing my eye around, remarked the singular effects produced by the phosphorescent qualities of the large decayed trunks which lay in all directions around me. How easy, I thought, would it be for the confused and agitated mind of a person bewildered in a swamp like this, to imagine in each of these luminous masses some wondrous and fearful being, the very sight of which might make the hair stand erect on his head. The thought of being myself placed in such a predicament burst over my mind, and I hastened to join my companions, beside whom I laid me down and slept, assured that no enemy could approach us without first rousing the dogs, which were growling in fierce dispute over the remains of the cougar.

At daybreak we left our camp, the squatter bearing on his shoulder the skin of the late destroyer of his stock, and retraced our steps until we found our horses, which had not strayed far from the place where we had left them. These we soon saddled, and jogging along in a direct course guided by the sun, congratulating each other on the destruction of so formidable a neighbor as the panther had been, we soon arrived at my host's cabin. The five neighbors partook of such refreshment as the house could afford, and dispersing, returned to their homes, leaving me to follow my favorite pursuits.

Ornithological Biography, Volume I

The Swallow-Tailed Kite *(Elanoides forficatus)*

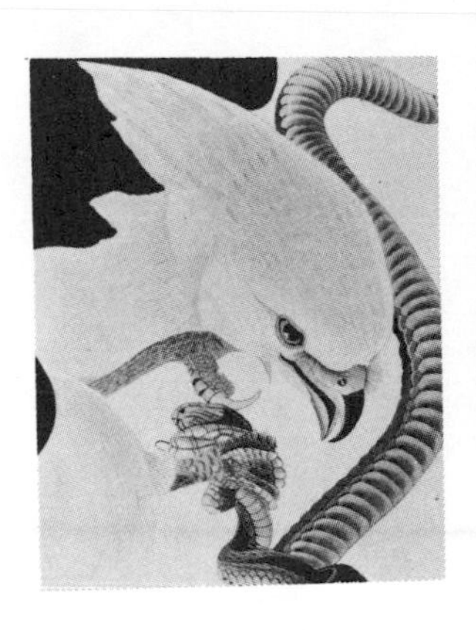

The flight of this elegant species of hawk is singularly beautiful and protracted. It moves through the air with such ease and grace that it is impossible for any individual who takes the slightest pleasure in observing the manners of birds not to be delighted by the sight of it whilst on wing. Gliding along in easy flappings, it rises in wide circles to an immense height, inclining in various ways its deeply forked tail to assist the direction of its course, dives with the rapidity of lightning, and, suddenly checking itself, reascends, soars away, and is soon out of sight.

At other times a flock of these birds, amounting to fifteen or twenty individuals, is seen hovering around the trees. They dive in rapid succession amongst the branches, glancing along the trunks, and seizing in their course the insects and small lizards of which they are in quest. Their motions are astonishingly rapid, and the deep curves which they describe, their sudden doublings and crossings, and the extreme ease with which they seem to cleave the air, excite the admiration of him who views them while thus employed in searching for food.

A solitary individual of this species has once or twice been seen in Pennsylvania. Farther to the eastward, the swallowtailed hawk has never, I believe, been observed. Traveling southward, along the Atlantic Coast, we find it in Virginia, although in very small numbers. Beyond that State it becomes more abundant. Near the Falls of the Ohio, a pair had a nest and reared four young ones in 1820. In the lower parts of Kentucky it begins to become numerous; but in the States farther to the south, and particularly in parts near the sea, it is abundant. In the large prairies of the Attacapas and Oppellousas, it is extremely common.

In the States of Louisiana and Mississippi, where the birds are abundant, they arrive in large companies in the beginning of April, and are heard uttering a sharp plaintive note. At this period I generally remarked that they came from the westward, and have counted upward of a hundred in the space of an hour, passing over me in a direct easterly course. At that season, and in the beginning of September, when they all retire from the United States, they are easily approached when they have alighted, being then apparently fatigued, and busily engaged in preparing themselves for continuing their journey, by dressing and oiling their feathers. At all other times, however, it is extremely difficult to get near them, as they are generally on wing through the day, and at night rest on the highest pines and cypresses, bordering the river bluffs, the lakes, or the swamps of that district of country.

They always feed on the wing. In calm and warm weather, they soar to an immense height, pursuing the large insects called "mosquito hawks," and performing the most singular evolutions that can be conceived, using their tails with an elegance of motion peculiar to themselves. Their principal food, however, is large grasshoppers, grass caterpillars, small snakes, lizards, and frogs. They sweep close over the fields, sometimes seeming to alight for a moment to secure a snake, and holding it fast by the neck, carry it off, and devour it in the air. When searching for grasshoppers and caterpillars, it is not difficult to approach them under cover of a fence or tree. When one of them is killed and falls to the ground, the whole flock comes over the dead bird, as if intent upon carrying it off. An excellent opportunity is thus afforded of shooting as many as may be wanted, and I have killed several of these hawks in this manner, firing as fast as I could load my gun.

The fork-tailed hawks are also very fond of frequenting the creeks, which, in that country, are much encumbered with drifted logs and accumulations of sand, in order to pick up some of the numerous water snakes which lie basking in the sun. At other times, they dash along the trunks of trees and snap off the pupae of the locust, or that insect itself. Although when on wing they move with a grace and ease which it is impossible to describe, yet on the ground they are scarcely able to walk.

I kept for several days one which had been slightly wounded in the wing. It refused to eat, kept the feathers of the head and rump constantly erect, and vomited several times part of the contents of its stomach. It never threw itself on its back, nor attempted to strike with its talons, unless when taken up by the tip of the wing. It died from inanition, as it constantly refused the food placed before it in profusion, and instantly vomited what had been thrust down its throat.

The swallow-tailed hawk pairs immediately after its arrival in the Southern States, and as its courtships take place on the wing, its motions are then more beautiful than ever. The nest is usually placed on the top branches of the tallest oak or pine tree, situated on the margin of a stream or pond. It resembles that of the common crow externally, being formed of dry sticks, intermixed with Spanish moss, and is lined with coarse grasses and a few feathers. The eggs are from four to six, of a greenish-white color, with a few irregular blotches of dark brown at the larger end.

The male and female sit alternately, the one feeding the other. The young are at first covered with buff-colored down. Their next covering exhibits the pure white and black of the old birds, but without any of the glossy purplish tints of the latter. The tail, which at first is but slightly forked, becomes more so in a few weeks, and at the approach of autumn exhibits little difference from that of the adult birds. The plumage is completed the first spring. Only one brood is raised in the season. The species leaves the United States in the beginning of September, moving off in flocks, which are formed immediately after the breeding season is over.

Ornithological Biography, Volume I

The Clapper Rail *(Rallus longirostris)*

During ebb, the clapper rail advances toward the edge of the waters as they recede, and searches, either among the grasses, or along the deep furrows made by the ebb and flow of the tides, for its food, which consists principally of small crabs, a species of saltwater snail attached to the rushes, the fry of fishes, aquatic insects, and plants. When the tide flows, they gradually return, and at high water they resort to the banks, where they remain concealed until the waters begin to retreat. This species is by no means exclusively nocturnal, for it moves about in search of food during the whole of the day, in this respect resembling the gallinules. Their courage is now and then brought to the test by the sudden approach of some of their winged enemies, such as a hawk or an owl, especially the marsh hawk, which is often attacked by them while sailing low over the grass in which they are commonly concealed.

On such occasions, the rail rises a few yards into the air, strikes at the marauder with bill and claws, screaming aloud all the while, and dives again among the grass, to the astonishment of the bird of prey, which usually moves off at full speed. They are not so fortunate in their encounters with such hawks as pounce from on high on their prey, such as the red-tailed and red-shouldered hawks, against which they have no chance of defending themselves. Minks, raccoons, and wildcats destroy a great number of them during the night, and many are devoured by turtles and ravenous fishes; but their worst enemy is man. My friend Bachman has shot as many as sixty in the course of four hours, and others have killed double that number in double the time.

The saltwater marsh hen swims with considerable ease, though not swiftly or gracefully. While in this act, it extends its neck forward, and strikes the water with its feet, as if unwilling to move far at a time, the motion of its neck resembling that of the gallinules. It dives well, remains a considerable time under water, and in this manner dexterously eludes its pursuers, although it certainly does not possess the powers of holding fast to the bottom, as some persons have alleged. When hard pressed, it often sinks just below the surface, keeping the bill above in order to breathe, and in this position, if not detected, remains for a considerable time. If perceived and approached, it instantly dives, and uses its wings to accelerate its progress, but rises as soon as it comes to a place of safety.

Their movements on the ground, or over the partially submerged or floating beds of weeds, are extremely rapid, and they run swiftly off before a dog, the utmost exertions of which are required to force them on wing. Such an attempt by man would prove utterly futile, unless he were to come upon them unawares. When not pursued, and feeling secure, they walk in a deliberate manner, the body considerably inclined, now and then jerking the tail upward, although by no means so frequently as gallinules are wont to do. On the least appearance of danger, they lower the head, stretch out the neck, and move off with incomparable speed, always in perfect silence. They have thousands of paths among the rank herbage, crossing each other so often that they can very easily escape pursuit; and besides, they have a power of compressing their bodies to such a degree as frequently to force a passage between two stems so close that one could hardly believe it possible for them to squeeze themselves through. When put up, they fly slowly and generally straight before you, with their legs dangling, so that they are very easily shot by a quick sportsman, as they rarely fly far at a time on such occasions, but prefer pitching down again into the first tuft of rank grass in their way. When on their migrations, however, they pass low and swiftly over the marshes, or the water, stretched to their full extent, and with constant beat of the wings.

The young, which are at first covered with down of a black color, obtain their full plumage before the winter arrives, and after this undergo little change of color, although they increase in size for a year after. In the Eastern States, this species is not held in much estimation as an article of food, perhaps in a great measure on account of the quantity of soras met with there during early autumn, and which are certainly more delicate; but in the Southern States, especially during winter, they are considered good for the table, and a great number are killed and offered for sale in the markets. Numbers are destroyed by torchlights, which so dazzles their eyes as to enable persons fond of the sport to knock them down with poles or paddles during high tides. It is by day, however, that they are usually shot, and as this kind of sport is exceedingly pleasant, I will attempt to describe it.

About Charleston, in South Carolina, the shooting of marsh hens takes place from September to February, a few days in each month during the spring tides. A light skiff or canoe is procured, the latter being much preferable, and paddled by one or two experienced persons, the sportsman standing in the bow, and his friend, if he has one with him, taking his station in the stern. At an early hour they proceed to the marshes, amid many boats containing parties on the same errand. There is no lack of shooting grounds, for every creek of salt water swarms with marsh hens. The sportsman who leads has already discharged his barrels, and on either side of his canoe a bird has fallen. As the boat moves swiftly toward them, more are raised, and although he may not be ready, the safety of the bird is in imminent jeopardy, for now from another bark double reports are heard in succession. The tide is advancing apace, the boats merely float along, and the birds, driven from place to place, seek in vain for safety.

Here, on a floating mass of tangled weeds, stands a small group side by side. The gunner has marked them, and presently nearly the whole covey is prostrated. Now, onward to that great bunch of tall grass all the boats are seen to steer; shot after shot flies in rapid succession; dead and dying lie all around on the water; the terrified survivors are trying to save their lives by hurried flight; but their efforts are unavailing—one by one they fall, to rise no more. It is a sorrowful sight, after all: see that poor thing gasping hard in the agonies of death, its legs quivering in convulsive twitches, its bright eyes fading into glazed obscurity. In a few hours, hundreds have ceased to breathe the breath of life; hundreds that erst reveled in the joys of careless existence, but which can never behold their beloved marshes again. The cruel sportsman, covered with mud and mire, drenched to the skin by the splashing of the paddles, his face and hands besmeared with powder, stands amid the wreck which he has made, exultingly surveys his slaughtered heaps, and with joyous feelings returns home with a cargo of game more than enough for a family thrice as numerous as his own.

How joyful must be the congratulations of those which have escaped, without injury to themselves or their relatives! With what pleasure, perhaps, have some of them observed the gun of one of their murderers, or the powder flask of another, fall overboard! How delighted have they been to see a canoe overturned by an awkward movement, and their enemies struggling to reach the shore, or sticking fast in the mud! Nor have the mink and raccoon come off well, for notwithstanding the expertness of the former at diving, and the cunning of the latter, many have been shot, and the boatmen intend to make caps of their fur.

In the Carolinas there are some most expert marksmen, of whom I know two who probably were never surpassed. One of them I have seen shoot fifty marsh hens at fifty successive shots, and the other, I am assured, had killed a hundred without missing one. I have heard or read of a French king, who, on starting a partridge, could take a pinch of snuff, then point his gun, and shoot the bird; but whether this be true or not I cannot say, although I have witnessed as remarkable a feat, for I have seen a Carolinian, furnished with two guns, shoot at and kill four marsh hens as they flew off at once around him! On speaking once to a friend of the cruelty of destroying so many of these birds, he answered me as follows: "It gives variety to life; it is good exercise, and in all cases affords a capital dinner, besides the pleasure I feel when sending a mess of marsh hens to a friend such as you."

Ornithological Biography, Volume III

The Pied-Billed Grebe *(Podilymbus podiceps)*

There go the little dobchicks among the tall rushes and aquatic grasses that border the marsh. They have seen me, and now I watch them as they sink gently backward into the deep water, in the manner of frightened frogs. Cunning things! "Water witches," as they call you, I clearly see your bills, although you have withdrawn all of you save those parts, and sneak off toward yon bunch of bulrushes. Well, speed on, and may safety attend you! Nature has granted you means of eluding your enemies,

and I am heartily glad to see that you have profited by her instructions. I know you can fly too. How happy must you be, to be thus enabled to migrate through the air, instead of being obliged to labor for months with your curiously scolloped feet, in removing from one country to another, as *authors* say you do. Ah! you have reached a small secluded pool, where you intend to breed in peace and security; there you are, collecting rushes and weeds to form a large matted bed, on which you intend to deposit your pearly eggs. Labor on, mind me not, I am a true friend and admirer of your race.

I see that among these plants you have fixed your tenement, in which there will soon be five eggs, which, although tinged with green, will look as if pure white. I wish I knew how many days of constant heat from your bodies it will require to hatch them. Some other time perhaps you may tell me. Miniatures of yourselves I now see swimming gaily, skipping, springing, gliding, dipping, just like yourselves. So, you snatch the crawling bug, and gorge yourself with leeches, fish, and herbage. How fast your young ones grow, changing from downy to hairy, and again to feathery and silky. On winglets they now cross the clear pool and crawl on the opposite shore, there enjoying the warmth of the bright sunbeams. September has come; plump and strong, seven of you there are; the evening is calm and beautiful; you spread out your wings, reach with some difficulty a proper height, and swift as meteors glide through the air, until, meeting with warmer waters, you alight on them and there remain for a season.

The pied-billed dobchick may be met with in almost every part of the United States, at one season or other: in the South and West during autumn and winter, in the East and Northwest in spring and summer, mostly on fresh waters of all descriptions, yet when these are covered with ice, on bays and estuaries, where it searches for shrimps and fry, although under other circumstances such haunts are not congenial to it. It is found in New Brunswick and Nova Scotia, but I did not meet with it in Labrador or Newfoundland.

I had the good fortune, on the twenty-eighth of June, to stumble upon a nest of this bird near the banks of the Wabash River, above Vincennes. It was large for the bird, raised several inches above the muddy and reedy shores of a pond, only a few feet from the water, and composed of decayed weeds, rushes, and earth. On being discovered, the sitting bird slid over the mud, along a path that led directly to the water, in which it immediately dived, and I saw no more of it for about twenty minutes. The eggs, which were five, measured an inch and a quarter, by seven-and-a-half-eighths, were smooth, rather rounded, and of a light greenish-white color. On breaking one of them, I found it to contain a chick considerably advanced, which induced me to leave the nest untouched, and before I departed I saw the bird, which I believed to be female, swimming low at a distance. I watched it for some time, but could not discover another, and walked away to allow it to resume its occupation. The nest was fixed among the stalks of strong reeds, but was not attached to any of them. In the month of August, while on the Cayuga Lakes, I saw one of these birds with a brood of young about half grown, but could not obtain a single specimen, as they dived with extreme quickness, and eluded all pursuit.

Few birds plunge with more rapidity than this species, which, during submersion, employs its wings, as I had an opportunity of observing while some were passing under a boat when I was in pursuit of them. On the water it is almost impossible to catch them, unless they have been injured in the wing, when they are unable to dive without difficulty. The curious habit which they have of sinking gradually backward in the water, at the sight of an enemy, is very pleasing to observe. Not a ripple do they leave on the spot where they have disappeared, and one unacquainted with them can hardly conceive that a bird could have escaped in so dexterous a manner. My friend, Thomas MacCulloch, gave me an account of one which, having been observed on a small milldam, was pursued by the miller's sons, who, after chasing it fully an hour, could not even drive it on shore. Their father, however, who was as anxious as themselves to see the curious creature, drained the pond, when the little thing was seen crawling over the mud in a manner not unlike that of a turtle. It was now easily caught, as it was not able to rise on wing, the species, it seems, being incapable of springing from the ground, and was afterward given to my young friend, who presented it beautifully prepared to me.

While I was at Philadelphia, my learned and staunch friend, Dr. Richard Harlan, received two pied-billed grebes alive, which had been caught in a fishing net on Brandywine Creek. We placed them in a large tub of water, where we could see all their subaqueous movements. They swam round the sides of the tub in the manner of the

NOTES ON THE PLATES

121. SWALLOW-TAILED KITE *(Elanoides forficatus)*. In Audubon's time, this bird bred as far north as Minnesota and as far west as Texas. Now it is largely confined to southern Florida and a few areas along the Gulf Coast. Its favored haunts are river bottoms, marshes, and swampy forests. It also hunts for its prey —lizards, snakes, insects, frogs—over open land.

122–123. LEAST BITTERN *(Ixobrychus exilis)*. No larger than a flicker, this is the smallest of our herons. It is a shy, secretive bird of fresh-water marshes, usually hidden among dense stands of cattails. When alarmed, it tends to escape by running rather than by taking wing.

124–125. LITTLE BLUE HERON *(Florida caerulea)*. This heron is associated with both fresh-water and coastal marshes in the South. When young, it has white plumage. It spends the night in large communal roosts and nests in colonies with other herons. After the breeding season is over, it tends to wander widely.

126–127. SHOVELER *(Spatula clypeata)*. The enormous bill of this duck has fine "teeth" running along the sides of the mandibles. Through this comblike structure, the waterfowl strains minute crustacea and other food from the water of ponds and marshes. The shoveler is a duck that migrates south early in fall and comes north late in the spring.

128. IVORY-BILLED WOODPECKER *(Campephilus principalis)*. Even in Audubon's day, this spectacular woodpecker, with its large cream-white bill, was widely shot by hunters. The subsequent felling of river-bottom forests, where it made its home in the South, hastened the species along the road to extinction.

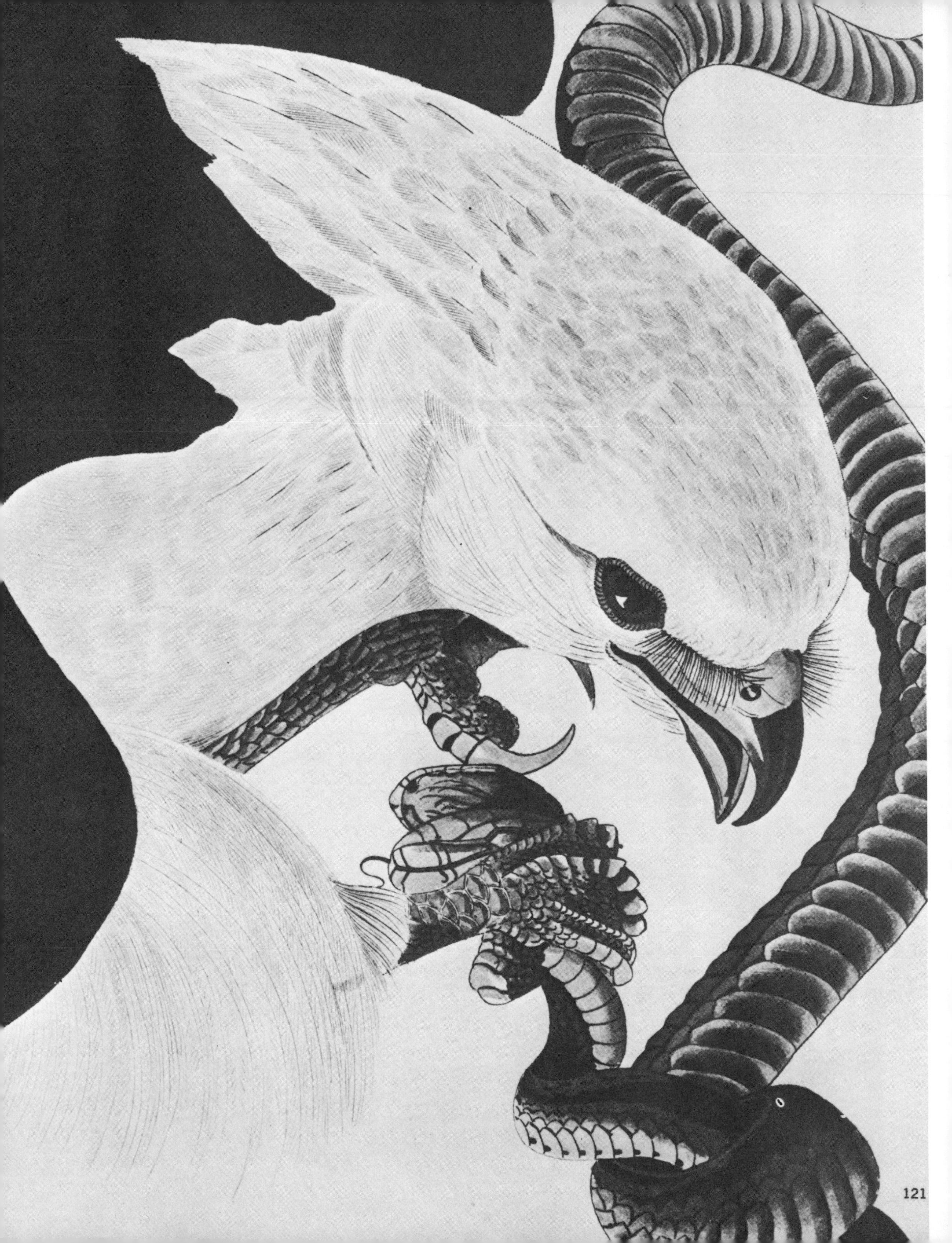

puffin, moving their wings in accordance with their feet, and continued so a much longer time than one could suppose it possible for them to remain under water, coming up to breathe, and plunging again with astonishing celerity. When placed on the carpet, they ran awkwardly half erect, for a distance of a few feet, tumbled over, and scrambled along with the aid of their wings. Nothing could induce them to eat, and after a day or two of captivity, the little creatures were taken to the Delaware, and set at liberty.

This bird retires to rest on the floating beds of rushes met with in ponds, or on the edges of the shores; and in such places you may see it sitting upright and dressing its plumage in the sunshine. They are extremely unwilling to rise on wing, unless during their migrations, or when chasing each other at the pairing season, which commences in March, when they manifest a good deal of pugnacity. On such occasions, the males fly, dive, and rise again on wing, in the manner of the foolish guillemot. While traveling, they pass rapidly through the air, at times at a considerable elevation, when the movements of their wings produce a sound like that of a hawk stooping on its prey. They are seldom found in parties of more than six or seven. The idea of their migrating by water is quite absurd. How long would it take a dobchick to swim from the mouths of the Mississippi to the headwaters of the Ohio; and when arrived there, after six or seven weeks of constant paddling, how is he to proceed farther? Yet it is well known that they breed farther north, and are general on the southern waters early in October.

The food of the pied-billed dobchick consists of small fry, plants, seeds, aquatic insects, and snails; along with which they swallow gravel. On opening several individuals, in different parts of the Union, I observed in their gizzards a quantity of hair and featherlike substance, for which I could not account, but which I at length found to be the down of certain plants, such as thistles, the seeds remaining undigested and attached to it. My friend, Thomas MacCulloch, made the same observation on examining some at Pictou, in Nova Scotia, and I have found similar substances in the stomach of many individuals of *Podiceps cristatus.*

The pied-billed dobchicks seem to form particular attachments to certain ponds or small lakes, where, until they are closed by ice, you may always observe a pair or a family. Opposite Henderson I regularly saw a couple every autumn, and my friend, the Reverend John Bachman, has observed a group of them for many winters in a small pond a few miles distant from Charleston. They seem to have a dislike to swift-running streams, and when on them keep to the eddies along the shores. The curious double pectination on the hind part of their tarsi seems to aid them greatly while sitting upright on the broad leaves of water lilies, on the surface of which I have observed indented impressions after the birds had plunged into the water from them.

Ornithological Biography, Volume III

The Carolina Parakeet (*Conuropsis carolinensis*)

The flight of the parakeet is rapid, straight, and continued through the forests, or over fields and rivers, and is accompanied by inclinations of the body which enable the observer to see alternately their upper and under parts. They deviate from a direct course only when impediments occur, such as the trunks of trees or houses, in which case they glance aside in a very graceful manner, merely as much as may be necessary. A general cry is kept up by the party, and it is seldom that one of these birds is on the wing for ever so short a space without uttering its cry. On reaching a spot which affords a supply of food, instead of alighting at once, as many other birds do, the parakeets take a good survey of the neighborhood, passing over it in circles of great extent, first above the trees, and then gradually lowering until they almost touch the ground, then suddenly reascending, they all settle on the tree that bears the fruit of which they are in quest, or on one close to the field in which they expect to regale themselves.

They are quite at ease on trees or any kind of plant, moving sidewise, climbing or hanging in every imaginable posture, assisting themselves very dexterously in all their motions with their bills. They usually alight extremely close together. I have seen branches of trees as completely covered by them as they could possibly be. If approached before they begin their plundering, they appear shy and distrustful, and often at a single cry from one of them, the whole take wing, and probably may not return to the same place that day. Should a person shoot at them as they go and wound an individual, its cries are sufficient to bring back the whole flock, when the sportsman may kill as many as he pleases. If the bird falls dead, they make a short round, and then fly off.

On the ground these birds walk slowly and awkwardly, as if their tails incommoded them. They do not attempt to run off when approached by the sportsman, should he come upon them unawares; but when he is seen at a distance, they lose no time in trying to hide, or in scrambling up the trunk of the nearest tree, in doing which they are greatly aided by their bills.

Their roosting place is in hollow trees, and the holes excavated by the larger species of woodpeckers, as far as these can be filled by them. At dusk, a flock of parakeets may be seen alighting against the trunk of a large sycamore or any other tree, when a considerable excavation exists within it. Immediately below the entrance the birds all cling to the bark and crawl into the hole to pass the night. When such a hole does not prove sufficient to hold the whole flock, those around the entrance hook themselves on by their claws, and the tip of the upper mandible, and look as if hanging by the bill. I have frequently seen them in such positions by means of a glass, and am satisfied that the bill is not the only support used in such cases.

When wounded and laid hold of, the parakeet opens its bill, turns its head to seize and bite, and, if it succeed, is capable of inflicting a severe wound. It is easily tamed by being frequently immersed in water, and eats as soon as it is placed in confinement. Nature seems to have implanted in these birds a propensity to destroy, in consequence of which they cut to atoms pieces of wood, books, and, in short, everything that comes in their way. They are incapable of articulating words, however much care and attention may be bestowed upon their education; and their screams are so disagreeable as to render them at best very indifferent companions. The woods are the habitation best fitted for them, and there the richness of their plumage, their beautiful mode of flight, and even their screams, afford welcome intimation that our darkest forests and most sequestered swamps are not destitute of charms.

They are fond of sand in a surprising degree, and on that account are frequently seen to alight in flocks along the gravelly banks about the creeks and rivers, or in the ravines of old fields in the plantations, when they scratch with bill and claws, flutter and roll themselves in the sand, and pick up and swallow a certain quantity of it. For the same purpose, they also enter the holes dug by our kingfisher. They are fond of saline earth, for which they visit the different licks interspersed in our woods.

Our parakeets are very rapidly diminishing in number; and in some districts, where twenty-five years ago they were plentiful, scarcely any are now to be seen. At that period, they could be procured as far up the tributary waters of the Ohio as the Great Kenhawa, the Scioto, the heads of the Miami, the mouth of the Manimee at its junction with Lake Erie, on the Illinois River, and sometimes as far northeast as Lake Ontario, and along the eastern districts as far as the boundary line between Virginia and Maryland. At the present day, very few are to be found higher than Cincinnati, nor is it until you reach the mouth of the Ohio that parakeets are met with in considerable numbers. I should think that along the Mississippi there is not now half the number that existed fifteen years ago.

Ornithological Biography, Volume I

The Wood Ibis *(Mycteria Americana)*

The wood ibis is rarely met with single, even after the breeding season, and it is more easy for a person to see a hundred together at any period of the year than to meet with one by itself. Nay, I have seen flocks composed of several thousands, and that there is a natural necessity for their flocking together I shall explain to you. This species feeds entirely on fish and aquatic reptiles, of which it destroys an enormous quantity, in fact more than it eats; for if they have been killing fish for half an hour and have gorged themselves, they suffer the rest to lie on the water untouched, when it becomes food for alligators, crows, and vultures, whenever these animals can lay hold of it. To procure its food, the wood ibis walks through shallow muddy lakes or bayous in numbers. As soon as they have discovered a place abounding in fish, they dance as it were all through it, until the water becomes thick with the mud stirred from the bottom by their feet. The fishes, on rising to the surface, are instantly struck by the beaks of the ibises, which, on being deprived of life, they turn over and so remain. In the course of ten or fifteen minutes, hundreds of fishes, frogs, young alligators, and water snakes cover the surface, and the birds greedily swallow them until they are completely gorged, after which they walk to the nearest margins, place themselves in long rows, with their breasts all turned toward the sun, in the manner of pelicans and vultures, and thus remain for an hour or so. When digestion is partially accomplished, they all take to wing, rise in spiral circlings to an immense height, and sail about for an hour or more, performing the most beautiful evolutions that can well be conceived. Their long necks and legs are stretched out to their full extent, the pure white of their plumage contrasts beautifully with the jetty black of the tips of their wings. Now in large circles they seem to ascend toward the upper regions of the atmosphere; now, they pitch toward the earth; and again, gently rising, they renew their gyrations. Hunger once more induces them to go in search of food, and, with extended front, the band sails rapidly toward another lake or bayou.

Mark the place, Reader, and follow their course through canebrake, cypress swamp, and tangled wood. Seldom do they return to the same feeding place on the same day. You have reached the spot, and are standing on the margin of a dark-watered bayou, the sinuosities of which lead your eye into a labyrinth ending in complete darkness. The tall canes bow to each other from the shores; the majestic trees above them, all hung with funereal lichen, gently wave in the suffocating atmosphere; the bullfrog, alarmed, shrinks back into the water; the alligator raises his head above the surface, probably to see if the birds have arrived, and the wily cougar is stealthily advancing toward one of the ibises, which he expects to carry off into the thicket. Through the dim light your eye catches a glimpse of the white-plumaged birds, moving rapidly like specters to and fro. The loud clacking of their mandibles apprises you of the havoc they commit among the terrified inhabitants of the waters, while the knell-like sounds of their feet come with a feeling of dread. Move, gently or not, move at all, and you infallibly lose your opportunity of observing the actions of the birds. Some old male has long marked you; whether it has been with eye or with ear, no matter. The first stick your foot cracks, his hoarse voice sounds the alarm. Off they all go, battering down the canes with their powerful pinions and breaking the smaller twigs of the trees as they force a passage for themselves.

Talk to me of the stupidity of birds, of the dullness of the wood ibis! Say it is fearless, easily approached, and easily shot. I listen, but it is merely through courtesy; for I have so repeatedly watched its movements, in all kinds of circumstances, that I am quite convinced we have not in the United States a more shy, wary, and vigilant bird than the wood ibis. In the course of two years spent, I may say, among them, for I saw some whenever I pleased during that period, I never succeeded in surprising one, not even under night, when they were roosting on trees at a height of nearly a hundred feet, and sometimes rendered farther secure by being over extensive swamps.

My Journal informs me, that one autumn while residing near Bayou Sara, being intent on procuring eight or ten of these birds to skin for my learned and kind friend the Prince of Musignano, I took with me two servants, who were first-rate woodsmen, and capital hands at the rifle, and that notwithstanding our meeting with many hundreds of wood ibises, it took us three days to shoot fifteen, which were for the most part killed on wing with rifle balls, at a distance of about a hundred yards. On that occasion we discovered that a flock roosted regularly over a large cornfield covered with huge girted trees, the tops of which were almost all decayed. We stationed ourselves apart in the field, concealed among the tall ripened corn, and in silence awaited the arrival of the birds. After the sun had disappeared, the broad front of a great flock of ibises was observed advancing toward us. They soon alighted in great numbers on the large branches of the dead trees; but whenever one of the branches gave way under their weight, all at once rose in the air, flew about several times, and alighted again. One of my companions, having a good opportunity, fired, and brought two down with a single bullet; but here the sport was ended. In five minutes after, not an ibis was within a mile of the place, nor did any return to roost there for more than a month. When on the margin of a lake, or even in the center of it—for all the lakes they frequent are exceedingly shallow—the first glimpse they have of a man induces them to exert all their vigilance; and should he after this advance a few steps, the birds fly off.

One of the most curious circumstances connected with this species is, that although the birds are, when feeding, almost constantly within the reach of alligators, of which they devour the young, these reptiles never attack them; whereas if a duck or a heron comes within the reach of their tails, it is immediately killed and swallowed. The wood ibis will wade up to its belly in the water, round the edges of "alligator holes," without ever being injured; but should one of these birds be shot, an alligator immediately makes toward it and pulls it under water. The garfish is not so courteous, but gives chase to the ibises whenever an opportunity occurs. The snapping turtle is also a great enemy to the young birds of this species.

The flight of the wood ibis is heavy at its rising from the ground. Its neck at that moment is deeply curved downward, its wings flap heavily but with great power, and its long legs are not stretched out behind until it has proceeded many yards. But as soon as it has attained a height of eight or ten feet, it ascends with great celerity, generally in a spiral direction, in silence if not alarmed, or, if frightened, with a rough croaking guttural note. When fairly on wing, they proceed in a direct flight, with alternate flappings and sailings of thirty or forty yards, the sailings more prolonged than the flappings. They alight on trees with more ease than herons generally do, and either stand erect or crouch on the branches, in the manner of the wild turkey, the herons seldom using the latter attitude. When they are at rest, they place their bill against the breast, while the neck shrinks as it were between the shoulders. In this position you may see fifty on the same tree, or on the ground, reposing in perfect quiet for hours at a time, although some individual of the party will be constantly on the lookout, and ready to sound the alarm.

In the spring months, when these birds collect in large flocks, before they return to their breeding places, I have seen thousands together, passing over the woods in a line more than a mile in extent, and moving with surprising speed at the height of only a few yards above the trees. When a breeding place has once been chosen, it is resorted to for years in succession; nor is it easy to make them abandon it after they have deposited their eggs, although, if much annoyed, they never return to it after that season.

Besides the great quantity of fishes that these ibises destroy, they also devour frogs, young alligators, wood rats, young rails and grackles, fiddlers and other crabs, as well as snakes and small turtles. They never eat the eggs of the alligator, as has been alleged, although they probably would do so, could they demolish the matted nests of that animal, a task beyond the power of *any* bird known to me. I never saw one eat anything which either it or some of its fellows had not killed. Nor will it eat any animal that had been dead for some time, even although it may have been killed by itself. When eating, the clacking of their mandibles may be heard at the distance of several hundred yards.

When wounded, it is dangerous to approach them, for they bite severely. They may be said to be very tenacious of life. Although usually fat, they are very tough and oily, and therefore are not fit for food. The Negroes, however, eat them, having, previous to cooking them, torn off the skin, as they do with pelicans and cormorants. My own attempts, I may add, were not crowned with success. Many of the Negroes of Louisiana destroy these birds when young, for the sake of the oil which their flesh contains, and which they use in greasing machines.

The French Creoles of that State name them "grands flammans," while the Spaniards of East Florida know them by the name of "gannets." When in the latter country, at St. Augustine, I was induced to make an excursion, to visit a large pond or lake, where I was assured there were gannets in abundance, which I might shoot off the trees, provided I was careful enough. On asking the appearance of the gannets, I was told that they were large white birds, with wings black at the end, a long neck, and a large sharp bill. The description so far agreeing with that of the common gannet or solan goose, I proposed no questions respecting the legs or tail, but went off. Twenty-three miles, I trudged through the woods, and at last came in view of the pond; when, lo! its borders and the trees around it were covered with wood ibises. Now, as the good people who gave the information spoke according to their knowledge, and agreeably to their custom of calling the ibises gannets, had I not gone to the pond, I might have written this day that gannets are found in the interior of the woods in the Floridas, that they alight on trees, &c. which, if *once* published, would in all probability have gone down to future times through the medium of compilers, and all perhaps without acknowledgment.

Ornithological Biography, Volume III

3. Lake and River

Introduction

The streams that Audubon knew in his earlier years became, as the population grew and cities expanded, no longer rivers of pure water, no longer streams teeming with fish. As decade followed decade, they carried an ever-increasing burden of sewage and waste and pollution toward the sea. Along the bed of the historic Potomac River today, there are places where the sewage sludge has been deposited ten feet deep. The rivers of the Midwest have carried—and continue to carry—the silt of rich farmlands. In eastern Pennsylvania, waterways run black with coal-mine debris. And in Maine, many miles from inland pulpwood factories, beautiful, winding streams now give off the nauseous smell of waste chemicals dumped into their current.

On the south shore of Lake Erie at the present time, bathers must travel twenty miles from one large city in order to find lake water pure enough for swimming. And in Michigan, another community has so polluted the bay on which it is situated that it has to pipe drinking water miles overland from another part of the same lake of which its bay is a part. Since Audubon's time, the story of streams and lakes has changed—and not for the better.

And so has the story of the wildlife that inhabited many of the waterways of the country. To a greater and greater extent, man has upset the balance of nature here. At each change some forms of wildlife have suffered. To cite one example, as the forest trees came down, more sunlight reached the water of woodland streams. Some grew slightly warmer. In consequence, the eggs of certain game fish, delicately adjusted to water temperatures, failed to hatch or hatched in reduced numbers.

It was during the Indian Summer of the autumn of 1810 that the Audubons descended the frontier river, the Ohio, on their way back to Henderson after a visit in Pennsylvania. At the time, their infant son, Victor, was slightly more than one year old. Shippingport, a village just below Louisville, was located at the foot of the falls, or rapids, of the Ohio. Here lived Audubon's brother-in-law, Nicholas A. Berthoud. The adventure in the great Florida storm, during the St. Johns River trip, occurred in February 1832.

Today beavers and otters exist in greatly reduced numbers. Both, however, appear able to thrive and increase wherever they are provided with protection in their natural habitat. It was while Audubon was busy at Henderson painting an otter that Thomas W. Bakewell appeared, told him of the failure of the commission house they had started, and disappeared again, leaving him still painting the otter.

One striking creature familiar to lakes and waterways of former times has fallen upon particularly evil days. This is the bald eagle, symbol of the nation. A common sight not many decades ago, it has been decreasing in numbers since soon after the turn of the century. In 1904, John Burroughs wrote in *Far and Near:* "I see fewer eagles along the Hudson than I used to see fifteen years ago." The great birds were shot by hunters for fun or to produce a stuffed trophy or in a self-righteous war on "vermin." Their nests were robbed by egg collectors. Numerous factors, including the rapid growth of the human population and the expansion of mechanized civilization, have worked against the eagles.

In Florida, for example, many nesting trees have been felled during building booms and widespread real-estate developments. Another and potent factor in the bird's decrease—undreamed of in Audubon's day—apparently is DDT. Eggs that failed to hatch in eagle nests have been examined in the laboratory and found to contain concentrations of this lethal insecticide. Only a small proportion of modern Americans have ever seen the emblem of their country soaring high above them, wild and free. Today, in all the United States, exclusive of Alaska, there are probably far fewer than two thousand pairs of bald eagles.

The Canada Goose *(Branta canadensis)*

It is extremely amusing to witness the courtship of the Canada goose in all its stages; and let me assure you, Reader, that although a gander does not strut before his beloved with the pomposity of a turkey or the grace of a dove, his ways are quite as agreeable to the female of his choice. I can imagine before me one who has just accomplished the defeat of another male after a struggle of half an hour or more. He advances gallantly toward the object of contention, his head scarcely raised an inch from the ground, his bill open to its full stretch, his fleshy tongue elevated, his eyes darting fiery glances, and as he moves he hisses loudly, while the emotion which he experiences causes his quills to shake and his feathers to rustle. Now he is close to her who in his eyes is all loveliness; his neck bending gracefully in all directions, passes all round her, and occasionally touches her body; and as she congratulates him on his victory, and acknowledges his affection, they move their necks in a hundred curious ways. At this moment fierce jealousy urges the defeated gander to renew his efforts to obtain his love; he advances apace, his eyes glowing with the fire of rage; he shakes his broad wings, ruffles up his whole plumage, and as he rushes on the foe, hisses with the intensity of anger. The whole flock seems to stand amazed, and opening up a space, the birds gather round to view the combat. The bold bird who has been caressing his mate, scarcely deigns to take notice of his foe, but seems to send a scornful glance toward him. He of the mortified feelings, however, raises his body, half opens his sinewy wings, and with a powerful blow, sends forth his defiance. The affront cannot be borne in the presence of so large a company, nor indeed is there much disposition to bear it in any circumstances; the blow is returned with vigor, the aggressor reels for a moment, but he soon recovers, and now the combat rages. Were the weapons more deadly, feats of chivalry would now be performed; as it is, thrust and blow succeed each other like the strokes of hammers driven by sturdy forgers. But now, the mated gander has caught hold of his antagonist's head with his bill; no bulldog could cling faster to his victim; he squeezes him with all the energy of rage, lashes him with his powerful wings, and at length drives him away, spreads out his pinions, runs with joy to his mate, and fills the air with cries of exultation.

But now, see yonder, not a couple, but half a dozen of ganders are engaged in battle! Some desperado, it seems, has fallen upon a mated bird, and several bystanders, as if sensible of the impropriety of such conduct, rush to the assistance of the wronged one. How they strive and tug, biting, and striking with their wings! And how their feathers fly about! Exhausted, abashed, and mortified, the presumptious intruder retreats in disgrace—there he lies almost breathless on the sand!

Such are the conflicts of these ardent lovers, and so full of courage and of affection toward their females are they that the approach of a male invariably ruffles their tempers as well as their feathers. No sooner has the goose laid her first egg than her bold mate stands almost erect by her side, watching even the rustling sound of the breeze. The least noise brings from him a sound of anger. Should he spy a raccoon making his way among the grass, he walks up to him undauntedly, hurls a vigorous blow at him, and drives him instantly away. Nay I doubt if a man himself, if unarmed, would come off unscathed in such an encounter. The brave gander does more; for, if imminent danger excite him, he urges his mate to fly off, and resolutely remains near the nest until he is assured of her safety, when he also betakes himself to flight, mocking as it were by his notes his disappointed enemy.

Suppose all be peace and quiet around the fond pair, and the female to be sitting in security upon her eggs. The nest is placed near the bank of a noble stream or lake; the clear sky is spread over the scene, the bright beams glitter on the waters, and a thousand odorous flowers give beauty to the swamp which of late was so dismal. The gander passes to and fro over the liquid element, moving as if lord of the waters; now he inclines his head with a graceful curve, now sips to quench his thirst; and, as noontide has arrived, he paddles his way toward the shore, to relieve for a while his affectionate and patient consort.

The lisping sounds of their offspring are heard through the shell; their little bills have formed a breach in the inclosing walls; full of life, and bedecked with beauty, they come forth, with tottering steps and downy covering. Toward the water they now follow their careful parent, they reach the border of the stream, their mother already floats on the loved element, one after another launches forth, and now the flock glides gently along. What a beautiful sight! Close by the grassy margin the mother slowly leads her innocent younglings; to one she shows the seed of the floating grass, to another points out the crawling slug. Her careful eye watches the cruel turtle, the garfish, and the pike, that are lurking for their prey, and, with head inclined, she glances upward to the eagle or the gull that are hovering over the water in search of food. A ferocious bird dashes at her young ones; she instantly plunges beneath the surface, and, in the twinkling of an eye, her brood disappear after her; now they are among the thick rushes, with nothing above water but their little bills. The mother is marching toward the land, having lisped to her brood in accents so gentle that none but they and her mate can understand their import, and all are safely lodged under cover until the disappointed eagle or gull bears away.

More than six weeks have now elapsed. The down of the goslings, which was at first soft and tufty, has become coarse and hairlike. Their wings are edged with quills, and their bodies bristled with feathers. They have increased in size, and, living in the midst of abundance, they have become fat, so that on shore they make their way with difficulty, and as they are yet unable to fly, the greatest care is required to save them from their numerous enemies. They grow apace, and now the burning days of August are over. They are able to fly with ease from one shore to another, and as each successive night the hoarfrosts cover the country, and the streams are closed over by the ice, the family joins that in their neighborhood, which is also joined by others. At length they spy the advance of a snowstorm, when the ganders with one accord sound the order for their departure.

After many wide circlings, the flock has risen high in the thin air, and an hour or more is spent in teaching the young the order in which they are to move. But now, the host has been marshaled, and off it starts, showing, as it proceeds, at one time an extended front, at another a single lengthened file, and now arraying itself in an angular form. The old males advance in front, the females follow, the young come in succession according to their strength, the weakest forming the rear. Should one feel fatigued, his position is changed in the ranks, and he assumes a place in the wake of another, who cleaves the air before him; perhaps the parent bird flies for a while by his side to encourage him.

Two, three, or more days elapse before they reach a secure resting place. The fat with which they were loaded at their departure has rapidly wasted; they are fatigued, and experience the keen gnawings of hunger; but now they spy a wide estuary, toward which they direct their course. Alighting on the water, they swim to the beach, stand, and gaze around them; the young full of joy, the old full of fear, for well are they aware that many foes have been waiting their arrival. Silent all night remains the flock, but not inactive; with care they betake themselves to the grassy shores, where they allay the cravings of appetite, and recruit their wasted strength. Soon as the early dawn lightens the surface of the deep they rise in the air, extend their lines, and proceed southward, until arriving in some place where they think they may be enabled to rest in security, they remain during the winter. At length, after many annoyances, they joyfully perceive the return of spring, and prepare to fly away from their greatest enemy, man.

The Canada goose, when it remains with us to breed, begins to form its nest in March, making choice of some retired place not far from the water, generally among the rankest grass, and not unfrequently under a bush. It is carefully formed of dry plants of various kinds, and is of a large size, flat, and raised to the height of several inches. Only once did I find a nest elevated above the ground. It was placed on the stump of a large tree, standing in the center of a small pond, about twenty feet high, and contained five eggs. As the spot was very secluded, I did not disturb the birds, anxious as I was to see in what manner they should convey the young to the water. But in this I was disappointed, for, on going to the nest, near the time at which I expected the process of incubation to terminate, I had the mortification to find that a raccoon, or some other animal, had destroyed the whole of the eggs, and that the birds had abandoned the place. The greatest number of eggs which I have found in the nest of this species was nine, which I think is more by three than these birds usually lay in a wild state. In the nests of those which I have had in a domesticated state, I have sometimes counted as many as eleven, several of them, however, usually proving unproductive. The eggs measure, on an average, three and a half inches by two and a half, are thick shelled, rather smooth, and of a very dull yellowish-green color. The period of incubation is twenty-eight days. They never have more than one brood in a season, unless their eggs are removed or broken at an early period.

The young follow their parents to the water a day or two after they have issued from the egg, but generally return to land to repose in the sunshine in the evening, and pass the night there under their mother, who employs all imaginable care to ensure their comfort and safety, as does her mate, who never leaves her during incubation for a longer time than is necessary for procuring food, and takes her place at intervals. Both remain with their brood until the following spring.

It is during the breeding season that the gander displays his courage and strength to the greatest advantage. I knew one that appeared larger than usual, and of which all the lower parts were of a rich cream color. It returned three years in succession to a large pond a few miles from the mouth of Green River in Kentucky and whenever I visited the nest, it seemed to look upon me with utter contempt. It would stand in a stately attitude, until I reached within a few yards of the nest, when suddenly lowering its head, and shaking it as if it were dislocated from the neck, it would open its wings, and launch into the air, flying directly at me. So daring was this fine fellow that in two instances he struck me a blow with one of his wings on the right arm, which, for an instant, I thought, was broken. I observed that immediately after such an effort to defend his nest and mate, he would run swiftly toward them, pass his head and neck several times over and around the female, and again assume his attitude of defiance.

Always intent on making experiments, I thought of endeavoring to conciliate this bold son of the waters. For this purpose I always afterward took with me several ears of corn, which I shelled, and threw toward him. It remained untouched for several days; but I succeeded at last, and before the end of a week both birds fed freely on the grain even in my sight! I felt much pleasure on this occasion, and repeating my visit daily, found that before the eggs were hatched, they would allow me to approach within a few feet of them, although they never suffered me to touch them. Whenever I attempted this the male met my fingers with his bill, and bit me so severely that I gave it up.

The great beauty and courage of the male rendered me desirous of obtaining possession of him. I had marked the time at which the young were likely to appear, and on the preceding day I baited with corn a large coop made of twine, and waited until he should enter. He walked in, I drew the string, and he was my prisoner. The next morning the female was about to lead her offspring to the river, which was distant nearly half a mile, when I caught the whole of the young birds, and with them the mother too, who came within reach in attempting to rescue one of her brood, and had them taken home. There I took a cruel method of preventing their escape, for with a knife I pinioned each of them on the same side, and turned them loose in my garden, where I had a small but convenient artificial pond. For more than a fortnight, both the old birds appeared completely cowed. Indeed, for some days I felt apprehensive that they would abandon the care of the young ones. However, with much attention, I succeeded in rearing the latter by feeding them abundantly with the larvae of locusts, which they ate greedily, as well as with corn meal moistened with water, and the whole flock, consisting of eleven individuals, went on prosperously.

In December the weather became intensely cold, and I observed that now and then the gander would spread his wings, and sound a loud note, to which the female first, and then all the young ones in succession, would respond, when they would all run as far as the ground allowed them in a southerly direction, and attempt to fly off. I kept the whole flock three years. The old pair never bred while in my possession, but two pairs of the young ones did, one of them raising three, the other seven. They all bore a special enmity to dogs and showed dislike to cats; but they manifested a still greater animosity toward an old swan and a wild turkey cock which I had. I found them useful in clearing the garden of slugs and snails; and although they now and then nipped the vegetables, I liked their company. When I left Henderson, my flock of geese was given away, and I have not since heard how it has fared with them.

On one of my shooting excursions in the same neighborhood, I chanced one day to kill a wild Canada goose, which, on my return, was sent to the kitchen. The cook, while dressing it, found in it an egg ready for being laid, and brought it to me. It was placed under a common hen, and in due time hatched. Two years afterward the bird thus raised, mated with a male of the same species, and produced a brood. This goose was so gentle that she would suffer any person to caress her, and would readily feed from the hand. She was smaller than usual, but in every other respect as perfect as any I have ever seen. At the period of migration she showed by her movements less desire to fly off than any other I have known; but her mate, who had once been free, did not participate in this apathy.

The flight of this species of goose is firm, rather rapid, and capable of being protracted to a great extent. When once high in the air, they advance with extreme steadiness and regularity of motion. In rising from the water or from the ground, they usually run a few feet with outspread wings; but when suddenly surprised and in full plumage, a single spring on their broad webbed feet is sufficient to enable them to get on wing. While traveling to some considerable distance, they pass through the air at the height of about a mile, steadily following a direct course toward the point to which they are bound. Their notes are distinctly heard, and the various changes made in the disposition of their ranks are easily seen. But although on these occasions they move with the greatest regularity, yet when they are slowly advancing from south to north at an early period of the season, they fly much lower, alight more frequently, and are more likely to be bewildered by suddenly formed banks of fog, or by passing over cities or arms of the sea where much shipping may be in sight.

On such occasions great consternation prevails among them, they crowd together in a confused manner, wheel irregularly, and utter a constant cackling resembling the sounds from a disconcerted mob. Sometimes the flock separates, some individuals leave the rest, proceed in a direction contrary to that in which they came, and after a while, as if quite confused, sail toward the ground, once alighted on which they appear to become almost stupefied, so as to suffer themselves to be shot with ease, or even knocked down with sticks. This I have known to take place on many occasions, besides those of which I have myself been a witness. Heavy snowstorms also cause them great distress, and in the midst of them some have been known to fly againt beacons and lighthouses, dashing their heads against the walls in the middle of the day.

In the night they are attracted by the lights of these buildings, and now and then a whole flock is caught on such occasions. At other times their migrations northward are suddenly checked by a change of weather, the approach of which seems to be well known to them, for they will suddenly wheel and fly back in a southern direction several hundred miles. In this manner I have known flocks to return to the places which they had left a fortnight before. Nay even during the winter months, they are keenly sensible to changes in temperature, flying north or south in search of feeding grounds with so much knowledge of the future state of the weather that one may be assured when he sees them proceeding southward in the evening that the next morning will be cold, and vice versa.

If feeding in the fields or meadows, they nip the blades of grass sidewise, in the manner of the domestic goose, and after rainy weather, they are frequently seen rapidly patting the earth with both feet, as if to force the earthworms from their burrows. If they dabble at times with their bills in muddy water in search of food, this action is by no means so common with them as it is with ducks, the mallard for example. They are extremely fond of alighting in cornfields covered with tender blades, where they often remain through the night and commit great havoc.

Wherever you find them, and however remote from the haunts of man the place may be, they are at all times so vigilant and suspicious that it is extremely rare to surprise them. In keenness of sight and acuteness of hearing, they are perhaps surpassed by no bird whatever. They act as sentinels toward each other, and during the hours at which the flock reposes, one or more ganders stand on the watch. At the sight of cattle, horses, or animals of the deer kind, they are seldom alarmed, but a bear or a cougar is instantly announced, and if on such occasions the flock is on the ground near water, the birds immediately betake themselves in silence to the latter, swim to the middle of the pond or river, and there remain until danger is over. Should their enemies pursue them in the water, the males utter loud cries, and the birds arrange themselves in close ranks, rise simultaneously in a few seconds, and fly off in a compact body, seldom at such times forming lines or angles, it being in fact only when the distance they have to travel is great that they dispose themselves in those forms.

So acute is their sense of hearing that they are able to distinguish the different sounds or footsteps of their foes with astonishing accuracy. Thus the breaking of a dry stick by a deer is at once distinguished from the same accident occasioned by a man. If a dozen of large turtles drop into the water, making a great nose in their fall, or if the same effect is produced by an alligator, the wild goose pays no regard to it; but however faint and distant may be the sound of an Indian's paddle, that may by accident have struck the side of his canoe, it is at once marked, every individual raises its head and looks intently toward the place from which the noise has proceeded, and in silence all watch the movements of their enemy.

These birds are extremely cunning also, and should they conceive themselves unseen, they silently move into the tall grasses by the margin of the water, lower their heads, and lie perfectly quiet until the boat has passed by. I have seen them walk off from a large frozen pond into the woods to elude the sight of the hunter, and return as soon as he had crossed the pond. But should there be snow on the ice or in the woods, they prefer watching the intruder, and take to wing long before he is within shooting distance, as if aware of the ease with which they could be followed by their tracks over the treacherous surface.

When I first went to the Falls of the Ohio, the rocky shelvings of which are often bare for fully half a mile, thousands of wild geese of this species rested there at night. The breadth of the various channels that separate the rocky islands from either shore, and the rapidity of the currents which sweep along them, render this place of resort more secure than most others. The wild geese still betake themselves to these islands during winter for the same purpose, but their number has become very small; and so shy are these birds at present in the neighborhood of Louisville that the moment they are disturbed at the ponds where they go to feed each morning, were it but by the report of a single gun, they immediately return to their rocky asylums.

Even there, however, they are by no means secure, for it not unfrequently happens that a flock alights within half gunshot of a person concealed in a pile of drifted wood, whose aim generally proves too true for their peace. Nay, I knew a gentleman, who had a large mill opposite Rock Island, and who used to kill the poor geese at the distance of about a quarter of a mile by means of a small cannon heavily charged with rifle bullets; and, if I recollect truly, Mr. Tarascon in this manner not unfrequently obtained a dozen or more geese at a shot. This was done at dawn, when the birds were busily engaged in trimming their plumage with the view of flying off in a few minutes to their feeding grounds. This war of extermination could not last long; the geese deserted the fatal rock, and the great gun of the mighty miller was used only for a few weeks.

Ornithological Biography, Volume III

The Mink *(Mustela vison)*

Next to the ermine, the mink is the most active and destructive little depredator that prowls around the farmyard, or the farmer's duckpond, where the presence of one or two of these animals will soon be made known by the sudden disappearance of sundry young ducks and chickens. The vigilant farmer may perhaps see a fine fowl moving in a singular and most involuntary manner, in the clutches of a mink, toward a fissure in a rock or a hole in some pile of stones, in the gray of the morning, and should he rush to the spot to ascertain the fate of the unfortunate bird, he will see it suddenly twitched into a hole too deep for him to fathom and wish he had carried with him his double-barreled gun, to have ended at once the life of the voracious destroyer of his carefully tended poultry. Our friend, the farmer, is not, however, disposed to allow the mink to carry on the sport long, and therefore straightway repairs to the house for his gun, and if it be loaded and ready for use (as it always should be in every well-regulated farmhouse) he speedily returns with it to watch for the reappearance of the mink and shoot him ere he has the opportunity to depopulate his poultry yard. The farmer now takes a stand facing the retreat into which the mink has carried his property, and waits patiently until it may please him to show his head again. This, however, the cunning rogue will not always accommodate him by doing, and he may lose much time to no purpose. Let us introduce you to a scene on our own little place near New York.

There is a small brook, fed by several springs of pure water, which we have caused to be stopped by a stone dam to make a pond for ducks in the summer and ice in the winter; above the pond is a rough bank of stones through which the water filters into the pond. There is a little space near this where the sand and gravel have formed a diminutive beach. The ducks descending to the water are compelled to pass near this stony bank. Here a mink had fixed his quarters with certainly a degree of judgment and audacity worthy of high praise, for no settlement could promise to be more to his mind. At early dawn the crowing of several fine cocks, the cackling of many hens and chickens, and the paddling, splashing, and quacking of a hundred old and young ducks would please his ears; and by stealing to the edge of the bank of stones, with his body nearly concealed between two large pieces of broken granite, he could look around and see the unsuspecting ducks within a yard or two of his lurking place. When thus on the lookout dodging his head backward and forward, he waits until one of them has approached close to him, and then with a rush seizes the bird by the neck, and in a moment disappears with it between the rocks. He has not, however, escaped unobserved, and like other rogues deserves to be punished for having taken what did not belong to him. We draw near the spot, gun in hand, and after waiting some time in vain for the appearance of the mink, we cause some young ducks to be gently driven down to the pond—diving for worms or food of various kinds while danger so imminent is near them—intent only on the objects they are pursuing, they turn not a glance toward the dark crevice where we can now see the bright eyes of the mink as he lies concealed. The unsuspecting birds remind us of some of the young folks in that large pond we call the world, where, alas! they may be in greater danger than our poor ducks or chickens. Now we see a fine hen descend to the water; cautiously she steps on the sandy margin and dipping her bill in the clear stream, sips a few drops and raises her head as if in gratitude to the Giver of all good; she continues sipping and advancing gradually; she has now approached the fatal rocks, when with a sudden rush the mink has seized her; ere he can regain his hole, however, our gun's sharp crack is heard and the marauder lies dead before us.

We acknowledge that we have little inclination to say anything in defense of the mink. We must admit, however, that although he is a cunning and destructive rogue, his next-door neighbor, the ermine or common weasel, goes infinitely beyond him in his mischievous propensities. Whilst the mink is satisfied with destroying one or two fowls at a time, on which he makes a hearty meal, the weasel, in the very spirit of wanton destructiveness, sometimes in a single night puts to death every tenant of the poultry house!

Whilst residing at Henderson, on the banks of the Ohio River, we observed that minks were quite abundant, and often saw them carrying off rats which they caught like the weasel or ferret, and conveyed away in their mouths, holding them by the neck in the manner of a cat.

Along the trout streams of our Eastern and Northern States, the mink has been known to steal fish that, having been caught by some angler, had been left tied together with a string while the fisherman proceeded farther in quest of more. An angler informed us that he had lost in this way thirty or forty fine trout, which a mink dragged off the bank into the stream and devoured; and we have been told that by looking carefully after them, the minks could be seen watching the fisherman and in readiness to take his fish, should he leave it at any distance behind him. Mr. Hutson of Halifax informed us that he had a salmon weighing four pounds carried off by one of them.

We have observed that the mink is a tolerably expert fisher. On one occasion, whilst seated near a trout brook in the northern part of the State of New York, we heard a sudden splashing in the stream and saw a large trout gliding through the shallow water and making for some long overhanging roots on the side of the bank. A mink was in close pursuit, and dived after it; in a moment afterward it reappeared with the fish in its mouth. By a sudden rush we induced it to drop the trout, which was upward of a foot in length.

We are disposed to believe, however, that fishes are not the principal food on which the mink subsists. We have sometimes seen it feeding on frogs and crayfish. In the Northern States we have often observed it with a Wilson's meadow mouse in its mouth, and in Carolina the very common cotton rat furnishes no small proportion of its food. We have frequently remarked it coursing along the edges of the marshes, and found that it was in search of this rat, which frequents such localities, and we discovered that it was not an unsuccessful mouser. We once saw a mink issuing from a hole in the earth, dragging by the neck a large Florida rat.

This species has a good nose, and is able to pursue its prey like a hound following a deer. A friend of ours informed us that once while standing on the border of a swamp near the Ashley River, he perceived a marsh hare dashing by him; a moment after came a mink with its nose near the ground, following the frightened animal, apparently by the scent, through the marsh.

The Viviparous Quadrupeds of North America, Volume I

Frontier River

When my wife, my eldest son (then an infant), and myself were returning from Pennsylvania to Kentucky, we found it expedient, the waters being unusually low, to provide ourselves with a skiff, to enable us to proceed to our abode at Henderson. I purchased a large, commodious, and light boat of that denomination. We procured a mattress, and our friends furnished us with ready prepared viands. We had two stout Negro rowers, and in this trim we left the village of Shippingport, in expectation of reaching the place of our destination in a very few days.

It was in the month of October. The autumnal tints already decorated the shores of that queen of rivers, the Ohio. Every tree was hung with long and flowing festoons of different species of vines, many loaded with clustered fruits of varied brilliancy, their rich bronzed carmine mingling beautifully with the yellow foliage, which now predominated over the yet green leaves, reflecting more lively tints from the clear stream than ever landscape painter portrayed, or poet imagined.

The days were yet warm. The sun had assumed the rich and glowing hue which at that season produces the singular phenomenon called there the "Indian Summer." The moon had rather passed the meridian of her grandeur. We glided down the river, meeting no other ripple of the water than that formed by the propulsion of our boat. Leisurely we moved along, gazing all day on the grandeur and beauty of the wild scenery around us.

Now and then a large catfish rose to the surface of the water in pursuit of a shoal of fry, which, starting simultaneously from the liquid element like so many silver arrows, produced a shower of light, while the pursuer with open jaws seized the stragglers, and, with a splash of his tail, disappeared from our view. Other fishes we heard, uttering beneath our bark a rumbling noise, the strange sound of which we discovered to proceed from the white perch, for on casting our net from the bow, we caught several of that species, when the noise ceased for a time.

Nature, in her varied arrangements, seems to have felt a partiality toward this portion of our country. As the traveler ascends or descends the Ohio, he cannot help remarking that alternately, nearly the whole length of the river, the margin, on one side, is bounded by lofty hills and a rolling surface, while on the other, extensive plains of the richest alluvial land are seen as far as the eye can command the view. Islands of varied size and form rise here and there from the bosom of the water, and the winding course of the stream frequently brings you to places where the idea of being on a river of great length changes to that of floating on a lake of moderate extent. Some of these islands are of considerable size and value; while others, small and insignificant, seem as if intended for contrast, and as serving to enhance the general interest of the scenery. These little islands are frequently overflowed during great freshets or floods, and receive at their heads prodigious heaps of drifted timber. We foresaw with great concern the alterations that cultivation would soon produce along those delightful banks.

As night came, sinking in darkness the broader portions of the river, our minds became affected by strong emotions, and wandered far beyond the present moments. The tinkling of bells told us that the cattle which bore them were gently roving from valley to valley in search of food, or returning to their distant homes. The hooting of the great owl or the muffled noise of its wings as it sailed smoothly over the stream were matters of interest to us; so was the sound of the boatman's horn, as it came

145. OSPREY *(Pandion haliaetus)*. The huge stick nests of the fish hawk are familiar along the seacoast and near inland waters. Increasingly, as a result of pesticide poisons obtained through the fish that are eaten, ospreys are being reduced in numbers and nests are producing no young. Fish form their only food. These are obtained by plunges into the water, sometimes from a height of as much as 100 feet. When carrying a captured fish in its talons, an osprey always holds it head first, in the most streamlined position.

146–147. PACIFIC LOON *(Gavia arctica)*. On inland waters of the far north, large lakes, small ponds, sloughs, the Pacific loon nests and raises its young. During the breeding season, its wild, far-carrying call is repeated frequently. Afterward the bird is largely silent. When winter comes and ice forms, it flies to the open salt water of the coast. Its main wintering ground appears to be offshore along southern and Lower California.

148–149. COMMON GOLDENEYE *(Bucephala clangula)*. This diving duck feeds at depths of as much as twenty feet. Animal food makes up the bulk of its diet. Among old-time hunters, it was known as the "whistler" because of the high-pitched sound produced by its wings. Nests are generally made in tree cavities, some as high as sixty feet. The light, newly hatched ducklings drop unharmed to the ground. The goldeneye winters on salt water, usually flying offshore at dusk to sleep on the open sea.

150–151. TRUMPETER SWAN *(Olor buccinator)*. A giant among North American birds, with a wingspread of more than eight feet, the great trumpeter swan once bred from James Bay to Missouri. By the early years of the present century, it was reduced almost to extinction. From a comparatively few birds, living in such sanctuaries as Yellowstone National Park, the trumpeter swan is now gradually increasing in numbers.

152. CANADA GOOSE *(Branta canadensis)*. Ever since the days of the pioneers, the sight of Vs of Canada geese flying north has been considered a sign of spring. Many of these waterfowl nest on the Arctic tundra. The Canada goose mates for life and the families remain together during the flight south to the wintering ground and until after the return north the following spring. In spite of continual hunting pressure, this wild goose survives through its wary intelligence.

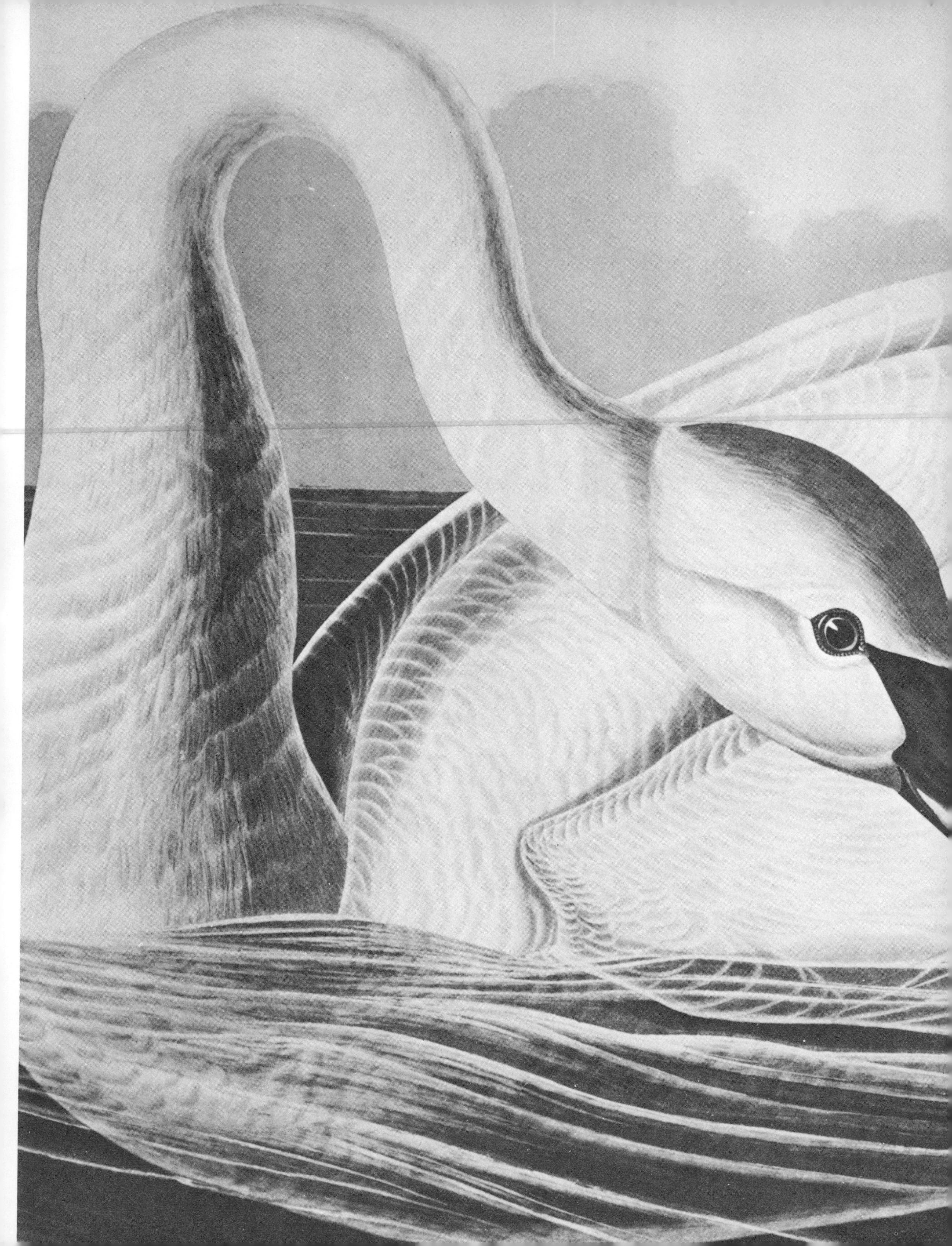

winding more and more softly from afar. When daylight returned, many songsters burst forth with echoing notes, more and more mellow to the listening ear. Here and there the lonely cabin of a squatter struck the eye, giving note of commencing civilization. The crossing of the stream by a deer foretold how soon the hills would be covered with snow.

Many sluggish flatboats we overtook and passed; some laden with produce from the different headwaters of the small rivers that pour their tributary streams into the Ohio; others, of less dimensions, crowded with emigrants from distant parts, in search of a new home. Purer pleasures I never felt; nor have you, Reader, I ween, unless indeed you have felt the like, and in such company.

The margins of the shores and of the river were, at this season, amply supplied with game. A wild turkey, a grouse, or a blue-winged teal could be procured in a few moments; and we fared well, for, whenever we pleased we landed, struck up a fire, and provided as we were with the necessary utensils, procured a good repast.

Several of these happy days passed, and we neared our home, when, one evening, not far from Pigeon Creek (a small stream which runs into the Ohio from the State of Indiana), a loud and strange noise was heard, so like the yells of Indian warfare that we pulled at our oars, and made for the opposite side as fast and as quietly as possible. The sounds increased, we imagined we heard cries of "murder"; and as we knew that some depredations had lately been committed in the country by dissatisfied parties of aborigines, we felt for a while extremely uncomfortable. Ere long, however, our minds became more calmed, and we plainly discovered that the singular uproar was produced by an enthusiastic set of Methodists, who had wandered thus far out of the common way for the purpose of holding one of their annual camp meetings, under the shade of a beech forest. Without meeting with any other interruption, we reached Henderson, distant from Shippingport, by water, about two hundred miles.

When I think of these times, and call back to my mind the grandeur and beauty of those almost uninhabited shores; when I picture to myself the dense and lofty summits of the forests, that everywhere spread along the hills and overhung the margins of the stream, unmolested by the ax of the settler; when I know how dearly purchased the safe navigation of that river has been, by the blood of many worthy Virginians; when I see that no longer any aborigines are to be found there, and that the vast herds of elk, deer, and buffaloes which once pastured on these hills, and in these valleys, making for themselves great roads to the several salt springs, have ceased to exist; when I reflect that all this grand portion of our Union, instead of being in a state of nature, is now more or less covered with villages, farms, and towns, where the din of hammers and machinery is constantly heard; that the woods are fast disappearing under the ax by day, and the fire by night; that hundreds of steamboats are gliding to and fro over the whole length of the majestic river, forcing commerce to take root and to prosper at every spot; when I see the surplus population of Europe coming to assist in the destruction of the forest, and transplanting civilization into its darkest recesses; when I remember that these extraordinary changes have all taken place in the short period of twenty years, I pause, wonder, and, although I know all to be fact, can scarcely believe its reality.

Ornithological Biography, Volume I

Catfish of the Ohio

Several species or varieties of catfish are found in the Ohio, namely, the blue, the white, and the mud cats, which differ considerably in their form and color, as well as in their habits. The mud cat is the best, although it seldom attains so great a size as the rest. The blue cat is the coarsest, but when not exceeding from four to six pounds it affords tolerable eating. The white cat is preferable to the last, but not so common; and the yellow mud cat is the best and rarest. Of the blue kind some have been caught that weighed a hundred pounds. Such fish, however, are looked upon as monsters.

The form in all the varieties inclines to the conical, the head being disproportionately large, while the body tapers away to the root of the tail. The eyes, which are small, are placed far apart, and situated as it were on the top of the forehead, but laterally. The mouth is wide and armed with numerous small and very sharp teeth, while it is defended by single-sided spines, which, when the fish is in the agonies of death, stand out at right angles, and are so firmly fixed as sometimes to break before you can loosen them. The catfish has also feelers of proportionate length, apparently intended to guide its motions over the bottom, whilst its eyes are watching the objects passing above.

When the waters are rising fast and have become muddy, a single line is used for catching catfish. It is fastened to the elastic branch of some willow several feet above the water, and must be twenty or thirty feet in length. The entrails of a wild turkey, or a piece of fresh venison furnish good bait; and if, when you visit your line the next morning after you have set it, the water has not risen too much, the swinging of the willow indicates that a fish has been hooked, and you have only to haul the prize ashore.

One evening I saw that the river was rising at a great rate, although it was still within its banks. I knew that the white perch were running, that is, ascending the river from the sea, and, anxious to have a tasting of that fine fish, I baited a line with a crayfish and fastened it to the bough of a tree. Next morning as I pulled in the line, it felt as if fast at the bottom, yet on drawing it slowly I found that it came. Presently I felt a strong pull, the line slipped through my fingers, and next instant a large catfish leaped out of the water. I played it for a while until it became exhausted, when I drew it ashore. It had swallowed the hook, and I cut off the line close to its head. Then passing a stick through one of the gills, I and a servant tugged the fish home. On cutting it open, we, to our surprise, found in its stomach a fine white perch, dead, but not in the least injured. The perch had been lightly hooked, and the catfish, after swallowing it, had been hooked in the stomach, so that, although the instrument was small, the torture caused by it no doubt tended to disable the catfish. The perch we ate, and the cat, which was fine, we divided into four parts, and distributed among our neighbors.

My most worthy friend and relative, Nicholas Berthoud, Esq., who formerly resided at Shippingport in Kentucky, but now in New York, a better fisher than whom I never knew, once placed a trotline in the basin below Tarascon's Mills, at the foot of the rapids of the Ohio. I cannot recollect the bait which was used, but on taking up the line we obtained a remarkably fine catfish, in which was found the greater part of a sucking pig.

Ornithological Biography, Volume III

The Otter (Lutra canadensis)

Fresh and pleasant in our mind is the recollection of our early expeditions among the wild woods, and along the unvisited shores of our new country; and although more

than forty years of varied and busy life have passed since the otter was shot and drawn, whose figure we have given, we will try to take you with us to a spot on the eastern banks of the fair Ohio. It is a cold wintry morning: the earth concealed by a slight covering of snow, and the landscape in all its original wildness. Here let us proceed cautiously, followed by that constant companion, our faithful dog. Whilst we are surveying the quiet waters as they roll onward toward the great Mississippi, in whose muddy current they will lose their clear and limpid character, and become as opaque and impetuous as the waves of that mighty river of the West, we see a dark object making its way toward the spot on which we stand, through the swiftly dividing element. It has not observed us: we remain perfectly still, and presently it is distinctly visible; it is an otter, and now within the range of our old gun "Tear Jacket," we take but one moment to raise our piece and fire; the water is agitated by a violent convulsive movement of the animal, our dog plunges into the river, and swimming eagerly to the otter, seizes it, but the latter dives, dragging the dog with it beneath the surface, and when they reappear, the otter has caught the dog by the nose and is struggling violently. The brave dog, however, does not give up, but in a few moments drags the wounded otter to the shore, and we immediately dispatch it. Being anxious to figure the animal, we smooth its disordered fur and proceed homeward with it, where, although at that time we had not drawn many quadrupeds, we soon select a position in which to figure the otter, and accordingly draw it with one foot in a steel trap, and endeavor to represent the pain and terror felt by the creature when its foot is caught by the sharp sawlike teeth of the trap.

Not far from the town of Henderson, Kentucky, but on the opposite side of the Ohio River, in the State of Indiana, there is a pond nearly one mile in length, with a depth of water varying from twelve to fifteen feet. Its shores are thickly lined with cane, and on the edge of the water stand many large and lofty cypress trees. We often used to seat ourselves on a fallen trunk, and watch in this secluded spot the actions of the birds and animals which resorted to it, and here we several times observed otters engaged in catching fishes and devouring them. When pursuing a fish, they dived expertly and occasionally remained for more than a minute below the surface. They generally held their prey when they came to the top of the water by the head, and almost invariably swam with it to a half-sunken log, or to the margin of the pond, to eat the fish at their ease, having done which, they returned again to the deep water to obtain more.

One morning we observed that some of these animals resorted to the neighborhood of the root of a large tree which stood on the side of the pond opposite to us, and with its overhanging branches shaded the water. After a fatiguing walk through the tangled canebrake and thick underwood which bordered the sides of this lonely place, we reached the opposite side of the pond near the large tree, and moved cautiously through the mud and water toward its roots; but the hearing or sight of the otters was attracted to us, and we saw several of them hastily make off at our approach. On sounding the tree with the butt of our gun, we discovered that it was hollow, and then having placed a large stick in a slanting position against the trunk, we succeeded in reaching the lowest bough, and thence climbed up to a broken branch from which an aperture into the upper part of the hollow enabled us to examine the interior. At the bottom there was quite a large space or chamber to which the otters retired, but whether for security or to sleep we could not decide.

Next morning we returned to the spot, accompanied by one of our neighbors, and having approached and stopped up the entrance under water as noiselessly as possible, we cut a hole in the side of the tree four or five feet from the ground, and as soon as it was large enough to admit our heads, we peeped in and discovered three otters on a sort of bed composed of the inner bark of trees and other soft substances, such as water grasses. We continued cutting the hole we had made larger, and when sufficiently widened, took some green saplings, split them at the butt end, and managed to fix the head of each animal firmly to the ground by passing one of these split pieces over his neck, and then pressing the stick forcibly downward. Our companion then crept into the hollow, and soon killed the otters, with which we returned home.

The American otter frequents running streams, large ponds, and more sparingly the shores of some of our great lakes. It prefers those waters which are clear, and makes a hole or burrow in the banks, the entrance to which is under water.

This species has a singular habit of sliding off the wet sloping banks into the water, and the trappers take advantage of this habit to catch the animal by placing a steel trap near the bottom of their sliding places, so that the otters occasionally put their foot into it as they are swiftly gliding toward the water.

In Carolina, a very common mode of capturing the otter is by tying a pretty large fish on the pan of a steel trap, which is sunk in the water where it is from five to ten feet deep. The otter dives to the bottom to seize the fish, is caught either by the nose or foot, and is generally found drowned. At other times the trap is set under the water, without bait, on a log, one end of which projects into the water, whilst the other rests on the banks of a pond or river; the otter, in endeavoring to mount the log, is caught in the trap.

Mr. Godman, in his account of these singular quadrupeds, states that "their favorite sport is sliding, and for this purpose in winter the highest ridge of snow is selected, to the top of which the otters scramble, where, lying on the belly with the forefeet bent backward, they give themselves an impulse with their hind legs and swiftly glide headforemost down the declivity, sometimes for the distance of twenty yards. This sport they continue apparently with the keenest enjoyment until fatigue or hunger induces them to desist."

This statement is confirmed by Cartwright, Hearne, Richardson, and more recent writers who have given the history of this species, and is in accordance with our own personal observations.

The otters ascend the bank at a place suitable for their diversion, and sometimes where it is very steep, so that they are obliged to make quite an effort to gain the top; they slide down in rapid succession where there are many at a sliding place. On one occasion we were resting on the bank of Canoe Creek, a small stream near Henderson, which empties into the Ohio, when a pair of otters made their appearance, and not observing our proximity, began to enjoy their sliding pastime. They glided down the soaplike muddy surface of the slide with the rapidity of an arrow from a bow, and we counted each one making twenty-two slides before we disturbed their sportive occupation.

This habit of the otter of sliding down from elevated places to the borders of streams is not confined to cold countries, or to slides on the snow or ice, but is pursued in the Southern States, where the earth is seldom covered with snow or the waters frozen over. Along the reserve dams of the rice fields of Carolina and Georgia these slides are very common. From the fact that this occurs in most cases during winter, about the period of the rutting season, we are inclined to the belief that this propensity may be traced to those instincts which lead the sexes to their periodical associations.

The Viviparous Quadrupeds of North America, Volume II

Wildlife on the St. Johns

On the tide we proceeded apace. Myriads of cormorants covered the face of the waters, and over it fish crows innumerable were already arriving from their distant roosts. We landed at one place to search for the birds whose charming melodies had engaged our attention, and here and there some young eagles we shot, to add to our store of fresh provisions! The river did not seem to me equal in beauty to the fair Ohio; the shores were in many places low and swampy, to the great delight of the numberless herons that moved along in gracefulness, and the grim alligators that swam in sluggish sullenness. In going up a bayou, we caught a great number of the young of the latter for the purpose of making experiments upon them.

After sailing a considerable way, during which our commander and officers took the soundings as well as the angles and bearings of every nook and crook of the sinuous stream, we anchored one evening at a distance of fully one hundred miles from the mouth of the river. The weather, although it was the twelfth of February, was quite warm, the thermometer on board standing at 75°, and on the shore at 90°. The fog was so thick that neither of the shores could be seen, and yet the river was not a mile in breadth. The "blind mosquitoes" covered every object, even in the cabin, and so wonderfully abundant were these tormentors that they more than once fairly extinguished the candles whilst I was writing my journal, which I closed in despair, crushing between the leaves more than a hundred of the little wretches. Bad as they are, however, these blind mosquitoes do not bite. As if purposely to render our situation doubly uncomfortable, there was an establishment for jerking beef, on the nearer shores to the windward of our vessel, from which the breeze came laden with no sweet odors.

In the morning when I arose, the country was still covered with thick fogs, so that although I could plainly hear the notes of the birds on shore, not an object could I see beyond the bowsprit, and the air was as close and sultry as on the previous evening. Guided by the scent of the jerkers' works, we went on shore where we found the vegetation already far advanced. The blossoms of the jessamine, ever pleasing, lay steeped in dew; the humming bee was collecting her winter's store from the snowy flowers of the native orange; and the little warblers frisked along the twigs of the smilax. Now, amid the tall pines of the forest, the sun's rays began to force their way, and as the dense mists dissolved, the bright luminary at length shone forth.

We explored the woods around, guided by some friendly live-oakers who had pitched their camp in the vicinity. After a while the *Spark* again displayed her sails, and as she silently glided along, we spied a Seminole Indian approaching us in his canoe. The poor dejected son of the woods, endowed with talents of the highest order, although rarely acknowledged by the proud usurpers of his native soil, has spent the night in fishing, and the morning in procuring the superb-feathered game of the swampy thickets; and with both he comes to offer them for our acceptance. Alas! thou fallen one, descendant of an ancient line of freeborn hunters, would that I could restore to thee thy birthright, thy natural independence, the generous feelings that were once fostered in thy brave bosom. But the irrevocable deed is done, and I can merely admire the perfect symmetry of his frame, as he dexterously throws on our deck the trouts and turkeys which he has captured. He receives a recompense, and without smile or bow, or acknowledgment of any kind, off he starts with the speed of an arrow from his own bow.

Alligators were extremely abundant, and the heads of the fishes which they had snapped off lay floating around on the dark waters. A rifle bullet was now and then sent through the eye of one of the largest, which, with a tremendous splash of its tail, expired. One morning we saw a monstrous fellow lying on the shore. I was desirous of obtaining him to make an accurate drawing of his head, and, accompanied by my assistant and two of the sailors, proceeded cautiously toward him. When within a few yards, one of us fired and sent through his side an ounce ball, which tore open a hole large enough to receive a man's hand. He slowly raised his head, bent himself upward, opened his huge jaws, swung his tail to and fro, rose on his legs, blew in a frightful manner, and fell to the earth. My assistant leaped on shore, and, contrary to my injunctions, caught hold of the animal's tail, when the alligator, awakening from its trance, with a last effort crawled slowly toward the water, and plunged heavily into it.

Had he thought of once flourishing his tremendous weapon there might have been an end to his assailant's life, but he fortunately went in peace to his grave, where we left him, as the water was too deep. The same morning, another of equal size was observed swimming directly for the bows of our vessel, attracted by the gentle rippling of the water there. One of the officers, who had watched him, fired and scattered his brains through the air, when he tumbled and rolled at a fearful rate, blowing all the while most furiously. The river was bloody for yards around, but although the monster passed close by the vessel, we could not secure him, and after a while he sank to the bottom.

Early one morning I hired a boat and two men, with the view of returning to St. Augustine by a short cut. Our baggage being placed on board, I bade adieu to the officers, and off we started. About four in the afternoon we arrived at the short cut, forty miles distant from our point of departure, and where we had expected to procure a wagon but were disappointed. So we laid our things on the bank, and, leaving one of my assistants to look after them, I set out, accompanied by the other, and my Newfoundland dog. We had eighteen miles to go; and as the sun was only two hours high, we struck off at a good rate. Presently we entered a pine barren. The country was as level as a floor; our path, although narrow, was well beaten, having been used by the Seminole Indians for ages, and the weather was calm and beautiful. Now and then a rivulet occurred, from which we quenched our thirst, while the magnolias and other flowering plants on its banks relieved the dull uniformity of the woods. When the path separated into two branches, both seemingly leading the same way, I would follow one, while my companion took the other, and unless we met again in a short time, one of us would go across the intervening forest.

The sun went down behind a cloud, and the southeast breeze that sprung up at this moment sounded dolefully among the tall pines. Along the eastern horizon lay a bed of black vapor, which gradually rose, and soon covered the heavens. The air felt hot and oppressive, and we knew that a tempest was approaching. Plato was now our guide, the white spots of his skin being the only objects that we could discern amid the darkness, and as if aware of his utility in this respect, he kept a short way before us on the trail. Had we imagined ourselves more than a few miles from the town, we would have made a camp, and remained under its shelter for the night; but conceiving that the distance could not be great, we resolved to trudge along.

Large drops began to fall from the murky mass overhead; thick, impenetrable darkness surrounded us, and to my dismay, the dog refused to proceed. Groping with my hands on the ground, I discovered that several trails branched out at the spot where he lay down; and when I had selected one, he went on.

Vivid flashes of lightning streamed across the heavens, the wind increased to a gale, and the rain poured down upon us like a torrent. The water soon rose on the level ground so as almost to cover our feet, and we slowly advanced, fronting the tempest. Here and there a tall pine on fire presented a magnificent spectacle, illuminating the trees around it, and surrounded by a halo of dim light, abruptly bordered with the deep black of the night. At one time we passed through a tangled thicket of low trees, at another crossed a stream flushed by the heavy rain, and again proceeded over the open barrens.

How long we thus, half lost, groped our way, is more than I can tell you; but at length the tempest passed over, and suddenly the clear sky became spangled with stars. Soon after we smelled the salt marshes, and walking directly toward them, like pointers advancing on a covey of partridges, we at last to our great joy descried the light of the beacon near St. Augustine. My dog began to run briskly around, having met with ground on which he had hunted before, and taking a direct course, led us to the great causeway that crosses the marshes at the back of the town. We refreshed ourselves with the produce of the first orange tree that we met with, and in half an hour more arrived at our hotel. Drenched with rain, steaming with perspiration, and covered to the knees with mud, you may imagine what figures we cut in the eyes of the good people whom we found snugly enjoying themselves in the sitting room. Next morning, Major Gates, who had received me with much kindness, sent a wagon with mules and two trusty soldiers for my companion and luggage.

Ornithological Biography, Volume II

The Beaver *(Castor canadensis)*

The following account was noted down by us as related by a trapper named Prevost, who had been in the service of the American Fur Company for upward of twenty years, in the region adjoining the spurs of the Rocky Mountains, and who was the "Patroon" that conveyed us down the Missouri River in the summer and autumn of 1843. As it confirms the statements of Hearne, Richardson, and other close observers of the habits of the beaver, we trust that although it may present little that is novel, it will from its truth be acceptable and interesting to our readers. Mr. Prevost states in substance as follows.

Beavers prefer small clear-water rivers and creeks, and likewise resort to large springs. They, however, at times frequent great rivers and lakes. The trappers believe that they can have notice of the approach of winter weather, and of its probable severity, by observing the preparations made by the beavers to meet its rigors, as these animals always cut their wood in good season, and if this be done early, winter is at hand.

The beaver dams, where the animal is at all abundant, are built across the streams to their very headwaters. Usually these dams are formed of mud, mosses, small stones, and branches of trees cut about three feet in length and from seven to twelve inches round. The bark of the trees in all cases is taken off for winter provender, before the sticks are carried away to make up the dam. The largest tree cut by the beaver, seen by Prevost, measured eighteen inches in diameter; but so large a trunk is very rarely cut down by this animal. In the instance just mentioned, the branches only were used, the trunk not having been appropriated to the repairs of the dam or aught else by the beavers.

In constructing the dams, the sticks, mud, and moss are matted and interlaced together in the firmest and most compact manner; so much so that even men cannot destroy them without a great deal of labor. The mud and moss at the bottom are rooted up with the animal's snout, somewhat in the manner hogs work in the earth, and clay and grasses are stuffed and plastered in between the sticks, roots, and branches in so workmanlike a way as to render the structure quite watertight. The dams are sometimes seven or eight feet high, and are from ten to twelve feet wide at the bottom, but are built up with the sides inclining toward each other, so as to form a narrow surface on the top. They are occasionally as much as three hundred yards in length, and often extend beyond the bed of the stream in a circular form, so as to overflow all the timber near the margin, which the beavers cut down for food during winter, heap together in large quantities, and so fasten to the shore under the surface of the water that even a strong current cannot tear it away, although they generally place it in such a position that the current does not pass over it. These piles or heaps of wood are placed in front of the lodges, and when the animal wishes to feed he proceeds to them, takes a piece of wood, and drags it to one of the small holes near the principal entrance running above the water, although beneath the surface of the ground. Here the bark is devoured at leisure, and the wood is afterward thrust out, or used in repairing the dam. These small galleries are more or less abundant according to the number of animals in the lodges. The larger lodges are, in the interior, about seven feet in diameter, and between two and three feet high, resembling a great oven. They are placed near the edge of the water, although actually built on or in the ground. In front, the beavers scratch away the mud to secure a depth of water that will enable them to sink their wood deep enough to prevent its being impacted in the ice when the dam is frozen over, and also to allow them always free egress from their lodges, so that they may go to the dam and repair it if necessary. The top of the lodge is formed by placing branches of trees matted with mud, grasses, moss, &c., together, until the whole fabric measures on the outside from twelve to twenty feet in diameter, and is six or eight feet high, the size depending on the number of inhabitants. The outward coating is entirely of mud or earth, and smoothed off as if plastered with a trowel. As beavers, however, never work in the daytime, no person we believe has yet seen how they perform their task, or give this hard finish to their houses. This species does not use its forefeet in swimming, but for carrying burthens: this can be observed by watching the young ones, which suffer their forefeet to drag by the side of the body, using only the hind feet to propel themselves through the water. Before diving, the beaver gives a smart slap with its tail on the water, making a noise that may be heard a considerable distance, but in swimming the tail is not seen to work, the animal being entirely submerged except the nose and part of the head; it swims fast and well, but with nothing like the speed of the otter (*Lutra canadensis*).

The beavers cut a broad ditch all around their lodge, so deep that it cannot freeze to the bottom, and into this ditch they make the holes already spoken of, through which they go in and out and bring their food. The beds of these singular animals are separated slightly from each other, and are placed around the wall or circumference of the interior of the lodge; they are formed merely of a few grasses or the tender bark of trees, the space in the center of the lodge being left unoccupied. The beavers usually go to the dam every evening to see if repairs are needed, and to deposit their ordure in the water near the dam, or at least at some distance from their lodge.

They rarely travel by land, unless their dams have been carried away by the ice, and even then they take the beds of the rivers or streams for their roadway. In cutting down trees they are not always so fortunate as to have them fall into the water, or even toward it, as the trunks of trees cut down by these animals are observed lying in various positions; although as most trees on the margin of a stream or river lean somewhat toward the water, or have their largest branches extended over it, many of those cut down by the beavers naturally fall in that direction.

It is a curious fact, says our trapper, that among the beavers there are some that are lazy and will not work at all, either to assist in building lodges or dams or to cut down wood for their winter stock. The industrious ones beat these idle fellows and drive them away, sometimes cutting off a part of their tail and otherwise injuring them. These *paresseux* are more easily caught in traps than the others, and the trapper rarely misses one of them. They only dig a hole from the water running obliquely toward the surface of the ground twenty-five or thirty feet, from which they emerge when hungry to obtain food, returning to the same hole with the wood they procure to eat the bark.

They never form dams, and are sometimes to the number of five or seven together; all are males. It is not at all improbable that these unfortunate fellows have, as is the case with the males of many species of animals, been engaged in fighting with others of their sex, and after having been conquered and driven away from the lodge, have become idlers from a kind of necessity. The working beavers, on the contrary, associate, males, females, and young together.

Beavers are caught and found in good order at all seasons of the year in the Rocky Mountains; for in those regions the atmosphere is never warm enough to injure the fur; in the lowlands, however, the trappers rarely begin to capture them before the first of September, and they relinquish the pursuit about the last of May. This is understood to be along the Missouri, and the so-called Spanish country.

Cartwright found a beaver that weighted forty-five pounds; and we were assured that they have been caught weighing sixty-one pounds before being cleaned. The only portions of their flesh that are considered fine eating, are the sides of the belly, the rump, the tail, and the liver. The tail, so much spoken of by travelers and by various authors, as being very delicious eating, we did not think equaled their descriptions. It has nearly the taste of beef marrow but is rather oily, and cannot be partaken of unless in a very moderate quantity, except by one whose stomach is strong enough to digest the most greasy substances.

Beavers become very fat at the approach of autumn; but during winter they fall off in flesh, so that they are generally quite poor by spring, when they feed upon the bark of roots, and the roots of various aquatic plants, some of which are at that season white, tender, and juicy. During winter, when the ice is thick and strong, the trappers hunt the beaver in the following manner. A hole is cut in the ice as near as possible to the aperture leading to the dwelling of the animal, the situation of which is first ascertained; a green stick is placed firmly in front of it, and a smaller stick on each side, about a foot from the stick of green wood; the bottom is then patted or beaten smooth and even, and a strong stake is set into the ground to hold the chain of the trap, which is placed within a few inches of the stick of green wood, well baited, and the beaver, attracted either by the fresh bark or the bait, is almost always caught. Although when captured in this manner, the animal struggles, diving and swimming about in its efforts to escape, it never cuts off a foot in order to obtain its liberty; probably because it is drowned before it has had time to think of this method of saving itself from the hunter. When trapping under other circumstances, the trap is placed within five or six inches of the shore, and about the same distance below the surface of the water, secured and baited as usual. If caught, the beavers now and then cut off the foot by which they are held, in order to make their escape.

A singular habit of the beaver was mentioned to us by the trapper, Prevost, of which we do not recollect having before heard. He said that when two beaver lodges are in the vicinity of each other, the animals proceed from one of them at night to a certain spot, deposit their castoreum, and then return to their lodge. The beavers in the other lodge, scenting this, repair to the same spot, cover it over with earth, and then make a similar deposit on the top. This operation is repeated by each party alternately, until quite a mound is raised, sometimes to the height of four or five feet.

The strong musky substance contained in the glands of the beaver is called castoreum—by trappers, bark-stone—with this the traps are baited. A small stick, four or five inches long, is chewed at one end, and that part dipped in the castoreum, which is generally kept in a small horn. The stick is then placed with the anointed end above water and the other end downward. The beaver can smell the castoreum at least one hundred yards, makes toward it at once, and is generally caught.

Where beavers have not been disturbed or hunted, and are abundant, they rise nearly half out of water at the first smell of the castoreum, and become so excited that they are heard to cry aloud, and breathe hard to catch the odor as it floats on the air. A good trapper used to catch about eighty beavers in the autumn, sixty or seventy in the spring, and upward of three hundred in the summer in the mountains, taking occasionally as many as five hundred in one year. Sixty or seventy beaver skins are required to make a pack weighing one hundred pounds, which, when sent to a good market, is worth, even now, from three to four hundred dollars.

The Indians occasionally destroy beaver dams in order to capture these animals, and have good dogs to aid them in this purpose. The mountain Indians, however, are not trappers.

Sometimes the Indians of the prairies break open beaver lodges in the summertime, as, during winter they are usually frozen hard. The beaver is becoming very scarce in the Rocky Mountains, so much so that if a trapper now secures one hundred in the winter and spring hunt, he is considered fortunate.

Formerly, when the fur was high in price and the animals abundant, the trading companies were wont to send as many as thirty or forty men, each with from six to twelve traps and two good horses: when arrived at a favorable spot to begin their work, these men erected a camp, and each one sought alone for his game, the skins of which he brought to camp, where a certain number of men always remained to stretch and dry them.

The trappers subsist principally upon the animals they kill, having a rifle and a pair of pistols with them. After a successful hunt, on meeting each other at the camp, they have a "frolic" as they term it.

Some old and wary beavers are so cunning, that on finding the bait they cover it over, as if it were on the ground, with sticks, &c., deposit their own castoreum on the top, and manage to remove the trap. This is often the case when the beaver has been hunted previously. In places where they have remained undisturbed, but few escape the experienced trapper. The trappers are not very unfrequently killed by the Indians, and their occupation is one involving toil and hazard. They rarely gain a competence for their old age, to say nothing of a fortune, and in fact all the articles they are of necessity obliged to purchase in the Indian country cost them large sums, as their price is greatly increased by the necessary charges for transportation to the remote regions of the West.

When at Fort Union, we saw a trapper who had just returned from an unfortunate expedition to the mountains; his two horses had been stolen, and he lost his gun and rifle in coming down the river in a slender canoe, and was obliged to make for the shore, dig a hole wherein to deposit the few furs he had left, and travel several hundred miles on foot with only berries and roots for his food. He was quite naked when he reached the fort.

The beaver which we brought from Boston to New York was fed principally on potatoes and apples, which he contrived to peel as if assisted with a knife, although his lower incisors were his only substitute for that useful implement. While at this occupation the animal was seated on his rump, in the manner of a ground hog, marmot, or squirrel, and looked like a very large woodchuck, using his forefeet, as squirrels and marmots are wont to do.

This beaver was supplied every day with a large basin filled with water, and every morning his ordure was found to have been deposited therein. He generally slept on a good bed of straw in his cage, but one night having been taken out and placed at the back of the yard in a place where we thought he would be secure, we found next morning to our surprise that he had gnawed a large hole through a stout pine door which separated him from that part of the yard nearest the house, and had wandered about until he fell into the space excavated and walled up outside the kitchen window. Here he was quite entrapped, and having no other chance of escape from this pit, into which he had unluckily fallen, he gnawed away at the window sill and the sash, on which his teeth took such effect that on an examination of the premises we found that a carpenter and several dollars' worth of work were needed to repair damages. When turned loose in the yard in the daytime he would at times slap his tail twice or thrice on the brick pavement, after which he elevated this member from the ground, and walked about in an extremely awkward manner. He fell ill soon after we had received him, and when killed was examined by Dr. James Trudeau, who found that he would shortly have died of an organic disease.

It is stated by some authors that the beaver feeds on fish. We doubt whether he possesses this habit, as we in several occasions placed fish before those we saw in captivity, and although they were not very choice in their food, and devoured any kind of vegetable, and even bread, they in every case suffered fish to remain untouched in their cages.

The food of this species, in a state of nature, consists of the bark of several kinds of trees and shrubs, and of bulbous and other roots. It is particularly fond of the bark of the birch (*Betula*), the cottonwood (*Populus*), and of several species of willow (*Salix*); it feeds also with avidity on the roots of some aquatic plants, especially on those of the *Nuphair luteum*. In summer, when it sometimes wanders to a distance from the water, it eats berries, leaves, and various kinds of herbage.

The young are born in the months of April and May; those produced in the latter month are the most valuable, as they grow rapidly and become strong and large, not being checked in their growth, which is often the case with those that are born earlier in the season. Some females have been taken in July with young, but such an event is of rare occurrence. The eyes of the young beaver are open at birth. The dam at times brings forth as many as seven at a litter, but from two to five is the more usual number. The young remain with the mother for at least a year, and not unfrequently two years, and when they are in a place of security, where an abundance of food is to be procured, ten or twelve beavers dwell together.

About a month after their birth, the young first follow the mother, and accompany her in the water; they continue to suckle some time longer, although if caught at that tender age, they can be raised without any difficulty by feeding them with tender branches of willows and other trees. Many beavers from one to two months old are caught in traps set for old ones. The gravid female keeps aloof from the male until after the young have begun to follow her about. She resides in a separate lodge till the month of August, when the whole family once more dwell together.

The Viviparous Quadrupeds of North America, Volume I

The Bald Eagle *(Haliaeetus leucocephalus)*

The figure of this noble bird is well known throughout the civilized world, emblazoned as it is on our national standard, which waves in the breeze of every clime, bearing to distant lands the remembrance of a great people living in a state of peaceful freedom. May that peaceful freedom last forever!

The great strength, daring, and cool courage of the white-headed eagle, joined with his unequaled power of flight, render him highly conspicuous among his brethren. To these qualities did he add a generous disposition toward others, he might be looked up to as a model of nobility. The ferocious, overbearing, and tyrannical temper which is ever and anon displaying itself in his actions, is nevertheless, best adapted to his state, and was wisely given him by the Creator to enable him to perform the office assigned to him.

To give you, Kind Reader, some idea of the nature of this bird, permit me to place you on the Mississippi, on which you may float gently along, while approaching winter brings millions of waterfowl on whistling wings from the countries of the north, to seek a milder climate in which to sojourn for a season. The eagle is seen perched, in an erect attitude, on the highest summit of the tallest tree by the margin of the broad stream. His glistening but stern eye looks over the vast expanse. He listens attentively to every sound that comes to his quick ear from afar, glancing now and then on the earth beneath, lest even the light tread of the fawn may pass unheard. His mate is perched on the opposite side, and should all be tranquil and silent, warns him by a cry to continue patient. At this well-known call, the male partly opens his broad wings, inclines his body a little downward, and answers to her voice in tones not unlike the laugh of a maniac. The next moment, he resumes his erect attitude, and again all around is silent. Ducks of many species, the teal, the widgeon, the mallard, and others, are seen passing with great rapidity, and following the course of the current; but the eagle heeds them not: they are at that time beneath his attention.

The next moment, however, the wild trumpetlike sound of a yet distant but approaching swan is heard. A shriek from the female eagle comes across the stream—for she is fully as alert as her mate. The latter suddenly shakes the whole of his body, and with a few touches of his bill, aided by the action of his cuticular muscles, arranges his plumage in an instant. The snow-white bird is now in sight: her long neck is stretched forward, her eye is on the watch, vigilant as that of her enemy; her large wings seem with difficulty to support the weight of her body, although they flap incessantly. So irksome do her exertions seem that her very legs are spread beneath her tail, to aid her in her flight. She approaches, however. The eagle has marked her for his prey. As the swan is passing the dreaded pair, starts from his perch, in full preparation for the chase, the male bird, with an awful scream, that to the swan's ear brings more terror than the report of the large duck gun.

Now is the moment to witness the display of the eagle's powers. He glides through the air like a falling star, and, like a flash of lightning, comes upon the timorous quarry, which now, in agony and despair, seeks by various maneuvers to elude the grasp of his cruel talons. It mounts, doubles, and willingly would plunge into the stream, were it not prevented by the eagle, which, long possessed of the knowledge that by such a stratagem the swan might escape him, forces it to remain in the air by attempting to strike it with its talons from beneath. The hope of escape is soon given up by the swan. It has already become much weakened, and its strength fails at the sight of the courage and swiftness of its antagonist. Its last gasp is about to escape, when the ferocious eagle strikes with his talons the underside of its wing, and with unresisted power forces the bird to fall in a slanting direction upon the nearest shore.

It is then that you may see the cruel spirit of this dreaded enemy of the feathered race, whilst, exulting over his prey, he for the first time breathes at ease. He presses down his powerful feet, and drives his sharp claws deeper than ever into the heart of the dying swan. He shrieks with delight, as he feels the last convulsions of his prey, which has now sunk under his unceasing efforts to render death as painfully felt as it can possibly be. The female has watched every movement of her mate; and if she did not assist him in capturing the swan, it was not from want of will, but merely that she felt full assurance that the power and courage of her lord were quite sufficient for the deed. She now sails to the spot where he eagerly awaits her, and when she has arrived, they together turn the breast of the swan upward, and gorge themselves with gore.

At other times, when these eagles, sailing in search of prey, discover a goose, a duck, or a swan that has alighted on the water, they accomplish its destruction in a manner that is worthy of your attention. The eagles, well aware that waterfowl have it in their power to dive at their approach, and thereby elude their attempts upon them, ascend in the air in opposite directions over the lake or river, on which they have observed the object which they are desirous of possessing. Both eagles reach a certain height, immediately after which one of them glides with great swiftness toward the prey; the latter, meantime, aware of the eagle's intention, dives the moment before he reaches the spot. The pursuer then rises in the air, and is met by its mate, which glides toward the water bird that has just emerged to breathe, and forces it to plunge again beneath the surface, to escape the talons of this second assailant. The first eagle is now poising itself in the place where its mate formerly was, and rushes anew to force the quarry to make another plunge. By thus alternately gliding, in rapid and often repeated rushes over the ill-fated bird, they soon fatigue it, when it stretches out its neck, swims deeply, and makes for the shore, in the hope of concealing itself among the rank weeds But this is of no avail, for the eagles follow it in all its motions, and the moment it approaches the margin, one of them darts upon it and kills it in an instant, after which they divide the spoil.

During spring and summer, the white-headed eagle, to procure sustenance, follows a different course, and one much less suited to a bird apparently so well able to supply itself without interfering with other plunderers. No sooner does the fish hawk make its appearance along our Atlantic shores, or ascend our numerous and large rivers, than the eagle follows it, and like a selfish oppressor, robs it of the hard-earned fruits of its labor. Perched on some tall summit, in view of the ocean or of some watercourse, he watches every motion of the osprey while on wing. When the latter rises from the water, with a fish in its grasp, forth rushes the eagle in pursuit. He mounts above the fish hawk, and threatens it by actions well understood, when the latter, fearing perhaps that its life is in danger, drops its prey. In an instant, the eagle, accurately estimating the rapid descent of the fish, closes his wings, follows it with the swiftness of thought, and the next moment grasps it. The prize is carried off in silence to the woods, and assists in feeding the ever-hungry brood of the eagle.

This bird now and then procures fish himself, by pursuing them in the shallows of small creeks. I have witnessed several instances of this in the Perkioming Creek in Pennsylvania, where, in this manner, I saw one of them secure a number of redfins, by wading briskly through the water and striking at them with his bill. I have also observed a pair scrambling over the ice of a frozen pond to get at some fish below, but without success.

It does not confine itself to these kinds of food, but greedily devours young pigs, lambs, fawns, poultry, and the putrid flesh of carcasses of every description, driving off the vultures and carrion crows, or the dogs, and keeping a whole party at defiance until it is satiated. It frequently gives chase to the vultures. A ludicrous instance of this took place near the city of Natchez, on the Mississippi. Many vultures were engaged in devouring the body and entrails of a dead horse when a white-headed eagle accidentally passing by, the vultures all took to wing, one among the rest with a portion of the entrails partly swallowed, and the remaining part, about a yard in length, dangling in the air. The eagle instantly marked him, and gave chase. The poor vulture tried in vain to disgorge, when the eagle, coming up, seized the loose end of the gut, and dragged the bird along for twenty or thirty yards, much against its will, until both fell to the ground, when the eagle struck the vulture, and in a few moments killed it, after which he swallowed the delicious morsel.

The white-headed eagle seldom utters its piercing cry without throwing its head backward until it nearly touches the feathers of the back. It then opens its bill, and its tongue is seen to move as it emits its notes, of which four or five are delivered in rapid succession. Although loud and disagreeable when heard at hand, they have a kind of melancholy softness when listened to at a great distance. When these birds are irritated, and on the wing, they often thrust forth their talons, opening and closing them, as if threatening to tear the object of their anger in pieces.

Ornithological Biography, Volumes I and II

4. Prairie, Desert, and Mountain

Introduction

Nobody knows how many million bison roamed the western prairies, as nobody knows how many billion passenger pigeons moved across the sky, in the year Audubon came to America, But it is known that during one period more than a million bison a year were being slaughtered. It is known that in 1883 the last surviving herd on the Great Plains, by being blocked from water day after day along the Cannonball River, in North Dakota, was wiped out completely by a party of white and Cree Indian hunters. After that, only isolated survivors in remote sections remained. Hardly more than fifty years after Audubon's ascent of the Missouri River, the bison of the plains was so close to extinction in the United States that, of the unnumbered millions of a few decades before, only a score or so remained, all within the boundaries of the Yellowstone National Park. Since then, where these great animals have received protection, they have been increasing steadily in numbers.

The Missouri River journey, Audubon's last, carried him from St. Louis to Fort Union, an American Fur Company outpost at the mouth of the Yellowstone where North Dakota now joins Montana. He left Minnie's Land, his home near New York, on March 11, 1843, and returned to it on November 6. Accompanying him up the Missouri were his old friend, Edward Harris, for whom he named Harris's sparrow; John G. Bell, a taxidermist, for whom he named Bell's vireo; Isaac Sprague, an artist, whose name is commemorated in Sprague's pipit; and Lewis Squires, an athletic young man who acted as his assistant and secretary. The forty-eight day upstream journey was made in a wood-burning river steamer, the *Omeiga.* With its smokestack sending up a shower of hot cinders and once setting the vessel afire, it fought its way up against the current, loaded with trappers, Indians, and ten thousand pounds of gunpowder. At Fort Union, where he remained for two months, Audubon occupied the same room that had been used by Maximilian, Prince of Neuwied, ten years before. Men associated with the fur company at Fort Union who are frequently mentioned in the journal for this period include Culbertson, Provost, McKenzie, Bonaventure, Chardon, and Lafleur. The party started the return journey on August 16, floating downstream in a forty-foot Mackinaw barge. They reached St. Louis on October 19. This journey to the Yellowstone, on the Montana–North Dakota border, is the closest Audubon came to his dream of visiting the Rockies.

The serviceberries, which Audubon speaks of gathering near the river, were those of the shadbush or Juneberry, *Amelancher.* Its various species across the country usually grow as shrubs but in some instances it attains the stature of a tree, reaching a height of as much as seventy feet. About forty species of birds and twenty species of mammals eat its fruit.

During the early days of Audubon's wandering along the frontier, the whooping crane nested in lowland areas northward across the Great Plains and into Upper Canada. Today this shy bird is fighting an uncertain battle against extinction. Fewer than forty individuals are now alive. Of stately form and movement, it is the tallest of all North American species. Both its summer breeding area in far-northern Canada and its wintering grounds on the lower Gulf Coast of Texas have been set aside as sanctuaries. The struggle of the cranes to survive has attracted wide public interest. Each fall the number of birds returning to their Texas refuge is announced by the press in all parts of the country.

One bird that is now widely distributed across the open lands of the United States was not here at all in Audubon's day. This is the starling. From fewer than 100 individuals, released in New York's Central Park in the mid-1890s, the species has spread

NOTES ON THE PLATES

169. JAGUAR *(Felis onca).* Arid mountain regions of southern New Mexico and Arizona form the only home of the jaguar in the United States.

170–171. NINE-BANDED ARMADILLO *(Dasypus novemcinctus).* Mainly an animal of the dry Southwest, the burrowing armadillo is extending its range. It has been introduced into Florida.

172. BLACK-TAILED JACK RABBIT *(Lepus californicus).* The commonest jack rabbit of the West, it is confined mainly to arid plains.

173. KIT FOX *(Vulpes velox).* The smallest of our foxes. Mainly nocturnal. Western plains, foothills, deserts are its home. Now becoming rare, the kit fox is believed to be facing possible extinction.

174–175. MOUNTAIN BEAVER *(Aplodontia rufa).* Not a beaver, in habits more like a pocket gopher, this rodent is found from sea level to elevations of 9000 feet along the West Coast.

176–177. (1–2) AUDUBON'S WARBLER *(Dendroica auduboni).* (4) HERMIT WARBLER *(Dendroica occidentalis).* Both of these warblers breed in coniferous forests of the western mountains.

178. HOODED SKUNK *(Mephitis macroura).* The rarest of North American skunks, it is found only near the Mexican border in the Southwest.

179. PIKA *(Ochotona princeps).* The little pika inhabits rock slides of the western mountains at elevations up to 13,600 feet.

180. COLLARED PECCARY *(Pecari angulatus).* Once ranging to northern Arkansas, this wild pig is now confined to the arid Southwest.

181. LARK SPARROW *(Chondestes grammacus).* A bird of treeless prairies, orchards, and farms, this species breeds mainly in western states.

182. ELK *(Cervus canadensis).* The bulls of this highland deer weigh as much as 750 pounds. They are noted for their bugling call.

183. COLUMBIA BLACK-TAILED DEER *(Odocoileus columbianus).* The humid forests of the Northwest form the habitat of this dark-hued deer.

184. UPLAND PLOVER *(Bartramia longicauda).* Almost entirely insectivorous, these birds feed and nest on pasture land and prairies. In landing on a post, they characteristically lift their wings high before closing them.

from coast to coast and from Canada to Mexico. It has multiplied until today it is one of the most numerous birds in the country. The rather dubious honor of having given the starling to the New World might have gone to John James Audubon himself. More than half a century before the actual introduction was made, he was unsuccessful in his attempt to bring fifty of these birds from England to the United States.

The Coyote or Prairie Wolf *(Canis latrans)*

The prairie wolf hunts in packs, but is also often seen prowling singly over the plains in search of food. During one of our morning rambles near Fort Union, we happened to start one of these wolves suddenly. It made off at a very swift pace and we fired at it without any effect, our guns being loaded with small shot at the time; after running about one hundred yards, it suddenly stopped and shook itself violently, by which we perceived that it had been touched; in a few moments it again started and soon disappeared beyond a high range of hills, galloping along like a hare or an antelope.

The bark or howl of this wolf greatly resembles that of the dog, and on one occasion the party traveling with us were impressed by the idea that Indians were in our vicinity, as a great many of these wolves were about us and barked during the night like Indian dogs. We were all on the alert, and our guns were loaded with ball in readiness for an attack.

In Texas the prairie wolves are perhaps more abundant than the other species; they hunt in packs of six or eight, which are seen to most advantage in the evening in pursuit of deer. It is amusing to see them cut across the curves made by the latter when trying to escape, the hindmost wolves thus saving some distance and finally striking in ahead of the poor deer and surrounding it, when a single wolf would fail in the attempt to capture it. By its predatory and destructive habits, this wolf is a great annoyance to the settlers in the new territories of the West. Travelers and hunters on the prairies dislike it for killing the deer, which supply these wanderers with their best meals and furnish them with part of their clothing, the buckskin breeches, the most durable garment for the woods or plains. The bark or call note of this wolf, although a wild sound to the inhabitant of any settled and cultivated part of the country, is sometimes welcomed, as it often announces the near approach of daylight; and if the wanderer, aroused from his slumbers by the howling of this animal, raises his blanket and turns his head toward the east, from his camping ground underneath the branches of some broad spreading live oak, he can see the red glow, perchance, that fringes the misty morning vapors, giving the promise of a clear and calm sunrise in the mild climate of Texas, even in the depth of winter. Should daylight thus be at hand, the true hunter is at once afoot, short space of time does he require for the duties of the toilet, and soon he has made a fire, boiled his coffee, and broiled a bit of venison or wild turkey.

This wolf feeds on birds, small and large quadrupeds, and when hard pressed by hunger, even upon carrion or carcasses of buffaloes, &c. It is easily tamed when caught young, and makes a tolerable companion, though not gifted with the good qualities of the dog. We had one once, which was kept in a friend's store in the West, and we discovered it to be something of a ratcatcher. This individual was very desirous of being on friendly terms with all the dogs about the premises, especially with a large French poodle that belonged to our friend, but the poodle would not permit our half-savage barking wolf to play with him, and generally returned its attempted caresses with an angry snap, which put all further friendly demonstrations out of the question. One day we missed our pet from his accustomed place near the back part of the warehouse, and while we were wondering what had become of him, were attracted by an unusual uproar in the street. In a moment we perceived the noise was occasioned by a whole pack of curs of high and low degree, which were in full cry and in pursuit of our prairie wolf. The creature thus hard beset, before we could interfere, had reached a point opposite a raised window, and, to our surprise, made a sudden spring at it and jumped into the warehouse without touching the edges of the sills in the most admirable manner, while his foes were completely baffled.

After this adventure the wolf would no longer go out in the town and seemed to give up his wish to extend the circle of his acquaintance.

The barking or prairie wolf digs its burrows upon the prairies on some slight elevation, to prevent them from being filled with water. These dens have several entrances, like those of the red fox. The young, from five to seven and occasionally more in number, are brought forth in March and April. They associate in greater numbers than the larger wolves, hunt in packs, and are said by Richardson to be fleeter than the common wolf. A gentleman, an experienced hunter on the Saskatchewan, informed him that the only animal on the plains which he could not overtake when mounted on a good horse was the prong-horned antelope, and that the prairie wolf was next in speed.

All our travelers have informed us that on the report of a gun on the prairies, numbers of these wolves start from the earth and warily approach the hunter, under an expectation of obtaining the offal of the animal he has killed.

The Viviparous Quadrupeds of North America, Volume II

The Whooping Crane *(Grus americana)*

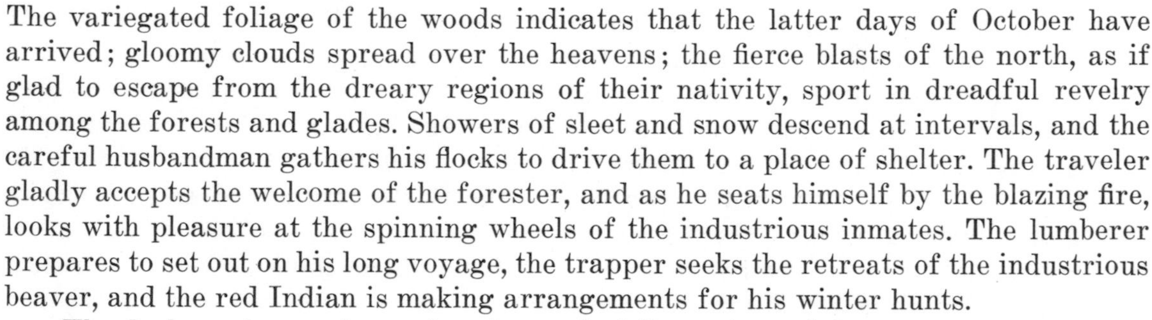

The variegated foliage of the woods indicates that the latter days of October have arrived; gloomy clouds spread over the heavens; the fierce blasts of the north, as if glad to escape from the dreary regions of their nativity, sport in dreadful revelry among the forests and glades. Showers of sleet and snow descend at intervals, and the careful husbandman gathers his flocks to drive them to a place of shelter. The traveler gladly accepts the welcome of the forester, and as he seats himself by the blazing fire, looks with pleasure at the spinning wheels of the industrious inmates. The lumberer prepares to set out on his long voyage, the trapper seeks the retreats of the industrious beaver, and the red Indian is making arrangements for his winter hunts.

The ducks and geese have already reached the waters of the western ponds; here a swan or two is seen following in their train, and as the observer of nature stands watching the appearances and events of this season of change, he hears from on high the notes of the swiftly traveling but unseen whooping crane. Suddenly the turbid atmosphere clears, and now he can perceive the passing birds. Gradually they descend, dress their extended lines, and prepare to alight on the earth. With necks outstretched and long bony legs extended behind, they proceed, supported by wings white as the snow but tipped with jet, until arriving over the great savannah, they wheel their circling flight and slowly approach the ground, on which with half-closed wings, and outstretched feet they alight, running along for a few steps to break the force of their descent.

Reader, see the majestic bird shake its feathers, and again arrange them in order. Proud of its beautiful form, and prouder still of its power of flight, it stalks over the withering grasses with all the majesty of a gallant chief. With long and measured steps he moves along, his head erect, his eye glistening with delight. His great journey is accomplished, and being well acquainted with a country which has often been visited by him, he at once commences his winter avocations.

The whooping crane reaches the western country about the middle of October or the beginning of November, in flocks of twenty or thirty individuals, sometimes of twice or thrice that number, the young by themselves, but closely followed by their parents. They spread from Illinois over Kentucky, and all the intermediate States, until they reach the Carolinas on the southern coast, the Floridas, Louisiana, and the countries bordering on Mexico, in all of which they spend the winter, seldom returning northward until about the middle of April or toward the beginning of May. They are seen on the edges of large ponds supplied with rank herbage, on fields or savannahs, now in swampy woods and again on extensive marshes.

The interior of the country and the neighborhood of the seashores suit them equally well so long as the temperature is sufficiently high. In the Middle States, it is very seldom indeed that they are seen; and to the eastward of these countries they are unknown; for all their migrations are performed far inland, and thus they leave and return to the northern retreats where, it is said, they breed and spend the summer. While migrating they appear to travel both by night and by day, and I have frequently heard them at the former and seen them at the latter time, as they were proceeding toward their destination.

Whether the weather is calm or tempestuous it makes no difference to them, their power of flight being such as to render them regardless of the winds. Nay, I have observed them urging their way during very heavy gales, shifting from high to low in the air with remarkable dexterity. The members of a flock sometimes arrange themselves in the form of an acute-angled triangle; sometimes they move in a long line; again they mingle together without order, or form an extended front, but in whatever manner they advance, each bird sounds his loud note in succession, and on all occasions of alarm these birds manifest the same habit. While with us they are also always met with in flocks.

When wounded, these birds cannot be approached without caution, as their powerful bill is capable of inflicting a severe wound. Knowing this as I do, I would counsel any sportsman not to leave his gun behind, while pursuing a wounded crane. One afternoon in winter, as I was descending the Mississippi on my way to Natchez, I saw several cranes standing on a large sand bar. The sight of these beautiful birds excited in me a desire to procure some of them. Accordingly, taking a rifle and some ammunition, I left the flat-bottomed boat in a canoe, and told the men to watch for me, as the current was rapid in that place, the river being there narrowed by the sand bar. I soon paddled myself to the shore, and having observed that by good management I might approach the cranes under cover of a huge stranded tree, I landed opposite to it, drew up my canoe, and laying myself flat on the sand, crawled the best way I could, pushing my gun before me. On reaching the log, I cautiously raised my head opposite to a large branch, and saw the birds at a distance somewhat short of a hundred yards. I took, as I thought, an excellent aim, although my anxiety to show the boatmen how good a marksman I was rendered it less sure than it might otherwise have been. I fired, when all the birds instantly flew off greatly alarmed, excepting one which leaped into the air but immediately came down again, and walked leisurely away with a drooping pinion. As I rose on my feet, it saw me, I believe, for the first time, cried out lustily, and ran off with the speed of an ostrich.

I left my rifle unloaded, and in great haste pursued the wounded bird, which doubtless would have escaped had it not made toward a pile of driftwood where I overtook it. As I approached it, panting and almost exhausted, it immediately raised itself to the full stretch of its body, legs, and neck, ruffled its feathers, shook them, and advanced toward me with open bill, and eyes glancing with anger. I cannot tell you whether it was from feeling almost exhausted with the fatigue of the chase; but, however it was, I felt unwilling to encounter my antagonist, and keeping my eye on him, moved backward.

The farther I removed, the more he advanced, until at length I fairly turned my back to him, and took to my heels, retreating with fully more speed than I had pursued. He followed, and I was glad to reach the river, into which I plunged up to the neck, calling out to my boatmen, who came up as fast as they could. The crane stood looking angrily on me all the while, immersed up to his belly in the water, and only a few yards distant, now and then making thrusts at me with his bill. There he stood until the people came up; and highly delighted they were with my situation. However, the battle was soon over, for, on landing, some of them struck the winged warrior on the neck with an oar, and carried him on board.

While in the Floridas, I saw only a few of these birds alive, but many which had

NOTES ON THE PLATES

189. COUGAR *(Felis concolor)*. North America's biggest cat, the cougar or mountain lion or puma may weigh as much as 260 pounds. At one time it ranged throughout the eastern United States. Except for a few in southern swamps and isolated cases in the wooded north, it is now confined to mountain country of the West.

190. BOBCAT *(Lynx rufus)*. About a yard long, weighing usually from a dozen to twenty-five pounds, the bobcat is found in swamps, deserts, and forests. It hunts mainly after dark. Hares and rodents make up the bulk of its diet, although on occasion bobcats have been known to attack and kill deer.

191. THIRTEEN-LINED GROUND SQUIRREL *(Citellus tridecemlineatus)*. In the central part of the United States this ground squirrel lives from sea level to 10,000-foot elevations in mountains. About half of its diet consists of grasshoppers and other insects. Sometimes it pounces on and devours mice.

192. RING-TAILED CAT *(Bassariscus astutus)*. Its legs are short, its ears large, its ringed tail almost as long as its body. It is found in cliffs, caves, and canyons in the Southwest. An agile climber, the ring-tailed cat roams abroad at night, hunting rodents, birds, insects, and berries.

been shot by the Spaniards and Indians for the sake of their flesh and beautiful feathers, of which latter they make fans and fly brushes. None of these birds remains there during summer; and William Bartram, when speaking of this species, must have mistaken the wood ibis for it.

In captivity the whooping crane becomes extremely gentle, and feeds freely on grain and other vegetable substances. A Mr. Magwood, residing near Charleston in South Carolina, kept one for some time feeding it on maize. It accidentally wounded one of its feet on the shell of an oyster, and although the greatest care was taken of it, died after lingering some weeks. Having myself kept one alive. I will give you an account of its habits.

It was nearly full grown when I obtained it, and its plumage was changing from grayish brown to white. I received it as a present from Captain Clack of the United States Navy, commander of the *Erie* sloop of war. It had been wounded in the wing, on the coast of Florida, but the fractured limb had been amputated and soon healed. During a voyage of three months, it became very gentle, and was a great favorite with the sailors. I placed it in a yard, in company with a beautiful snow goose. This was at Boston. It was so gentle as to suffer me to caress it with the hand, and was extremely fond of searching for worms and grubs about the woodpile, probing every hole it saw with as much care and dexterity as an ivory-billed woodpecker. It also watched with all the patience of a cat the motions of some mice which had burrows near the same spot, killed them with a single blow, and swallowed them entire, one after another, until they were extirpated. I fed it on corn and garbage from the kitchen, to which were added bits of bread and cheese, as well as some apples. It would pick up the straws intended to keep its feet from being soiled, and arrange them round its body, as if intent on forming a nest.

For hours at a time it would stand resting on one foot in a very graceful posture; but what appeared to me very curious was that it had a favorite leg for this purpose; and in fact none of my family ever found it standing on the other, although it is probable that this happened in consequence of the mutilation of the wing, the leg employed being that of the injured side. The stump of its amputated wing appeared to be a constant source of trouble, particularly at the approach of the winter: it would dress the feathers about it, and cover it with so much care that I really felt for the poor fellow. When the weather became intensely cold, it regularly retired at the approach of night under a covered passage, where it spent the hours of darkness; but it always repaired to this place with marked reluctance, and never until all was quiet and nearly dark, and it came out, even when the snow lay deep on the ground, at the first approach of day.

Now and then it would take a run, extend its only wing, and, uttering a loud cry, leap several times in the air, as if anxious to return to its haunts. At other times it would look upward, cry aloud as if calling to some acquaintance passing high in the air, and again use its ordinary note whenever its companion the snow goose sent forth her own signals. It seldom swallowed its food without first carrying it to the water and dipping it several times, and now and then it would walk many yards for that express purpose. Although the winter was severe, the thermometer some mornings standing as low as 10°, the bird fattened and looked extremely well. So strong was the natural suspicion of this bird that I frequently saw it approach some cabbage leaves with measured steps, look at each sideways before it would touch one of them, and after all, if it by accident tossed the leaf into the air when attempting to break it to pieces, it would run off as if some dreaded enemy were at hand.

On looking over my notes, I find that I have omitted to inform you that the extraordinary strength of the thighs, legs, and feet of the whooping crane tends greatly to make it more terrestrial than the herons; and that the great size of their nostrils, which so much resemble those of the vultures, is well adapted to keep the inner parts of the organ from the damp earth and other matters with which they are so often in contact while searching in the ground or mud for roots and other vegetable substances on which the bird principally feeds. I am convinced, also, that this species does not attain its full size or perfect plumage until it is four or five years old. The beauty of the plumage may be improved in brilliancy during the breeding season by a greater brightness in the color of the bill, as in the booby gannet and white ibis, as well as in the redness of the fleshy parts of the head.

Ornithological Biography, Volume III

The Turkey Vulture (*Carthartes aura*)

As soon as, like me, you shall have seen the turkey buzzard follow, with arduous closeness of investigation, the skirts of the forests, the meanders of creeks and rivers, sweeping over the whole of extensive plains, glancing his quick eye in all directions, with as much intentness as ever did the noblest of falcons, to discover where below him lies the suitable prey; when, like me, you have repeatedly seen that bird pass over objects calculated to glut his voracious appetite unnoticed, because unseen; and when you have also observed the greedy vulture, propelled by hunger, if not famine, moving like the wind suddenly round his course, as the carrion attracts his eye; then you will abandon the deeply rooted notion that this bird possesses the faculty of discovering, by his sense of smell, his prey at an immense distance.

This power of smelling so acutely I adopted as a fact from my youth. I had read of this when a child; and many of the theorists to whom I subsequently spoke of it repeated the same with enthusiasm, the more particularly as they considered it an extraordinary gift of nature. But I had already observed that nature, although wonderfully bountiful, had not granted more to any one individual than was necessary, and that no one was possessed of any two of the senses in a very high state of perfection; that if it had a good scent, it needed not so much acuteness of sight and vice versa. When I visited the Southern States, and had lived, as it were, amongst these vultures for several years, and discovered thousands of times that they did not smell me when I approached them, covered by a tree, until within a few feet; and that when so near, or at a greater distance, I showed myself to them, they instantly flew away much frightened; the idea evaporated, and I assiduously engaged in a series of experiments, to prove to *myself,* at least, how far this acuteness of smell existed, or if it existed at all.

I sit down to communicate to you the results of those experiments, and leave for *you* to conclude how far and how long the world has been imposed on by the mere assertions of men who had never seen more than the skins of our vultures, or heard the accounts from men caring little about observing nature closely.

My *First Experiment* was as follows: I procured a skin of our common deer, entire to the hoofs, and stuffed it carefully with dried grass until filled rather above the natural size, suffered the whole to become perfectly dry and as hard as leather, took it to the middle of a large open field, laid it down on its back with the legs up and apart, as if the animal was dead and putrid. I then retired about a hundred yards, and in the lapse of some minutes, a vulture, coursing round the field tolerably high, espied the skin, sailed directly toward it, and alighted within a few yards of it. I ran immediately, covered by a large tree, until within about forty yards, and from that place could spy the bird with ease. He approached the skin, looked at it with apparent suspicion, jumped on it, raised his tail, and voided freely (as you well know all birds of prey in a wild state generally do before feeding), then approaching the eyes, that were here solid globes of hard, dried, and painted clay, attacked first one and then the other with, however, no further advantage than that of disarranging them.

This part was abandoned; the bird walked to the other extremity of the pretended animal, and there, with much exertion, tore the stitches apart, until much fodder and hay was pulled out; but no flesh could the bird find or smell; he was intent on discovering some where none existed, and, after reiterated efforts, all useless, he took flight and coursed above the field, when, suddenly wheeling round and alighting, I saw him kill a small garter snake, and swallow it in an instant. The vulture rose again, sailed about, and passed several times quite low over the stuffed deerskin, as if loath to abandon so good looking a prey.

Judge of my feelings when I plainly saw that the vulture, which could not discover, through its *extraordinary* sense of smell, that no flesh, either fresh or putrid, existed about that skin, could at a glance see a snake, scarcely as thick as a man's finger, live, and destitute of odor, hundreds of yards distant. I concluded that, at all events, his ocular powers were much better than his sense of smell.

Second Experiment: I had a large dead hog hauled some distance from the house and put into a ravine, about twenty feet deeper than the surface of the earth around it, narrow and winding much, filled with briars and high cane. In this I made the Negroes conceal the hog by binding cane over it, until I thought it would puzzle either buzzards, carrion crows, or any other birds to see it, and left it for two days. This was early in the month of July when, in this latitude, a dead body becomes putrid and extremely fetid in a short time. I saw from time to time many vultures, in search of food, sail over the field and ravine in all directions, but none discovered the carcass, although during this time several dogs had visited it, and fed plentifully on it. I tried to go near it, but the smell was so insufferable when within thirty yards that I abandoned it, and the remnants were entirely destroyed at last through natural decay.

I then took a young pig, put a knife through its neck, and made it bleed on the earth and grass about the same place, and having covered it closely with leaves, also watched the result. The vultures saw the fresh blood, alighted about it, followed it down into the ravine, discovered by the blood the pig, and devoured it when yet quite fresh, within my sight.

Not contented with these experiments, which I already thought fully conclusive, having found two young vultures, about the size of pullets, covered yet with down, and looking more like quadrupeds than birds, I had them brought home and put into a large coop in the yard, in the view of everybody, and attended to their feeding myself. I gave them a great number of redheaded woodpeckers and parakeets, birds then easy to procure, as they were feeding daily on the mulberry trees in the immediate neighborhood of my orphans.

These the young vultures could tear to pieces by putting both feet on the body and applying the bill with great force. So accustomed to my going toward them were they in a few days that when I approached the cage with hands filled with game for them, they immediately began hissing and gesticulating very much like young pigeons, and putting their bills to each other, as if expecting to be fed mutually, as their parent had done.

Two weeks elapsed, black feathers made their appearance, and the down diminished. I remarked an extraordinary increase of their legs and bill, and thinking them fit for trial, I closed three sides of the cage with plank, leaving the front only with bars for them to see through, had the cage cleaned, washed, and sanded to remove any filth attached to it from the putrid flesh that had been in it, and turned its front immediately from the course I usually took toward it with food for them.

I approached it often barefooted, and soon perceived that if I did not accidentally make a noise, the young birds remained in their silent upright attitudes until I showed myself to them by turning to the front of their prison. I frequently fastened a dead squirrel or rabbit, cut open, with all the entrails hanging loosely, to a long pole, and in this situation would put it to the back part of the cage; but no hissing, no movement. was made; when, on the contrary, I presented the end of the pole thus covered over the cage, no sooner would it appear beyond the edge than my hungry birds would jump against the bars, hiss furiously, and attempt all in their power to reach the food. This was repeatedly done with fresh and putrid substances, all very congenial to their taste.

Satisfied within myself, I dropped these trials, but fed the birds until full grown,

NOTES ON THE PLATES

197. BAND-TAILED PIGEON *(Columba fasciata)*. In form, this bird of western foothills, canyons, chaparral, and mountain forests resembles the domestic pigeon. It feeds on buds, seeds, fruit. Sometimes acorns up to as much as an inch and a half long are swallowed whole.

198. BIGHORN *(Ovis canadensis)*. These wild sheep of the high western mountains sometimes weigh more than 300 pounds. Sure-footed and skillful climbers, they turn to rough terrain to escape pursuit. The female, which lacks the great curling horns of the male, is shown here.

199. FLYING SQUIRREL *(Glaucomys sabrinus)*. These nocturnal tree squirrels glide for considerable distances on the membranes stretched between their front and rear legs. They are gregarious, many often inhabiting the same tree cavity. They sometimes eat bird eggs and nestlings. But the main diet of these squirrels consists of a variety of nuts, buds, berries, and insects.

200–201. MUSK OX *(Ovibos moschatus)*. The treeless open land of the Arctic tundra is the main home of the hardy musk ox. Protected by its thick coat, moving about in herds, it endures all the rigors of the winter cold. When danger threatens, the herd forms a rough circle with calves inside and with all the horned heads of the adults facing outward.

202–203. BISON *(Bison bison)*. This huge animal, weighing up to a ton, once roamed the Great Plains in herds that totaled millions. In Colonial times, the bison ranged from close to the Atlantic seaboard across the plains and into the western mountains. Almost exterminated by the turn of the century, it has been slowly increasing in such sanctuaries as the Yellowstone National Park.

204. MOUNTAIN GOAT *(Oreamnos americanus)*. A mountain-climbing antelope, closely related to the chamois, this animal is most often found above timberline on western peaks. It is an expert climber, scaling almost perpendicular cliffs. Often it spends the winter on the exposed heights of the mountain slopes.

and then turned them out into the yard of the kitchen, for the purpose of picking up whatever substances might be thrown to them. Their voracity, however, soon caused their death: young pigs were not safe if within their reach; and young ducks, turkeys, or chickens were such a constant temptation that the cook, unable to watch them, killed them both, to put an end to their depredations.

I could enumerate many more instances, indicating that the power of smelling in these birds has been grossly exaggerated, and that, if they can smell objects at any distance, they can see the same objects much father. I would ask any observer of the habits of birds why, if vultures could smell at a great distance their prey, they should spend the greater portion of their lives hunting for it, when they are naturally so lazy that, if fed in one place, they never leave it, and merely make such a change as is absolutely necessary to enable them to reach it.

Ornithological Biography, Volume II

The Bison *(Bison bison)*

ALONG THE MISSOURI RIVER

June 9, Friday: Sprague and I went up to the top of the hills, bounding the beautiful prairie, by which we had stopped to repair something about the engine. We gathered some handsome lupines, of two different species, and many other curious plants. From this elevated spot we could see the wilderness to an immense distance; the Missouri looked as if only a brook, and our steamer a very small one indeed. At this juncture we saw two men running along the shore upward, and I supposed they had seen an elk or something else, of which they were in pursuit. Meantime, gazing around, we saw a large lake, where we are told that ducks, geese, and swans breed in great numbers; this we intend also to visit when we come down. At this moment I heard the report of a gun from the point where the men had been seen, and when we reached the steamboat we were told that a buffalo had been killed. From the deck I saw a man swimming round the animal; he got on its side, and floated down the stream with it. The captain sent a parcel of men with a rope; the swimmer fastened this round the neck of the buffalo, and with his assistance, for he now swam all the way, the poor beast was brought alongside; and as the tackle had been previously fixed, it was hauled up on the foredeck. Sprague took its measurements with me, which are as follows: length from nose to root of tail, eight feet; height of fore shoulder to hoof, four feet nine and one-half inches; height at the rump to hoof, four feet two inches. The head was cut off, as well as one fore and one hind foot. The head is so full of symmetry, and so beautiful, that I shall have a drawing of it tomorrow, as well as careful ones of the feet. Whilst the butchers were at work, I was highly interested to see one of our Indians cutting out the milk bag of the cow and eating it, quite fresh and raw, in pieces somewhat larger than a hen's egg. One of the stomachs was partially washed in a bucket of water, and an Indian swallowed a large portion of this. Mr. Chardon brought the remainder on the upper deck and ate it uncleaned. I had a piece well cleaned and tasted it; to my utter astonishment, it was very good, but the idea was repulsive to me; besides which, I am not a meat eater, as you know, except when other provisions fail. The animal was in good condition; and the whole carcass was cut up and dispersed among the men below, reserving the nicer portions for the cabin. This was accomplished with great rapidity; the blood was washed away in a trice, and half an hour afterward no one would have known that a buffalo had been dressed on deck.

June 11, Sunday: We have seen many wolves and some buffaloes. One young bull stood on the brink of a bluff, looking at the boat steadfastly for full five minutes; and as we neared the spot, he waved his tail, and moved off briskly. On another occasion, a young bull that had just landed at the foot of a very steep bluff was slaughtered without difficulty; two shots were fired at it, and the poor thing was killed by a rifle bullet. I was sorry, for we did not stop for it, and its happy life was needlessly ended.

AT FORT UNION

June 16, Friday: The buffalo, old and young, are fond of rolling on the ground in the manner of horses, and turn quite over; this is done not only to clean themselves, but also to rub off the loose old coat of hair and wool that hangs about their body like so many large dirty rags. Those about the fort are gentle, but will not allow a person to touch their bodies, not even the young calves of the last spring.

June 27, Tuesday: I am now going to take this book to Lewis Squires and ask him to write in it his account of the buffalo hunt.

(The following is in Mr. Squires's handwriting.)

By Mr. Audubon's desire I will relate the adventures that befell me in my first buffalo hunt, and I am in hopes that among the rubbish a trifle, at least, may be obtained which may be of use or interest to him. On the morning of Friday, the twenty-third, before daylight, I was up, and in a short time young McKenzie made his appearance. A few minutes sufficed to saddle our horses and be in readiness for our contemplated hunt. We were accompanied by Mr. Bonaventure the Younger, one of the hunters of the fort, and two carts to bring in whatever kind of meat might be procured. We were ferried across the river in a flatboat, and thence took our departure for the buffalo country. We passed through a wooded bottom for about one mile, and then over a level prairie for about one mile and a half, when we commenced the ascent of the bluffs that bound the western side of the Missouri Valley; our course then lay over an undulating prairie, quite rough, and steep hills with small ravines between, and over dry beds of streams that are made by the spring and fall freshets. Occasionally we were favored with a level prairie never exceeding two miles in extent.

When the carts overtook us, we exchanged our horses for them, and sat on buffalo robes on the bottom, our horses following on behind us. As we neared the place where the buffaloes had been killed on the previous hunt, Bonaventure rode alone to the top of a hill to discover, if possible, their whereabouts; but to our disappointment nothing living was to be seen. We continued on our way watching closely ahead, right and left. Three o'clock came and as yet nothing had been killed; as none of us had eaten anything since the night before, our appetites admonished us that it was time to pay attention to them. McKenzie and Bonaventure began to look about for antelopes; but before any were "comeatable," I fell asleep, and was awakened by the report of a gun. Before we in the carts arrived at the spot from whence this report proceeded, the hunters had killed, skinned, and nearly cleaned the game, which was a fine male antelope. I regretted exceedingly I was not awake when it was killed, as I might have saved the skin for Mr. Audubon, as well as the head, but I was too late.

It was now about five o'clock, and one may well imagine I was *somewhat* hungry. Owen McKenzie commenced eating the raw liver, and offered me a piece. What others can eat, I felt assured I could at least taste. I accordingly took it and ate quite a piece of it; to my utter astonishment, I found it not only palatable but very good; this experience goes far to convince me that our prejudices make things appear more disgusting than fact proves them to be. Our antelope cut up and in the cart, we proceeded on our "winding way," and scarcely had we left the spot where the entrails of the animal remained before the wolves and ravens commenced coming from all quarters, and from places where a minute before there was not a sign of one. We had not proceeded three hundred yards at the utmost, before eight wolves were about the spot, and others approaching.

On our way, both going and returning, we saw a cactus of a conical shape, having a light, straw-colored, double flower, differing materially from the flower of the flat cactus, which is quite common; had I had any means of bringing one in, I would most gladly have done so, but I could not depend on the carts, and as they are rather unpleasant companions, I preferred awaiting another opportunity, which I hope may come in a few days. We shot a young of Townsend's hare, about seven or eight steps from us, with about a dozen shot; I took good care of it until I left the cart on my return to the fort, but when the carts arrived it had carelessly been lost. This I regretted very much, as Mr. Audubon wanted it. It was nearly sunset when Bonaventure discovered a buffalo bull, so we concluded to encamp for the night, and run the buffaloes in the morning. We accordingly selected a spot near a pond of water, which in spring and fall is quite a large lake, and near which there was abundance of good pasture; our horses were soon unsaddled and hoppled, a good fire blazing, and some of the antelope meat roasting on sticks before it. As soon as a bit was done, we commenced operations, and it was soon gone "the way of all flesh." I never before ate meat without salt or pepper, and until then never fully appreciated these two *luxuries,* as they now seemed, nor can anyone until deprived of them and seated on a prairie as we were, or in some similar situation. On the opposite side of the lake we saw a grizzly bear, but he was unapproachable. After smoking our pipes we rolled ourselves in our robes, with our saddles for pillows, and were soon lost in a sound, sweet sleep.

During the night I was awakened by a crunching sound; the fire had died down, and I sat up, and looking about, perceived a wolf quietly feeding on the remains of our supper. One of the men awoke at the same time and fired at the wolf, but without effect, and the fellow fled; we neither saw nor heard more of him during the night. By daylight we were all up, and as our horses had not wandered far, it was the work of a few minutes to catch and saddle them. We rode three or four miles before we discovered anything, but at last saw a group of three buffaloes some miles from us. We pushed on, and soon neared them; before arriving at their feeding ground, we saw, scattered about, immense quantities of pumice stone in detached pieces of all sizes; several of the hills appeared to be composed wholly of it. As we approached within two hundred yards of the buffaloes they started, and away went the hunters after them. My first intention of being merely a looker-on continued up to this moment, but it was impossible to resist following; almost unconsciously I commenced urging my horse after them, and was soon rushing up hills and through ravines; but my horse gave out, and disappointment and anger followed, as McKenzie and Bonaventure succeeded in killing two, and wounding a third, which escaped. As soon as they had finished them, they commenced skinning and cutting up one, which was soon in the cart, the offal and useless meat being left on the ground. Again the wolves made their appearance as we were leaving; they seemed shy, but Owen McKenzie succeeded in killing one, which was old and useless. The other buffalo was soon skinned and in the cart.

In the meantime McKenzie and I started on horseback for water. The man who had charge of the keg had let it all run out, and most fortunately none of us had wanted water until now. We rode to a pond, the water of which was very salt and warm, but we had to drink this or none; we did so, filled our flasks for the rest of the party, and a few minutes afterward rejoined them. We started again for more meat to complete our load. I observed, as we approached the buffaloes, that they stood gazing at us with their heads erect, lashing their sides with their tails; as soon as they discovered what we were at, with the quickness of thought they wheeled, and with the most surprising speed, for an animal apparently so clumsy and awkward, flew before us. I could hardly imagine that these enormous animals could move so quickly, or realize that their speed was as great as it proved to be; and I doubt if in this country one horse in ten can be found that will keep up with them.

We rode five or six miles before we discovered any more. At last we saw a single bull, and while approaching him we started two others; slowly we wended our way toward them until within a hundred yards, when away they went. I had now begun to enter into the spirit of the chase, and off I started, full speed, down a rough hill in swift pursuit; at the bottom of the hill was a ditch about eight feet wide; the horse cleared this safely. I continued, leading the others by some distance, and rapidly approaching the buffaloes. At this prospect of success my feelings can better be imagined than described. I kept the lead of the others till within thirty or forty yards of the buffaloes, when I began making preparations to fire as soon as I was sufficiently near; imagine, if possible, my disappointment when I discovered that now, when all my hopes of success were raised to the highest pitch, I was fated to meet a reverse as mortifying as success would have been gratifying. My horse failed, and slackened his pace, despite every effort of mine to urge him on; the other hunters rushed by me at full speed, and my horse stopped altogether. I saw the others fire; the animal swerved a little, but still kept on. After breathing my horse a while, I succeeded in starting him up again, followed after them, and came up in time to fire one shot ere the animal was brought down. I think that I never saw an eye so ferocious in expression as that of the wounded buffalo; rolling wildly in its socket, inflamed as the eye was, it had the most frightful appearance that can be imagined; and in fact, the picture presented by the buffalo as a whole is quite beyond my powers of description. The fierce eyes, blood streaming from his sides, mouth, and nostrils, he was the wildest, most unearthly looking thing it ever fell to my lot to gaze upon. His sufferings were short; he was soon cut up and placed in the cart, and we retraced our steps homeward. (End of Squires's account.)

June 30, Friday: When a herd of buffaloes is chased, although the bulls themselves run very swiftly off, their speed is not to be compared to that of the cows and yearlings; for these latter are seen in a few minutes to leave the bulls behind them, and as cows and young buffaloes are preferable to the old males, when the hunters are well mounted they pursue the cows and young ones invariably. Last winter buffaloes were extremely abundant close to this fort, so much so that while the people were engaged in bringing hay in carts, the buffaloes during the night came close in, and picked up every wisp that was dropped. An attempt to secure them alive was made by strewing hay in such a manner as to render the bait more and more plentiful near the old fort, which is distant about two hundred yards, and which was once the property of Mr. Sublette and Co.; but as the hogs and common cattle belonging to the fort are put up there regularly at sunset, the buffaloes ate the hay to the very gates, but would not enter the enclosure, probably on account of the different smells issuing therefrom. At this period large herds slept in front of the fort, but just before dawn would remove across the hills about one mile distant, and return toward night. An attempt was made to shoot them with a cannon—a four-pounder; three were killed and several wounded. Still the buffaloes came to their sleeping ground at evening, and many were killed during the season. I saw the head of one Mr. Culbertson shot, and the animal must have been of unusual size.

July 16, Sunday: The weather pleasant with a fine breeze from the westward, and all eyes were bent upon the hills and prairie, which is here of great breadth, to spy if possible some object that might be killed and eaten. Presently a wolf was seen, and Owen went after it, and it was not until he had disappeared below the first low range of hills, and Owen also, that the latter came within shot of the rascal, which dodged in all sorts of manners; but Owen would not give up, and after shooting more than once, he killed the beast. A man had followed him to help bring in the wolf, and when near the river he saw a buffalo, about two miles off, grazing peaceably, as he perhaps thought, safe in his own dominions; but, alas! white hunters had fixed their eyes upon him, and from that moment his doom was pronounced. Mr. Culbertson threw down his hat, bound his head with a handkerchief, his saddle was on his mare, he was mounted and off and away at a swift gallop, more quickly than I can describe, not toward the buffalo, but toward the place where Owen had killed the wolf. The man brought the wolf on old Peter, and Owen, who was returning to the camp, heard the signal gun fired by Mr. Culbertson, and at once altered his course; his mare was evidently a little heated and blown by the wolf chase, but both hunters went after the buffalo, slowly at first, to rest Owen's steed, but soon, when getting within running distance, they gave whip, overhauled the bison, and shot at it twice with balls; this halted the animal; the hunters had no more balls, and now loaded with pebbles, with which the poor beast was finally killed.

The wagon had been sent from the camp. Harris, Bell, and Squires mounted on horseback, and traveled to the scene of action. They met Mr. Culbertson returning to camp, and he told Bell the buffalo was a superb one, and had better be skinned. A man was sent to assist in the skinning who had been preparing the wolf which was now cooking, as we had expected to dine upon its flesh; but when Mr. Culbertson returned covered with blood and looking like a wild Indian, it was decided to throw it away; so I cut out the liver, and old Provost and I went fishing and caught eighteen catfish. I hooked two tortoises, but put them back in the river. I took a good swim, which refreshed me much, and I came to dinner with a fine appetite. This meal consisted wholly of fish, and we were all fairly satisfied. Before long the flesh of the buffalo reached the camp, as well as the hide. The animal was very fat, and we have meat for some days. It was now decided that Squires, Provost, and Basil (one of the men) should proceed down the river to the Charbonneau, and there try their luck at otters and beavers, and the rest of us, with the cart, would make our way back to the fort. All was arranged, and at half-past three this afternoon we were traveling toward Fort Union. But hours previous to this, and before our scanty dinner, Owen had seen another bull, and Harris and Bell joined us in the hunt. The bull was shot at by McKenzie, who stopped its career, but as friend Harris pursued it with two of the hunters and finished it I was about to return, and thought sport over for the day.

However, at this stage of the proceedings Owen discovered another bull making his way slowly over the prairie toward us. I was the only one who had balls, and would gladly have claimed the privilege of running him, but fearing I might make out badly on my slower steed, and so lose meat which we really needed, I handed my gun and balls to Owen McKenzie, and Bell and I went to an eminence to view the chase. Owen approached the bull, which continued to advance, and was now less than a quarter of a mile distant; either it did not see or did not heed him, and they came directly toward each other, until they were about seventy or eighty yards apart, when the buffalo started at a good run, and Owen's mare, which had already had two hard runs this morning, had great difficulty in preserving her distance. Owen, perceiving this, breathed her a minute, and then applying the whip was soon within shooting distance, and fired a shot which visibly checked the progress of the bull, and enabled Owen to soon be alongside of him, when the contents of the secónd barrel were discharged into the lungs, passing through the shoulder blade. This brought him to a stand. Bell and I now started at full speed, and as soon as we were within speaking distance, called to Owen not to shoot again.

The bull did not appear to be much exhausted, but he was so stiffened by the shot on the shoulder that he could not turn quickly, and taking advantage of this, we approached him; as we came near he worked himself slowly round to face us, and then made a lunge at us; we then stopped on one side and commenced discharging our pistols with little or no effect, except to increase his fury with every shot. His appearance was now one to inspire terror had we not felt satisfied of our ability to avoid him. However, even so, I came very near being overtaken by him. Through my own imprudence, I placed myself directly in front of him, and as he advanced I fired at his head, and then ran *ahead* of him, instead of veering to one side, not supposing that he was able to overtake me; but turning my head over my shoulder, I saw to my horror Mr. Bull within three feet of me, prepared to give me a taste of his horns. The next instant I turned sharply off, and the buffalo being unable to turn quickly enough to follow me, Bell took the gun from Owen and shot him directly behind the shoulder blade. He tottered for a moment, with an increased jet of blood from the mouth and nostrils, fell forward on his horns, then rolled over on his side, and was dead. He was a very old animal, in poor case, and only part of him was worth taking to the fort.

July 20, Thursday: We were up early, and had our breakfast shortly after four o'clock, and before eight had left the landing of the fort, and were fairly under way for the prairies. As we neared the Fox River someone espied four buffaloes, and Mr. C., taking the telescope, showed them to me, lying on the ground. Our heads and carts were soon turned toward them, and we traveled within half a mile of them, concealed by a ridge or hill which separated them from us. The wind was favorable, and we moved on slowly round the hill, the hunters being now mounted. Harris and Bell had their hats on, but Owen and Mr. Culbertson had their heads bound with handkerchiefs. With the rest of the party I crawled on the ridge, and saw the bulls running away, but in a direction favorable for us to see the chase. On the word of command the horses were let loose, and away went the hunters, who soon were seen to gain on the game; two bulls ran together and Mr. C. and Bell followed after them, and presently one after another of the hunters followed them. Mr. C. shot first, and his bull stopped at the fire, walked toward where I was, and halted about sixty yards from me. His nose was within a few inches of the ground; the blood poured from his mouth, nose, and side, his tail hung down, but his legs looked as firm as ever, but in less than two minutes the poor beast fell on his side, and lay quite dead.

Bell and Mr. Culbertson went after the second. Harris took the third, and Squires the fourth. Bell's shot took effect in the buttock, and Mr. Culbertson shot, placing his ball a few inches above or below Bell's; after this Mr. Culbertson ran no more. At this moment Squires's horse threw him over his head, fully ten feet; he fell on his powder horn and was severely bruised; he cried to Harris to catch his horse, and was on his legs at once, but felt sick for a few minutes. Harris, who was as cool as a cucumber, neared his bull, shot it through the lungs, and it fell dead on the spot. Bell was now seen in full pursuit of his game, and Harris joined Squires, and followed the fourth, which, however, was soon out of my sight. I saw Bell shooting two or three times, and I heard the firing of Squires and perhaps Harris, but the weather was hot, and being afraid of injuring their horses, they let the fourth bull make his escape. Bell's bull fell on his knees, got up again, and rushed on Bell, and was shot again. The animal stood a minute with his tail partially elevated, and then fell dead; through some mishap Bell had no knife with him, so did not bring the tongue, as is customary. Mr. Culbertson walked toward the first bull and I joined him. It was a fine animal about seven years old; Harris's and Bell's were younger. The first was fat, and was soon skinned and cut up for meat. Mr. Culbertson insisted on calling it my bull, so I cut off the brush of the tail and placed it in my hatband. We then walked toward Harris, who was seated on his bull, and the same ceremony took place, and while they were cutting the animal up for meat, Bell, who said he thought his bull was about three quarters of a mile distant, went off with me to see it; we walked at least a mile and a half, and at last came to it. It was a poor one, and the tongue and tail were all we took away. . .

July 21, Friday: We were up at sunrise, and had our coffee, after which Lafleur a mulatto, Harris, and Bell went off after antelopes, for we cared no more about bulls; where the cows are, we cannot tell. Cows run faster than bulls, yearlings faster than cows, and calves faster than any of these. Squires felt sore, and his side was very black, so we took our guns and went after black-breasted lark buntings, of which we saw many, but could not near them. I found a nest of them, however, with five eggs. The nest is planted in the ground, deep enough to sink the edges of it. It is formed of dried fine grasses and roots, without any lining of hair or wool.

We returned to the camp and saw a wolf cross our path, and an antelope looking at us. We determined to stop and try to bring him to us; I lay on my back and threw my legs up, kicking first one and then the other foot, and sure enough the antelope walked toward us, slowly and carefully, however. In about twenty minutes he had come two or three hundred yards; he was a superb male, and I looked at him for some minutes; when about sixty yards off I could see his eyes, and being loaded with buckshot pulled the trigger without rising from my awkward position. Off he went; Harris fired, but he only ran the faster for some hundred yards, when he turned, looked at us again, and was off. When he reached camp we found Bell there; he had shot three times at antelopes without killing; Lafleur had also returned, and had broken the foreleg of one, but an antelope can run fast enough with three legs, and he saw no more of it. We now broke camp, arranged the horses, and turned our heads toward the Missouri, and in four and three-quarter hours reached the landing. On entering the wood we again broke branches of serviceberries, and carried a great quantity over the river. I much enjoyed the trip; we had our supper, and soon to bed in our hot room, where Sprague says the thermometer has been at 99° most of the day.

Mr. Culbertson tells me that Harris and Bell have done wonders, for persons who have never shot at buffaloes from on horseback. Harris had a fall too, during his second chase, and was bruised in the manner of Squires, but not so badly. I have but little doubt that Squires killed his bull, as he says he shot it three times, and Mr. Culbertson's must have died also. What a terrible destruction of life, as it were for nothing, or next to it, as the tongues only were brought in, and the flesh of these fine animals was left to beasts and birds of prey, or to rot on the spots where they fell. The prairies are literally covered with the skulls of the victims, and the roads the buffalo make in crossing the prairies have all the appearance of heavy wagon tracks.

July 26, Wednesday: We were all on foot before daybreak and had our breakfast by an early hour, and left on our trip for buffalo cows. The wagon was sent across by hauling it through the east channel, which is now quite low, and across the sand bars, which now reach seven-eighths of the distance across the river. We crossed in the skiff, and walked to the ferryboat—I barefooted, as well as Mr. Culbertson; others wore boots or moccasins, but my feet have been tender of late, and this is the best cure.

We soon saw a bull, and all agreed to give every chance possible to Squires. Mr. C., Owen, and Squires started, and Harris followed without a gun, to see the chase. The bull was wounded twice by Squires, but no blood came from the mouth, and now all three shot at it, but the bull was not apparently hurt seriously; he became more and more furious, and began charging upon them. Unfortunately, Squires ran between the bull and a ravine quite close to the animal, and it suddenly turned on him; his horse became frightened and jumped into the ravine, the bull followed, and now Squires lost his balance; however, he threw his gun down, and fortunately clung to the mane of his horse and recovered his seat. The horse got away and saved his life, for, from what Mr. C. told me, had he fallen, the bull would have killed him in a few minutes, and no assistance could be afforded him, as Mr. C. and Owen had, at that moment, empty guns. Squires told us all; he had never been so bewildered and terrified before. The bull kept on running, and was shot at perhaps twenty times, for when he fell he had *twelve balls* in his side, and had been shot twice in the head.

Another bull was now seen close by us, and Owen killed it after four shots. Whilst we were cutting up this one, Lafleur and someone else went to the other, which was found to be very poor, and, at this season smelling very rank and disagreeable. A few of the best pieces were cut away, and, as usual, the hunters ate the liver and fat quite raw, like wolves, and we were now on the move again. Presently we saw seven animals coming toward us, and with the glass discovered there were six bulls and one cow. The hunters mounted in quick time, and away after the cow, which Owen killed very soon. To my surprise the bulls did not leave her, but stood about one hundred yards from the hunters, who were cutting her in pieces; the best parts were taken for dried meat. Had we not been so many, the bulls would, in all probability, have charged upon the butchers, but after a time they went off at a slow canter.

July 27, Thursday: After traveling for a good while, Owen, who kept ahead of us, made signs from the top of a high hill that buffaloes were in sight. This signal is made by walking the rider's horse backward and forward several times. We hurried on toward him, and when we reached the place, he pointed to the spot where he had seen them, and said they were traveling fast, being a band of both cows and bulls. The hunters were mounted at once, and on account of Squires's soreness I begged him not to run; so he drove me in the wagon as fast as possible over hills, through plains and ravines of all descriptions, at a pace beyond belief. From time to time we saw the hunters, and once or twice the buffaloes, which were going toward the fort. At last we reached an eminence from which we saw both the game and the hunters approaching the cattle, preparatory to beginning the chase.

Off went the whole group, but the country was not as advantageous to the pursuers as to the pursued. The cows separated from the bulls, the latter making their way toward us, and six of them passed within one hundred yards of where I stood; we let them pass, knowing well how savage they are at these times, and turned our eyes again to the hunters. I saw Mr. C. pursuing one cow, Owen another, and Bell a third. Owen shot one and mortally wounded it; it walked up on a hill and stood there for some minutes before falling. Owen killed a second close by the one Mr. C. had now killed, Bell's dropped dead in quite another direction, nearly one mile off. Two bulls we saw coming directly toward us, so Lafleur and I went under cover of the hill to await their approach, and they came within sixty yards of us. I gave Lafleur the choice of shooting first, as he had a rifle; he shot and missed; they turned and ran in an opposite direction, so that I, who had gone some little distance beyond Lafleur, had no chance, and I was sorry enough for my politeness. Owen had shot a third cow, which went part way up a hill, fell, and kicked violently; she, however, rose and again fell, and kept kicking with all her legs in the air. Squires now drove to her, and I walked, followed by Moncrévier, a hunter; seeing Mr. C. and Harris on the bottom below, we made signs for them to come up, and they fortunately did, and by galloping to Squires probably saved that young man from more danger; for though I cried to him at the top of my voice, the wind prevented him from hearing me; he now stopped, however, not far from a badly broken piece of ground over which had he driven at his usual speed, which I doubt not he would have attempted, some accident must have befallen him.

The cow Mr. C. had killed was much the largest, and we left a cart and two men to cut up this, and the first two Owen had killed, and went to the place where the first lay, to have it skinned for me. Bell joined us soon, bringing a tongue with him, and he immediately began operations on the cow, which proved a fine one, and I have the measurements as follows: "Buffalo Cow, killed by Mr. Alexander Culbertson, July 27, 1843. Nose to root of tail, 96 inches. Height at shoulder, 60; at rump, 55½. Length of tail vertebrae, 13; to end of hair, 25; from brisket to bottom of feet, 21½; nose to anterior canthus, 10½; between horns at root, 11⅜; between tops of ditto, 17⅛; between nostrils, 2¼; length of ditto, 2½; height of nose, 3⅛; nose to opening of ear, 20; ear from opening to tip, 5; longest hair on head, 14 inches; from angle of mouth to end of underlip, 3½."

August 4, Friday: We were all under way this morning at half-past five, on a buffalo hunt; that is to say, the residue of *us,* Harris and I, for Bell was away with Owen, and Squires with Provost after bighorns, and Sprague at Fort Mortimer. We saw, after we had traveled ten miles, some buffalo bulls; some alone, others in groups of four or five, a few antelopes, but more shy than ever before. I was surprised to see how careless the bulls were of us, as some actually gave us chances to approach them within a hundred yards, looking steadfastly, as if not caring a bit for us. At last we saw one lying down immediately in our road, and determined to give him a chance for his life. Mr. C. had a white horse, a runaway, in which he placed a good deal of confidence; he mounted it, and we looked after him. The bull did not start till Mr. C. was within a hundred yards, and then at a gentle and slow gallop. The horse galloped too, but only at the same rate. Mr. C. thrashed him until his hands were sore, for he had no whip, the bull went off without even a shot being fired, and the horse is now looked upon as forever disgraced.

About two miles farther another bull was observed lying down in our way, and it was concluded to run him with the white horse, accompanied, however, by Harris. The chase took place, and the bull was killed by Harris, but the white horse is now scorned by everyone. A few pieces of meat, the tongue, tail, and head, were all that was taken from this very large bull. We soon saw that the weather was becoming cloudy, and we were anxious to reach a camping place; but we continued to cross ranges of hills, and hoped to see a large herd of buffaloes. The weather was hot "out of mind," and we continued till, reaching a fine hill, we saw in a beautiful valley below us seventy to eighty head, feeding peacefully in groups and singly, as might happen. The bulls were mixed in with the cows, and we saw one or two calves. Many bulls were at various distances from the main group, but as we advanced toward them they galloped off and joined the others. When the chase began it was curious to see how much swifter the cows were than the bulls, and how soon they divided themselves into parties of seven or eight, exerting themselves to escape from their murderous pursuers. All in vain, however; off went the guns and down went the cows, or stood bleeding through the nose, mouth, or bullet holes. Mr. C. killed three, and Harris one in about half an hour. We had quite enough, and the slaughter was ended. We had driven up to the nearest fallen cow, and approached close to her, and found that she was not dead, but trying to rise to her feet. I cannot bear to see an animal suffer unnecessarily, so begged one of the men to take my knife and stab her to the heart, which was done.

The animals were cut up and skinned, with considerable fatigue. To skin bulls and cows and cut up their bodies is no joke, even to such as are constantly in the habit of doing it. Whilst Mr. Culbertson and the rest had gone to cut up another at some distance, I remained on guard to save the meat from the wolves, but none came before my companions returned. We found the last cow quite dead. As we were busy about her the rain fell in torrents, and I found my blanket capote of great service. It was now nearly sundown, and we made up our minds to camp close by, although there was no water for our horses, neither any wood. Harris and I began collecting buffalo dung from all around, whilst the others attended to various other affairs. The meat was all unloaded and spread on the ground, the horses made fast, the fire burned freely, pieces of liver were soon cooked and devoured, coffee drunk in abundance, and we went to rest.

August 5, Saturday: It rained in the night; but this morning the weather was cool, wind at northwest, and cloudy, but not menacing rain. The white horse, which had gone out as a *hunter,* returned as a *pack horse,* loaded with the entire flesh of a buffalo cow; and our two mules drew three more and the heads of all four. This morning at daylight, when we were called to drink our coffee, there was a buffalo feeding within twenty steps of our tent, and it moved slowly toward the hills as we busied ourselves making preparations for our departure. We reached the fort at noon.

Provost tells me that buffaloes become so very poor during hard winters, when the snows cover the ground to the depth of two or three feet, that they lose their hair, become covered with scabs, on which the magpies feed, and the poor beasts die by hundreds. One can hardly conceive how it happens, notwithstanding these many deaths and the immense numbers that are murdered almost daily on these boundless wastes called prairies, besides the hosts that are drowned in the freshets, and the hundreds of young calves who die in early spring, so many are yet to be found. Daily we see so many that we hardly notice them more than the cattle in our pastures about our homes. But this cannot last; even now there is a perceptible difference in the size of the herds, and before many years the buffalo, like the great auk, will have disappeared; surely this should not be permitted.

The Missouri River Journals

The Snowy Owl *(Nyctea scandiaca)*

As the snowy owl is very seldom obtained alive, the following notices of the one which I had for a few weeks in my possession may perhaps prove interesting to you. The bird was purchased from an Indian the day upon which I sailed, and was at first so exceedingly timid that when I approached, it used to expand its wings and make every effort to escape, uttering at the same time a sharp shrill sound, which closely resembled the note of the little sparrow hawk. After a few days, however, it greedily devoured the fresh beef which was laid beside it, and became apparently quite reconciled to confinement. The disposition of the bird appeared to be exceedingly gentle. I never observed it attempt to strike with its claws, and it never used to bite unless when provoked. Nothing seemed to afford it so much pleasure as scratching its head and breastbone, and while this was being done, it would close its eyes and remain perfectly still, as if lulled to sleep by the agreeable sensation.

The captain put up a roost for the owl along one of the lockers, and often amused himself by shaking hands, as he called it, with the bird. This was done by placing one of his fingers among the strong talons of the owl, and shaking away, often very roughly, while the bird, apparently much delighted, used to support itself upon the other leg. At first, when the captain wished to withdraw his finger, he used to give the owl a sudden touch upon the shoulder with his left hand, which made the bird jump and scream most violently. For a short time this answered the purpose, but the owl got so cunning at length, that though the proffered finger was never refused, yet the slightest motion of the left arm was sufficient to make it tighten the grip and bite most furiously.

With the sailors it was a general favorite, and when upon deck they used to cram it with every bit of fresh meat they could obtain; and in course of time it became so accustomed to get scraps from them that frequently when dozing, by merely touching its bill or breast, it would take the pieces from their hands without opening its eyes. One morning the owl was dozing upon deck, and a sailor, by way of showing his cleverness, held his hands full of salt water directly in front of the bird. Without looking what his hands contained, it dipped its head into the water, much to its own discomfort, but to the great amusement of the sailors. The owl having apparently relapsed into a doze, the sailor, elated with the result of his first attempt, ventured to try the same trick again, but received a nip in return, which made him clap his finger into his mouth and retreat amid the laughter and jeers of the rest of the crew.

The roost which the captain had put up for the owl was directly behind the locker upon which the carpenter and mate usually sat at mess. During dinner, one very stormy day, by a sudden lurch of the vessel, the owl was thrown from its perch, and the first place it alighted upon was the bald pate of the carpenter, who was seated in front. It had, however, scarcely time to open its eyes upon its strange resting place ere it was dislodged by a stroke of the carpenter's arm, and obliged to seek a more secure footing, which it readily found among the bushy locks of the mate, who but an instant before was laughing at the strange predicament of his companion. For a short time every stroke which the mate gave his unwelcome visitor was quickly repaid by a closer grip, and a smart stroke upon each ear from a pair of powerful wings; but the vessel having at length settled, the bird retreated, apparently not a little astonished by the unusual uproar.

During the daytime it seemed a good deal inclined to doze, particularly after being fed, but not more so than I have seen hawks and some other birds. Toward evening, however, it certainly showed a stronger disposition to activity, its eyes became more bright and glaring, its motions more quick, and no movement in the cabin escaped its notice. Having repeatedly extinguished the candles in the cabin by attempts to fly, we were obliged to confine the bird whenever the daylight began to fade. Two things seemed to irritate it exceedingly: the first was to touch its wings, and the second to put water on it. The first might have originated from a wound, though I could not detect any injury; but the second seemed rather singular in a bird which was accustomed to obtain at least a part of its subsistence from the water. Before I parted with this bird, it seemed a good deal attached to me, though it took no notice of other persons. When it observed me even at a considerable distance, it would lower its head, watch me very closely, and seem much pleased when I approached.

Ornithological Biography, Volume V

5. Sea and Shore

Introduction

No longer do eggers in Labrador rob the nests of the sea birds. No longer do fishermen use the flesh of the puffins for bait. Protection is now provided—on Bonaventure Island and elsewhere—for the great bird cities of the northern coast. Yearly they are visited, not by eggers, but by nature students who feel the thrill that Audubon felt at the sight of storied cliffs white with nesting gannets. This advance, this gain in bird protection, is appreciated best of all when we consider it against the grim background of past conditions that pages of the *Ornithological Biography* preserve in graphic detail.

The journey to Labrador took place in the summer of 1833. By that time, well over a hundred of the double elephant folio plates and the first volume of the biographies had appeared. The second volume of the *Ornithological Biography* went to press the following year. It contained some of the Labrador material. Accompanying Audubon on his northern voyage were five young men: his son John; Joseph Coolidge; William Ingalls and George Cheyne Shattuck, of Boston; and Thomas Lincoln, of Dennisville, Maine, for whom he named a new bird discovered on the trip, the Lincoln's sparrow. The party sailed from Eastport, Maine, on June 6, in the *Ripley,* a chartered schooner of 106 tons. For two months they cruised along the wild Labrador coast. It was the last day of August when the ship returned to Eastport.

At the opposite end of the Atlantic coast from the gannet cliffs of the north, on the keys of Florida, the zenaida dove is now so rare a visitor that bird guides list it as "accidental" or "formerly Florida keys." However, this gentle creature is still found throughout the West Indies and along the coast of Yucatan.

Audubon first saw it in the spring of 1832, the year before his Labrador journey. On April 15 of that year, he set sail from St. Augustine in the government revenue cutter *Marion.* With him were two assistants, George Lehman, a Swiss landscape painter who helped with drawings, and Henry Ward, a young English taxidermist who had come to America and who assisted in preparing bird skins. For several weeks, the party wandered among remote and uninhabited keys, collecting specimens and observing the habits of the birds.

Down the Eastern shore of the United States today, all the way from above

Boston to below Baltimore, there extends an almost continuous community. Rarely are houses out of sight along the New England coast or on the New York, New Jersey, and Maryland shores. Sea meadows have been filled in for housing developments. Salt marshes have been drained by a maze of mosquito ditches. Vast changes have affected the wildlife of the coast since this Eastern shore was visited by Audubon.

And on the keys, as well as throughout Florida, the increase in buildings and human inhabitants has altered the character of the surroundings in many areas. But even in the present times, the abundance of life in varied and beautiful and interesting forms impresses the visitor. Shy creatures still have wild places to hide in, remote swamps to inhabit. But, except in sanctuaries such as the great Everglades National Park, these areas are being invaded or reduced year by year. Never again, the chances are, will human eyes witness the vast, teeming abundance of wildlife that Audubon encountered on the Florida shores in 1832.

The Gannet (*Morus bassanus*)

On the morning of the fourteenth of June, 1833, the white sails of the *Ripley* were spread before a propitious breeze, and onward she might be seen gaily wending her way toward the shores of Labrador. We had well explored the Magdalen Islands, and were anxious to visit the Great Gannet Rock, where, according to our pilot, the birds from which it derives its name bred. For several days I had observed numerous files proceeding northward, and marked their mode of flight while thus traveling. As our bark dashed through the heaving billows, my anxiety to reach the desired spot increased. At length, about ten o'clock, we discerned at a distance a white speck, which our pilot assured us was the celebrated rock of our wishes.

After a while I could distinctly see its top from the deck, and thought that it was still covered with snow several feet deep. As we approached it, I imagined that the atmosphere around was filled with flakes, but on my turning to the pilot, who smiled at my simplicity, I was assured that nothing was in sight but the gannets and their island home. I rubbed my eyes, took up my glass, and saw that the strange dimness of the air before us was caused by the innumerable birds, whose white bodies and black-tipped pinions produced a blended tint of light gray. When we had advanced to within half a mile, this magnificent veil of floating gannets was easily seen, now shooting upward as if intent on reaching the sky, then descending as if to join the feathered masses below, and again diverging toward either side and sweeping over the surface of the ocean. The *Ripley* now partially furled her sails and lay to, when all on board were eager to scale the abrupt sides of the mountain isle, and satisfy their curiosity.

Judge, Reader, of our disappointment. The weather, which hitherto had been beautiful, suddenly changed, and we were assailed by a fearful storm. However, the whaleboat was hoisted over and manned by four sturdy "down-easters," along with Thomas Lincoln and my son. I remained on board the *Ripley,* and commenced my distant observations, which I shall relate in due time.

An hour has elapsed; the boat, which had been hid from our sight, is now in view; the waves run high, and all around looks dismal. See what exertions the rowers make; it blows a hurricane, and each successive billow seems destined to overwhelm their fragile bark. My anxiety is intense, as you may imagine; in the midst of my friends and the crew I watch every movement of the boat, now balanced on the very crest of a rolling and foaming wave, now sunk far into the deep trough. We see how eagerly yet calmly they pull. My son stands erect, steering with a long oar, and Lincoln is bailing the water which is gaining on him, for the spray ever and anon dashes over the bow. But they draw near, a rope is thrown and caught, the whaleboat is hauled close under our leeboard; in a moment more all are safe on deck, the helm round, the schooner to, and away under bare poles she scuds toward Labrador.

Thomas Lincoln and my son were much exhausted, and the sailors required a double allowance of grog. A quantity of eggs of various kinds, and several birds, had been procured, for wherever sufficient room for a gannet's nest was not afforded on the rock, one or two guillemots occupied the spot, and on the ledges below the kittiwakes lay thick like snowflakes. The discharging of their guns produced no other effect than to cause the birds killed or severely wounded to fall into the water, for the cries of the countless multitudes drowned every other noise. The party had their clothes smeared with the nauseous excrements of hundreds of gannets and other birds, which in shooting off from their nests caused numerous eggs to fall, of which some were procured entire. The confusion on and around the rock was represented as baffling all description; and as we gazed on the mass now gradually fading on our sight, we all judged it well worth the while to cross the ocean to see such a sight. But yet it was in some measure a painful sight for me, for I had not been able to land on this great breeding place, of which, however, I here present a description given by our pilot Mr. Godwin.

"The top of the main rock is a quarter of a mile wide, from north to south, but narrower in the other direction. Its elevation is estimated at about four hundred feet. It stands in Lat. 47° 52′. The surf beats its base with great violence, unless after a long calm, and it is extremely difficult to land upon it, and still more so to ascend to the top or platform. The only point on which a boat may be landed lies on the south side, and the moment the boat strikes it must be hauled dry on the rocks. The whole surface of the upper platform is closely covered with nests, placed about two feet asunder, and in such regular order that a person may see between the lines, which run north and south, as if looking along the furrows of a deeply plowed field.

"The Labrador fishermen and others who annually visit this extraordinary resort of the gannets, for the purpose of procuring their flesh to bait their cod-hooks, ascend armed with heavy short clubs, in parties of eight, ten, or more, and at once begin their work of destruction. At sight of these unwelcome intruders, the affrighted birds rise on wing with a noise like thunder, and fly off in such a hurried and confused manner as to impede each other's progress, by which thousands are forced downward, and accumulate in a bank many feet high; the men beating and killing them with their clubs until fatigued, or satisfied with the number they have slain." Here Mr. Godwin assured us that he had visited the Gannet Rock ten seasons in succession, for the purpose just mentioned, and added that on one of these occasions, "six men had destroyed five hundred and forty gannets in about an hour, after which the party rested a while, and until most of the living birds had left their immediate neighborhood, for all around them, beyond the distance of about a hundred yards, thousands of gannets were yet sitting on their nests, and the air was filled with multitudes of others. The dead birds are now roughly skinned, and the flesh of the breast cut up into pieces of different sizes, which will keep good for bait for about a fortnight or three weeks. So great is the destruction of these birds for the purpose mentioned that the quantity of their flesh so procured supplies with bait upward of forty boats, which lie fishing close to the Island of Brion each season.

"By the twentieth of May the rock is covered with birds on their nests and eggs, and about a month afterward the young are hatched. The earth is scratched by the birds for a few inches deep, and the edges surrounded by seaweeds and other rubbish, to the height of eight or ten inches, tolerably well matted together. Each female gannet lays a single egg, which is pure white, but not larger than a good-sized hen's egg. When the young are hatched, they are bluish black, and for a fortnight or more their skin is not unlike that of the common dogfish. They gradually become downy and white, and when five or six weeks old look like great lumps of carded wool.''

I was well pleased with this plain statement of our pilot, as I had with my glass observed the regularity of the lines of nests, and seen many of the birds digging the earth with their strong bills, while hundreds of them were carrying quantities of that long seaweed called eelgrass, which they seem to bring from toward the Magdalen Islands. While the *Ripley* lay near the rock, thousands of the gannets constantly flew over our heads; and although I shot at and brought several to the water, neither the reports nor the sight of their dead companions seemed to make any impression on them.

On weighing several of the gannets brought on board, I found them to average rather more than seven pounds; but Mr. Godwin assured me that when the young birds are almost ready to fly, they weigh eight and sometimes nine pounds. This I afterward ascertained to be true, and I account for the difference exhibited at this period by the young birds by the great profusion of food with which their parents supply them, regardless in a great measure of their own wants. The pilot further told me that the stench on the summit of the rock was insupportable, covered as it is during the breeding season, and after the first visits of the fishermen, with the remains of carcasses of old and young birds, broken and rotten eggs, excrements, and multitudes of fishes. He added that the gannets, although cowardly birds, at times stand and await the approach of a man, with open bill, and strike furious and dangerous blows. Let me now, Reader, assure you that unless you had seen the sight witnessed by my party and myself that day, you could not form a correct idea of the impression it has to this moment left on my mind.

The flight of the gannet is powerful, well sustained, and at times extremely elegant. While traveling, whether in fine or foul weather, they fly low over the surface of the water, flapping their wings thirty or forty times in succession, in the manner of the ibis and the brown pelican, and then sailing about an equal distance, with the wings at right angles to the body, and the neck extended forward. But to judge of the elegance of this bird while on the wing, I would advise you to gaze on it from the deck of any of our packet ships, when her commander has first communicated the joyful news that you are less than three hundred miles from the nearest shore, whether it be that of merry England or of our own beloved country. You would then see the powerful fisher, on well-spread pinions and high over the water, glide silently along, surveying each swelling wave below, and coursing with so much ease and buoyancy as to tempt you to think that had you been furnished with equal powers of flight, you might perform a journey of eighty or ninety miles without the slightest fatigue in a single hour.

But perhaps at the very moment when these thoughts have crossed your mind, as they many times have crossed mine on such occasions, they are suddenly checked by the action of the bird, which, intent on filling its empty stomach, and heedless of your fancies, plunges headlong through the air, with the speed of a meteor, and instantaneously snatches the fish which its keen sight had discovered from on high. Now perchance you may see the snow-white bird sit buoyantly for a while on the

221. SNOWY OWL *(Nyctea scandiaca)*. Down the Atlantic seaboard, as well as inland across the country, this large white owl periodically makes its appearance. It is often seen resting on low dunes facing the ocean. These southward invasions from the tundras of the far north are a consequence of a scarcity of lemmings, the rodents which form the chief food of the snowy owl. The small mammals have cycles of abundance. At low points in the cycle, the owls turn south in search of other food. They have been found as far from their northern home as Texas.

222–223. COMMON MURRE *(Uria aalge)*. The common murre is the seabird that was preyed upon by the Labrador eggers. It nests, often in immense colonies, on rocky islands and sea cliffs. In obtaining its food—fish, crustacea, sea worms--it propels itself under water by using its wings as well as its webbed feet. It has been caught in the gill nets of fishermen at depths of more than 150 feet. The eggs, pale blue or green with black or brown markings, are strongly tapered, making them less likely to roll from ledges where they are laid.

224. GREAT BLUE HERON *(Ardea herodias)*. Coastal bays, marshes and mudflats, inland lakes and streams, all are chosen by this large heron in its hunt for food. It is a wide-ranging bird, breeding from Alaska to Nova Scotia and south to the West Indies.

225. AMERICAN FLAMINGO *(Phoenicopterus ruber)*. At the time of Audubon's visit to lower Florida in 1832, the brilliant red flamingo was a rather common bird. Now it is listed as a rarely-seen straggler. On islands of the Caribbean, where the flamingo is still numerous, it nests in huge colonies. Nests are made of mud and a single egg is laid in each.

226–227. BUFFLEHEAD *(Bucephala albeola)*. The "butterball" of the waterfowl hunters, this is the smallest of the sea ducks. Its breeding season is spent inland on fresh water. A curious feature of this period is the fact that this little duck often nests in the abandoned holes of flickers, sometimes more than fifty feet above the ground.

228. BROWN PELICAN *(Pelecanus occidentalis)*. On both the east and west coast, and along the Gulf, the brown pelican is a striking salt-water bird, skillful at soaring and adept at diving for fish. From a height of twenty or thirty feet, it plunges, hitting the water with a great splash, in the midst of a dense school of fish swimming near the surface.

bosom of its beloved element, either munching its prey, or swallowing it at once. Or perhaps, if disappointed in its attempt, you will see it rise by continued flappings, shaking its tail sidewise the while, and snugly covering its broad webbed feet among the undercoverts of that useful rudder, after which it proceeds in a straight course, until its wings being well supplied by the flowing air, it gradually ascends to its former height, and commences its search anew.

In severe windy weather, I have seen the gannet propelling itself against the gale by sweeps of considerable extent, placing its body almost sideways or obliquely, and thus alternately, in the manner of petrels and guillemots; and I have thought that the bird then moved with more velocity than at any other time, except when plunging after its prey. Persons who have seen it while engaged in procuring food must, like myself, have been surprised when they have read in books that gannets "are never known to dive," and yet are assured that they "have been taken by a fish fastened to a board sunk to the depth of two fathoms, in which case the neck has either been found dislocated, or the bill firmly fixed in the wood." With such statements before him, one might think that his own vision had been defective, had he not been careful to note down at once the results of his observations. And as this is a matter of habit with me, I will offer you mine, not caring one jot for what has been said to you before on the subject.

I have seen the gannet plunge, and afterward remain under the surface of the water for at least one minute at a time. On one occasion of this kind, I shot one just as it emerged, and which held a fish firmly in its bill, and had two others halfway down its throat. This has induced me to believe that it sometimes follows its prey in the water, and seizes several fishes in succession. At other times I have observed the gannet plunge amidst a shoal of launces so as scarcely to enter the water, and afterward follow them, swimming, or as it were running on the water, with its wings extended upward, and striking to the right and left until it was satiated. While on the Gulf of Mexico, I wounded a gannet, which, on falling to the water, swam so fast before the boat, that we rowed about a quarter of a mile before we reached it, when it suddenly turned toward us, opened its bill, as if intent on defending itself, but was killed with the stroke of an oar by one of the sailors.

When shot at without even being touched, these birds often disgorge their food in the manner of vultures; and this they always do when wounded, if their stomach and gullet happen to be full. Sometimes, after being wounded in the wings, they will float and allow you to take them, without making any attempt to escape. Nay, my young friend, George C. Shattuck, M.D., of Boston, while with me at Labrador, caught one which he found walking amongst a great number of guillemots on a low and rocky island.

When they are on their favorite breeding rocks and about to fly, they elevate their head, throw it backward, open the bill, and emit a loud prolonged cry, before launching themselves into the air, in doing which they waddle a few paces with their wings partially extended. After starting, their first motion is greatly inclined downward, but they presently recover, and seem to support themselves with ease. When they are twenty or thirty yards off, you observe them shaking the tail sideways, and then hiding their feet among the undercoverts of the tail. At other times they suddenly open their feet, moving them as if for the purpose of grasping some object below, in the same manner as some hawks, but only for a few moments, then again the tail is shaken, and the feet hidden as before. They beat their wings and sail alternately, even when flying around their breeding places.

On the ground the movements of the gannet are exceedingly awkward, and it marches with hampered steps, assisting itself with the wings, or keeping them partially open, to prevent its falling. Their walk, indeed, is merely a hobble. When the sun shines, they are fond of opening their wings and beating them in the manner of cormorants, shaking the head meanwhile rather violently, and emitting their usual uncouth guttural notes of *cara, karew, karow.* You may well imagine the effect of a concert performed by all the gannets congregated for the purpose of breeding on such a rock as that in the Gulf of St. Lawrence, where, amidst the uproar produced by the repetition of these notes, you now and then distinguish the loud and continued wolfish howling-like sounds of those about to fly off.

The young never leave the spot on which they have been reared until they are able to fly, when they separate from the old birds, and do not rejoin them until at least a year after. Although I have in a few instances found individuals yet patched with dark gray spots, and with most of their primary quills still black, I am confident that it is not until the end of two years that they acquire their full plumage. I have seen some with one wing almost pure black, and the tail of that color also; others with the tail only black; and several with pure black feathers interspersed among the general white plumage.

It is a curious fact that the gannets often procure mackerels or herring four or five weeks before the fishermen fall in with them on our coast; but this is easily explained by their extensive wanderings. Although this bird is easily kept in captivity, it is far from being a pleasant pet. Its ordure is abundant, disagreeable to the eye as well as the nose; its gait is awkward; and even its pale owl-like eyes glare on you with an unpleasant expression. Add to this the expense of its food, and I can easily conceive that you will not give it a place in your aviary, unless for the mere amusement of seeing it catch the food thrown to it, which it does like a dog.

The feathers of the lower parts of the gannet differ from those of most other birds, in being extremely convex externally, which gives the bird the appearance of being covered beneath with light shellwork, exceedingly difficult to be represented in a drawing.

Ornithological Biography, Volume IV

The Eggers of Labrador

The distinctive appellation of "eggers" is given to certain persons who follow, principally or exclusively, the avocation of procuring the eggs of wild birds, with the view of disposing of them at some distant port. Their great object is to plunder every nest, wherever they can find it, no matter where, and at whatever risk. They are the pest of the feathered tribes, and their brutal propensity to destroy the poor creatures after they have robbed them is abundantly gratified whenever an opportunity presents itself.

Much had been said to me respecting these destructive pirates before I visited the coast of Labrador, but I could not entirely credit all their cruelties until I had actually witnessed their proceedings, which were such as to inspire no small degree of horror. But you shall judge for yourself.

See yon shallop, shyly sailing along; she sneaks like a thief wishing, as it were, to shun the very light of heaven. Under the lee of every rocky isle someone at the tiller steers her course. Were his trade an honest one, he would not think of hiding his back behind the terrific rocks that seem to have been placed there as a resort to the myriads of birds that annually visit this desolate region of the earth, for the purpose of rearing their young at a distance from all disturbers of their peace. How unlike the open, the bold, the honest mariner, whose face needs no mask, who scorns to skulk under any circumstances. The vessel herself is a shabby thing; her sails are patched with stolen pieces of better canvas, the owners of which have probably been stranded on some inhospitable coast, and have been plundered, perhaps murdered, by the wretches before us. Look at her again! Her sides are neither painted nor even pitched; no, they are daubed over, plastered and patched with strips of sealskins laid along the seams. Her deck has never been washed or sanded; her hold—for no cabin has she—though at present empty, sends forth an odor pestilential as that of a charnel house. The crew, eight in number, lie sleeping at the foot of their tottering mast, regardless of the repairs needed in every part of her rigging. But see! she scuds along, and as I suspect her crew to be bent on the commission of some evil deed, let us follow her to the first harbor.

There rides the filthy thing! The afternoon is half over. Her crew have thrown their boat overboard, they enter and seat themselves, each with a rusty gun. One of them sculls the skiff toward an island for a century past the breeding place of myriads of guillemots, which are now to be laid under contribution. At the approach of the vile thieves, clouds of birds rise from the rock and fill the air around, wheeling and screaming over their enemies. Yet thousands remain in an erect posture, each covering its single egg, the hope of both parents. The reports of several muskets loaded with heavy shot are now heard, while several dead and wounded birds fall heavily on the rock or into the water. Instantly all the sitting birds rise and fly off affrighted to their companions above, and hover in dismay over their assassins, who walk forward exultingly, and with their shouts mingling oaths and execrations. Look at them! See how they crush the chick within its shell, how they trample on every egg in their way with their huge and clumsy boots. Onward they go, and when they leave the isle, not an egg that they can find is left entire. The dead birds they collect and carry to their boat. Now they have regained their filthy shallop; they strip the birds, by a single jerk, of their feathery apparel while the flesh is yet warm, and throw them on some coals, where in a short time they are broiled. The rum is produced when the guillemots are fit for eating, and after stuffing themselves with this oily fare, and enjoying the pleasure of beastly intoxication, over they tumble on the deck of their crazed craft, where they pass the short hours of night in turbid slumber.

The sun now rises above the snow-clad summit of the eastern mount. "Sweet is the breath of morn," even in this desolate land. The gay bunting erects his white crest, and gives utterance to the joy he feels in the presence of his brooding mate. The willow grouse on the rock crows his challenge aloud. Each floweret chilled by the night air expands its pure petals. The gentle breeze shakes from the blades of grass the heavy dewdrops. On the guillemot isle the birds have again settled, and now renew their loves. Startled by the light of day, one of the eggers springs to his feet and rouses his companions, who stare around them for a while, endeavoring to collect their senses. Mark them, as with clumsy fingers they clear their drowsy eyes! Slowly they rise on their feet. See how the filthy lubbers stretch out their arms and yawn; you shrink back, for verily "that throat might frighten a shark."

But the master soon recollecting that so many eggs are worth a dollar or a crown, casts his eye toward the rock, marks the day in his memory, and gives orders to depart. The light breeze enables them to reach another harbor a few miles distant, one which, like the last, lies concealed from the ocean by some other rocky isle. Arrived there, they re-act the scene of yesterday, crushing every egg they can find. For a week each night is passed in drunkenness and brawls, until, having reached the last breeding place on the coast, they return, touch at every isle in succession, shoot as many birds as they need, collect the fresh eggs, and lay in a cargo. At every step each ruffian picks up an egg so beautiful that any man with a feeling heart would pause to consider the motive which could induce him to carry it off. But nothing of this sort occurs to the egger, who gathers and gathers until he has swept the rock bare. The dollars alone chink in his sordid mind, and he assiduously plies the trade which no man would ply who had the talents and industry to procure subsistence by honorable means.

With a bark nearly half filled with fresh eggs they proceed to the principal rock, that on which they first landed. But what is their surprise when they find others there helping themselves as industriously as they can! In boiling rage they charge their guns and ply their oars. Landing on the rocks, they run up to the eggers, who, like themselves, are desperadoes. The first question is a discharge of musketry, the answer another. Now, man to man, they fight like tigers. One is carried to his boat with a fractured skull, another limps with a shot in his leg, and a third feels how many of his teeth have been driven through the hole in his cheek. At last, however, the quarrel is settled; the booty is to be equally divided; and now see them all drinking together. Oaths and curses and filthy jokes are all that you hear; but see, stuffed with food and reeling with drink, down they drop one by one; groans and execrations from the wounded mingle with the snoring of the heavy sleepers. There let the brutes lie.

Again it is dawn, but no one stirs. The sun is high; one by one they open their heavy eyes, stretch their limbs, yawn, and raise themselves from the deck. But see, here comes a goodly company. A hundred honest fishermen, who for months past have fed on salt meat, have felt a desire to procure some eggs. Gallantly their boats advance, impelled by the regular pull of their long oars. Each buoyant bark displays the flag of its nation. No weapons do they bring, nor anything that can be used as such save their oars and their fists. Cleanly clad in Sunday attire, they arrive at the desired spot, and at once prepare to ascend the rock. The eggers, now numbering a dozen, all armed with guns and bludgeons, bid defiance to the fishermen. A few angry words pass between the parties. One of the eggers, still under the influence of drink, pulls his trigger, and an unfortunate sailor is seen to reel in agony. Three loud cheers fill the air. All at once rush on the malefactors; a horrid fight ensues, the result of which is that every egger is left on the rock beaten and bruised. Too frequently the fishermen man their boats, row to the shallops, and break every egg in the hold.

The eggers of Labrador not only rob the birds in this cruel manner, but also the fishermen, whenever they can find an opportunity; and the quarrels they excite are numberless. While we were on the coast, none of our party ever ventured on any of the islands which these wretches call their own, without being well provided with means of defense. On one occasion when I was present, we found two eggers at their work of destruction. I spoke to them respecting my visit, and offered them premiums for rare birds and some of their eggs; but although they made fair promises, not one of the gang ever came near the *Ripley*.

These people gather all the eider down they can find; yet so inconsiderate are they that they that they kill every bird which comes in their way. The eggs of gulls, guillemots, and ducks are searched for with care; and the puffins and some other birds they massacre in vast numbers for the sake of their feathers. So constant and persevering are their depredations that these species, which, according to the accounts of the few settlers I saw in the country, were exceedingly abundant twenty years ago, have abandoned their ancient breeding places, and removed much farther north in search of peaceful security. Scarcely, in fact, could I procure a young guillemot before the eggers left the coast, nor was it until late in July that I succeeded, after the birds had laid three or four eggs each, instead of one, and when, nature having been exhausted, and the season nearly spent, thousands of these birds left the country without having accomplished the purpose for which they had visited it. This war of extermination cannot last many years more. The eggers themselves will be the first to repent the entire disappearance of the myriads of birds that made the coast of Labrador their summer residence, and unless they follow the persecuted tribes to the northward, they must renounce their trade.

Ornithological Biography, Volume III

The Great Auk *(Pinguinus impennis)*

The only authentic account of the occurrence of this bird on our coast that I possess was obtained from Mr. Henry Havell, brother of my engraver, who, when on his passage from New York to England, hooked a great auk on the banks of Newfoundland, in extremely boisterous weather. On being hauled on board, it was left at liberty on the deck, It walked very awkwardly, often tumbling over, bit everyone within reach of its powerful bill, and refused food of all kinds. After continuing several days on board, it was restored to its proper element.

When I was in Labrador, many of the fishermen assured me that the "penguin," as they name this bird, breeds on a low, rocky island to the southeast of Newfoundland, where they destroy great number of the young for bait; but as this intelligence came to me when the season was too far advanced, I had no opportunity of ascertaining its accuracy. In Newfoundland, however, I received similar information from several individuals. An old gunner residing on Chelsea Beach, near Boston, told me that he well remembered the time when the penguins were plentiful about Nahant and some other islands in the bay.

The egg is very large, measuring five inches in length, and three in its greatest breadth. In form it resembles that of the common guillemot; the shell is thick and rather rough to the touch; its color is yellowish white, with long irregular lines and blotches of brownish black, more numerous at the larger end.

Ornithological Biography, Volume IV

The Arctic Tern *(Sterna paradisaea)*

Light as a sylph, the Arctic tern dances through the air above and around you. The Graces, one might imagine, had taught it to perform those beautiful gambols which you see it display the moment you approach the spot which it has chosen for its nest. Over many a league of ocean has it passed, regardless of the dangers and difficulties that might deter a more considerate traveler. Now over some solitary green isle, a creek, or an extensive bay it sweeps, now over the expanse of the boundless sea; at length it has reached the distant regions of the north, and amidst the floating icebergs stoops to pick up a shrimp. It betakes itself to the borders of a lonely sandbank or a low rocky island; there side by side the males and the females alight, and congratulate each other on the happy termination of their long journey.

Little care is required to form a cradle for their progeny; in a short time the variegated eggs are deposited, the little terns soon burst the shell, and in a few days hobble toward the edge of the water, as if to save their fond parents trouble; feathers now sprout on their wings, and gradually invest their whole body; the young birds at length rise on wing, and follow their friends to sea. But now the brief summer of the north is ended, dark clouds obscure the sun, a snowstorm advances from the polar lands, and before it skim the buoyant terns, rejoicing at the prospect of returning to the southern regions.

The day after our arrival at the Magdalen Islands the weather was beautiful, although a stiff breeze blew from the southwest. I landed with my party at an early hour, and we felt as if at a halfway house on our journey from Nova Scotia to Labrador. Some of us ascended the more elevated parts of those interesting islands, while others walked along the shores. A clean sand beach lay before us, and we proceeded over it, until having reached a kind of peninsula, we were brought to a stand. The piping plover ran and flew swiftly before us, emitting its soft and mellow notes, while some dozens of Arctic terns were plunging into the waters, capturing a tiny fish or shrimp at every dash.

Until that moment this tern had not been familiar to me, and as I admired its easy and graceful motions, I felt agitated with a desire to possess it. Our guns were accordingly charged with mustard-seed shot, and one after another you might have seen the gentle birds come whirling down upon the waters. But previous to this I had marked their mode of flight, their manner of procuring their prey, and their notes, that I might be able to finish the picture from life. Alas, poor things! how well do I remember the pain it gave me, to be thus obliged to pass and execute sentence upon them. At that very moment I thought of those long-past times, when individuals of my own species were similarly treated; but I excused myself with the plea of necessity, as I recharged my double gun.

As soon as a sufficient number of males and females lay dead at our feet, we retired from the water's edge, to watch the motions of the survivors, among whom confusion and dismay prevailed, as they dashed close over our heads and vociferated their maledictions. We did not, however, depart until we had tried a curious experiment for the third time. A female had been shot and lay dead on the water for a considerable while. Her mate, whom I was unwilling to destroy, alighted upon her, and attempted to caress her, as if she had been alive. The same circumstance took place three different times, on our throwing the dead bird on the water. All this happened in the month of June 1833, when none of the Artic terns had yet produced eggs, although we found them nearly ready to lay, as were the piping plovers.

Our schooner now sailed onward, and carried us to the dreary shores of Labrador. There, after some search, we met with a great flock of Arctic terns breeding on a small island slightly elevated above the sea. Myriads of these birds were there sitting on their eggs. The individuals were older than those which we had seen on the Magdalen Islands; for the more advanced in life the individuals of any species are, the more anxious are they to reproduce, the sooner do they proceed to their summer residence, and the more extensive is the range of their migration northward. On the other hand, the younger the bird is, the farther south it removes during winter, both because it thus enjoys a milder climate and requires less exertion in procuring its food; whereas the older individuals not only have a stronger constitution, but are more expert in discovering and securing their prey, so that it is not necessary for them to extend their journey so far.

Ornithological Biography, Volume III

The Puffin *(Fratercula arctica)*

On my voyage to Labrador I observed puffins every day; but although we reached that country in the early part of June, none had then begun to breed. As we ap-

proached the shores of that inhospitable land, we every now and then saw them around the vessel, now floating on the swelling wave, now disappearing under the bow, diving with the swiftness of thought, and sometimes rising on wing and flying swiftly but low over the sea. The nearer we approached the coast the more abundant did we find the puffins, and sometimes they were so numerous as actually to cover the water to the extent of half an acre or more. At first we paid little attention to them, but as soon as I became aware that they had begun to breed, I commenced an investigation, of which I now proceed to lay before you the result.

The first breeding place which I and my party visited was a small island, a few acres in extent, and pleasant to the eye on account of the thick growth of green grass with which it was covered. The shores were exceedingly rugged, the sea ran high, and it required all the good management of our captain to effect a safe landing, which, however, was at length accomplished at a propitious moment, when, borne on the summit of a great wave, we reached the first rocks, leaped out in an instant, and held our boat, while the angry waters rolled back and left it on the land. After securing the boat, we reached with a few steps the greensward, and directly before us found abundance of puffins. Some already alarmed flew past us with the speed of an arrow, others stood erect at the entrance of their burrows, while some more timid withdrew within their holes as we advanced toward them.

In the course of half an hour we obtained a good number. The poor things seemed not at all aware of the effect of guns, for they would fly straight toward us as often as in any other direction; but after a while, they became more knowing, and avoided us with more care. We procured some eggs, and as no young ones were yet to be found, we went off satisfied. The soil was so light, and so easily dug, that many of the burrows extended to a depth of five or six feet, although not more than a few inches below the surface, and some of the poor birds underwent a temporary imprisonment in consequence of the ground giving way under our weight. The whole island was perforated like a rabbit warren, and every hole had its entrance placed due south, a circumstance which allowed the birds to emerge in our sight almost all at once, presenting a spectacle highly gratifying to us all. Our visit to this island took place on the twenty-eighth of June, 1833.

On the twelfth of August, our captain, my friends, George Shattuck and William Ingalls, with four sailors, and another boat in company, went on a visit to "Perroket Island," distant about two miles from the harbor of Bras d'Or. The place is known to all the codfishers and is celebrated for the number of puffins that annually breed there. As we rowed toward it, although we found the water literally covered with thousands of these birds, the number that flew over and around the green island seemed much greater, insomuch that one might have imagined half the puffins in the world had assembled there.

This far-famed isle is of considerable extent, its shores are guarded by numberless blocks of rock, and within a few yards of it the water is several fathoms in depth. The ground rises in the form of an amphitheater to the height of about seventy feet, the greatest length being from north to south, and its southern extremity facing the Strait of Belle Isle. For every burrow in the island previously visited by us there seemed to be a hundred here, on every crag or stone stood a puffin, at the entrance of each hole another, and yet the sea was covered and the air filled by them. I had two double-barreled guns and two sailors to assist me; and I shot for one hour by my watch, always firing at a single bird on wing. How many puffins I killed in that time I take the liberty of leaving you to guess.

The burrows were all inhabited by young birds, of different ages and sizes, and clouds of puffins flew over our heads, each individual holding a "lint" by the head. This fish, which measures four or five inches in length, and is of a very slender form, with a beautiful silvery hue, existed in vast shoals in the deep water around the island. The speed with which the birds flew made the fish incline by the side of their necks. When flying the puffins emitted a loud croaking noise, but they never dropped the fish, and many of them, when brought down by a shot, still held their prey fast.

I observed with concern the extraordinary affection manifested by these birds toward each other; for whenever one fell dead or wounded on the water, its mate or a stranger immediately alighted by its side, swam round it, pushed it with its bill as if to urge it to fly or dive, and seldom would leave it until an oar was raised to knock it on the head, when at last, aware of the danger, it would plunge below in an instant. Those which fell wounded immediately ran with speed to some hole, and dived into it, on which no further effort was made to secure them. Those which happened to be caught alive in the hand bit most severely and scratched with their claws at such a rate that we were glad to let them escape. The burrows here communicated in various ways with each other, so that the whole island was perforated as if by a multitude of subterranean labyrinths, over which one could not run without the risk of falling at almost every step. The voices of the young sounded beneath our feet like voices from the grave, and the stench was extremely disagreeable, so that as soon as our boats were filled with birds we were glad to get away.

During the whole of our visit, the birds never left the place, but constantly attended to their avocations. Here one would rise from beneath our feet, there, within a few yards of us, another would alight with a fish, and dive into its burrow, or feed the young that stood waiting at the entrance. The young birds were far from being friendly toward each other, and those which we carried with us kept continually fighting so long as we kept them alive. They used their yet extremely small and slender bills with great courage and pertinacity, and their cries resembled the wailings of young whelps. The smaller individuals were fed by the parents by regurgitation, or received little pieces of fish which were placed in their mouths; the larger picked up the fish that were dropped before them; but almost all of them seemed to crawl to the entrance of the holes for the purpose of being fed. In all the burrows that communicated with others a round place was scooped out on one side of the avenue, in the form of an oven; while in those which were single, this ovenlike place was found at the end, and was larger than the corridor. All the passages were flattish above, and rounded beneath as well as on the sides. In many instances we found two birds sitting each on its egg in the same hole.

The puffin never lays more than one egg, unless the first may have been destroyed or taken away; nor does it raise more than a single young one in the season. The time of incubation is probably from twenty-five to twenty-eight days, although I have not been able to ascertain the precise period. Both birds work in digging the hole, using their bills and feet; they also sit alternately on their egg, although the female engages more industriously in this occupation, while the male labors harder at the burrow. The egg is pure white when first deposited, but soon becomes soiled by the earth, as no nest is formed for its reception. It generally measures two and a half inches by one and three-fourths, but varies in size according to the age of the bird, as well as in shape, some being considerably more rounded at the smaller end than others. When boiled, the white is of a livid blue color. The captain and myself were the only persons of our party who tried to eat some. The eggs are certainly very bad, and are never collected by "The Eggers." The flesh of the birds is very dark, tough, and so fishy as to be eatable only in cases of great want. Two Italians who had come to Labrador to purchase codfish and were short of provisions fed upon puffins daily, to the great amusement of our party.

The fishermen at times, when bait is scarce along the coast, destroy a great number of these birds, which they skin like rabbits, and then cut the flesh into slices.

The flight of the puffin is firm, generally direct, now and then pretty well sustained. It is able to rise at once from the water or the land, although at times it runs on both before taking to wing. This depends much on necessity, for if pushed it flies at once from the ground, or plunges under the surface of the water. There they swim, with the wings partially opened, at a small depth, passing along in the manner of divers; and by this means they catch their prey; but at other times they dive to the bottom, many fathoms deep, for shellfish and other objects.

During the love season, the males chase each other in the air, on the water, or beneath its surface, with so much quickness as to resemble the ricochets of a cannon ball. Having kept several for about a week, I threw them overboard in the harbor where we were at anchor, and where the water was beautifully clear. On leaving my gloved hand, they plunged through the air, entered the water, and swam off, assisting themselves by their wings to the distance of from fifty to a hundred yards. On coming up, they washed their plumage for a long time, and then dived in search of food. While on board, they ran about from the dark toward the light, keeping themselves erect, and moving with great briskness, until at times close to my feet, when they would watch my motions like hawks, and if I happened to look toward them, would instantly make for some hiding place. They fed freely and were agreeable pets, only that they emitted an unpleasant grunting noise, and ran about incessantly during the night, when each footstep could be counted. When on rocky shores or islands with large stones, I observed that the puffins often flew from one crag or stone to another, alighting with ease, and then standing erect.

Ornithological Biography, Volume III

The Florida Keys

As the *Marion* neared the islet called Indian Key, which is situated on the eastern coast of the peninsula of Florida, my heart swelled with uncontrollable delight. Our vessel once over the coral reef that everywhere stretches along the shore like a great wall reared by an army of giants, we found ourselves in safe anchoring ground, within a few furlongs of the land. The next morning saw the oars of a boat propelling us toward the shore, and in a brief time we stood on the desired beach. With what delightful feelings did we gaze on the objects around us!—the gorgeous flowers, the singular and beautiful plants, the luxuriant trees. The balmy air which we breathed filled us with animation, so pure and salubrious did it seem to be. The birds which we saw were almost all new to us; their lovely forms appeared to be arrayed in more brilliant apparel than I had ever before seen, and as they gamboled in happy playfulness among the bushes, or glided over the light green waters, we longed to form a more intimate acquaintance with them.

Students of nature spend little time in introductions, especially when they present themselves to persons who feel an interest in their pursuits. This was the case with Mr. Thruston, the deputy collector of the island, who shook us all heartily by the hand, and in a trice had a boat manned at our service. Accompanied by him, his pilot and fishermen, off we went, and after a short pull landed on a large key. Few minutes had elapsed when shot after shot might be heard, and down came whirling through the air the objects of our desire. One thrust himself into the tangled groves that covered all but the beautiful coral beach that in a continued line bordered the island, while others gazed on the glowing and diversified hues of the curious inhabitants of the deep. I saw one of my party rush into the limpid element to seize on a crab that with claws extended upward awaited his approach, as if determined not to give way. A loud voice called him back to the land, for sharks are as abundant along these shores as pebbles, and the hungry prowlers could not have got a more savory dinner.

The pilot, besides being a first-rate shot, possessed a most intimate acquaintance with the country. He had been a "conch diver," and no matter what number of fathoms measured the distance between the surface of the water and its craggy bottom, to seek for curious shells in their retreat seemed to him more pastime than toil. Not a cormorant or pelican, a flamingo, an ibis, or heron had ever in his days formed its nest without his having marked the spot; and as to the keys to which the doves are wont to resort, he was better acquainted with them than many fops are with the contents of their pockets. In a word, he positively knew every channel that led to these islands, and every cranny along their shores. For years his employment had been to hunt those singular animals called sea cows or manatees, and he had conquered hundreds of them, "merely," as he said, because the flesh and hide bring "a fair price" at Havana. He never went anywhere to land without "Long Tom," which proved indeed to be a wonderful gun, and which made smart havoc when charged with "groceries," a term by which he designated the large shot which he used. In like manner, he never paddled his light canoe without having by his side the trusty javelin, with which he unerringly transfixed such fishes as he thought fit either for market or for his own use. In attacking turtles, netting, or overturning them, I doubt if his equal ever lived on the Florida coast. No sooner was he made acquainted with my errand than he freely offered his best services, and from that moment until I left Key West he was seldom out of my hearing.

While the young gentlemen who accompanied us were engaged in procuring plants, shells, and small birds, he tapped me on the shoulder, and with a smile said to me, "Come along, I'll show you something better worth your while." To the boat we betook ourselves, with the captain and only a pair of tars, for more, he said, would not answer. The yawl for a while was urged at a great rate, but as we approached a point, the oars were taken in, and the pilot alone sculling, desired us to make ready, for in a few minutes we should have "rare sport."

As we advanced, the more slowly did we move, and the more profound silence was maintained, until suddenly coming almost in contact with a thick shrubbery of mangroves, we beheld, right before us, a multitude of pelicans. A discharge of artillery seldom produced more effect—the dead, the dying, and the wounded fell from the trees upon the water, while those unscathed flew screaming through the air in terror and dismay. "There," said he, "did I not tell you so; is it not rare sport?" The birds, one after another, were lodged under the gunwales, when the pilot desired the captain to order the lads to pull away. Within about half a mile we reached the extremity of the key. "Pull away," cried the pilot, "never mind them on the wing, for those black rascals don't mind a little firing—now, boys, lay her close under the nests." And there we were, with four hundred cormorants' nests over our heads. The birds were sitting, and when we fired, the number that dropped as if dead and plunged into the water was such that I thought by some unaccountable means or other we had killed the whole colony. You would have smiled at the loud laugh and curious gestures of the pilot.

"Gentlemen," he said, "almost a blank shot!" And so it was, for, on following the birds as one after another peeped up from the water, we found only a few unable to take to wing. "Now," said the pilot, "had you waited until *I had spoken* to the black villains, you might have killed a score or more of them." On inspection, we found that our shots had lodged in the tough, dry twigs of which the birds form their nests and that we had lost the most favorable opportunity of hitting them by not waiting until they rose.

The sailors and other individuals to whom my name and pursuits had become known, carried our birds to the pilot's house. His good wife had a room ready for me to draw in, and my assistant might have been seen busily engaged in skinning, while George Lehman was making a sketch of the lovely isle.

Time is ever precious to the student of nature. I placed several birds in their natural attitudes and began to outline them. A dance had been prepared also, and no sooner was the sun lost to our eye than males and females, including our captain and others from the vessel, were seen advancing gaily toward the house in full apparel. The birds were skinned, the sketch was on paper, and I told the young men to amuse themselves. As to myself, I could not join in the merriment, for, full of the remembrance of you, Reader, and of the patrons of my work both in America and in Europe, I went on "grinding"—not on an organ, like the Lady of Bras d'Or, but on paper, to the finishing, not merely of my outlines but of my notes respecting the objects seen this day.

It was the end of April, when the nights were short and the days therefore long. Anxious to turn every moment to account, we were on board Mr. Thruston's boat at three next morning. Pursuing our way through the deep and tortuous channels that everywhere traverse the immense, muddy, soaplike flats that stretch from the outward keys to the main, we proceeded on our voyage of discovery. Here and there we met with great beds of floating seaweeds, which showed us that turtles were abundant there, these masses being the refuse of their feeding.

Coming under a key on which multitudes of frigate pelicans had begun to form their nests, we shot a good number of them and observed their habits. The boastings of our pilot were here confirmed by the exploits which he performed with his long gun, and on several occasions he brought down a bird from a height of fully a hundred yards. The poor birds, unaware of the range of our artillery, sailed calmly along, so that it was not difficult for "Long Tom," or rather for his owner, to furnish us with as many as we required. The day was spent in this manner, and toward night we returned, laden with booty, to the hospitable home of the pilot.

The next morning was delightful. The gentle sea breeze glided over the flowery isle, the horizon was clear, and all was silent save the long breakers that rushed over the distant reefs. As we were proceeding toward some keys seldom visited by men, the sun rose from the bosom of the waters with a burst of glory that flashed on my soul the idea of that power which called into existence so magnificent an object. The moon, thin and pale, as if ashamed to show her feeble light, concealed herself in the dim west. The surface of the waters shone in its tremulous smoothness and the deep blue of the clear heavens was pure as the world that lies beyond them. The heron heavily flew toward the land, like the glutton retiring at daybreak with well-lined paunch from the house of some wealthy patron of good cheer. The night heron and the owl, fearful of day, with hurried flight sought safety in the recesses of the deepest swamps; while the gulls and terns, ever cheerful, gamboled over the water, exulting in the prospect of abundance. I also exulted in hope, my whole frame seemed to expand;

and our sturdy crew showed by their merry faces that nature had charms for them too. How much of beauty and joy is lost to them who never view the rising sun, and of whose waking existence the best half is nocturnal!

Twenty miles our men had to row before we reached "Sandy Island," and as on its level shores we all leaped, we plainly saw the southernmost cape of the Floridas. The flocks of birds that covered the shelly beaches, and those hovering overhead, so astonished us that we could for a while scarcely believe our eyes. The first volley procured a supply of food sufficient for two days' consumption. Such tales, you have already been told, are well enough at a distance from the place to which they refer; but you will doubtless be still more surprised when I tell you that our first fire among a crowd of the great godwits laid prostrate sixty-five of these birds. Rose-colored curlews stalked gracefully beneath the mangroves; purple herons rose at almost every step we took, and each cactus supported the nest of a white ibis. The air was darkened by whistling wings, while on the waters floated gallinules and other interesting birds. We formed a kind of shed with sticks and grass, the sailor cook commenced his labors, and ere long we supplied the deficiencies of our fatigued frames. The business of the day over, we secured ourselves from insects by means of mosquito nets, and were lulled to rest by the cacklings of the beautiful purple gallinules!

When we laid ourselves down in the sand to sleep, the waters almost bathed our feet; when we opened our eyes in the morning, they were at an immense distance. Our boat lay on her side, looking not unlike a whale reposing on a mudbank. The birds in myriads were probing their exposed pasture ground. There great flocks of ibises fed apart from equally large collections of godwits, and thousands of herons gracefully paced along, ever and anon thrusting their javelin bills into the body of some unfortunate fish confined in a small pool of water. Of fish crows I could not estimate the number, but from the havoc they made among the crabs, I conjecture that these animals must have been scarce by the time of next ebb. Frigate pelicans chased the jaeger, which himself had just robbed a poor gull of its prize, and all the gallinules ran with spread wings from the mudbanks to the thickets of the island, so timorous had they become when they perceived us.

Surrounded as we were by so many objects that allured us, not one could we yet attain, so dangerous would it have been to venture on the mud; and our pilot having assured us that nothing could be lost by waiting, spoke of our eating, and on this hint told us he would take us to a part of the island where "our breakfast would be abundant although uncooked." Off we went, some of the sailors carrying baskets, others large tin pans and wooden vessels, such as they use for eating their meals in. Entering a thicket of about an acre in extent, we found on every bush several nests of the ibis, each containing three large and beautiful eggs, and all hands fell to gathering. The birds gave way to us and ere long we had a heap of eggs that promised delicious food. Nor did we stand long in expectation, for, kindling a fire, we soon prepared, in one way or other, enough to satisfy the cravings of our hungry maws. Breakfast ended, the pilot, looking at the gorgeous sunrise, said, "Gentlemen, prepare yourselves for fun, the tide is acoming."

Over the enormous mud flats, a foot or two of water is quite sufficient to drive all the birds ashore, even the tallest heron or flamingo, and the tide seems to flow at once over the whole expanse. Each of us, provided with a gun, posted himself behind a bush, and no sooner had the water forced the winged creatures to approach the shore than the work of destruction commenced. When it at length ceased, the collected mass of birds of different kinds looked not unlike a small haycock. Who could not with a little industry have helped himself to a few of their skins? Why, Reader, surely no one as fond of these things as I am. Everyone assisted in this, and even the sailors themselves tried their hands at the work.

Having filled our cask from a fine well long since dug in the sand of Cape Sable, either by Seminole Indians or pirates, no matter which, we left Sandy Isle about full tide and proceeded homeward, giving a call here and there at different keys, with the view of procuring rare birds, and also their nests and eggs. We had twenty miles to go "as the birds fly," but the tortuosity of the channels rendered our course fully a third longer. The sun was descending fast when a black cloud suddenly obscured the majestic orb. Our sails swelled by a breeze that was scarcely felt by us, and the pilot, requesting us to sit on the weather gunwale, told us that we were "going to get it." One sail was hauled in and secured and the other was reefed, although the wind had not increased. A low murmuring noise was heard and across the cloud that now rolled along in tumultuous masses shot vivid flashes of lightning. Our experienced guide steered directly across a flat toward the nearest land. The sailors passed their quids from one cheek to the other, and our pilot having covered himself with his oil jacket, we followed his example. "Blow, sweet breeze," cried he at the tiller, and, "we'll reach land before the blast overtakes us, for, Gentlemen, it is a furious cloud yon."

A furious cloud indeed was the one which now, like an eagle on outstretched wings, approached so swiftly that one might have deemed it in haste to destroy us. We were not more than a cable's length from the shore when, with imperious voice, the pilot calmly said to us, "Sit quite still, Gentlemen, for I should not like to lose you overboard just now; the boat can't upset, my word for that, if you will but sit still—here we have it!"

Persons who have never witnessed a hurricane, such as not unfrequently desolates the sultry climates of the South, can scarcely form an idea of its terrific grandeur. One would think that, not content with laying waste all on land, it must needs sweep the waters of the shallows quite dry to quench its thirst. No respite for an instant does it afford to the objects within the reach of its furious current. Like the scythe of the destroying angel, it cuts everything by the roots, as it were with the careless ease of the experienced mower. Each of its revolving sweeps collects a heap that might be likened to the full sheaf which the husbandman flings by his side.

On it goes with a wildness and fury that are indescribable; and when at last its frightful blasts have ceased, nature, weeping and disconsolate, is left bereaved of her beauteous offspring. In some instances, even a full century is required before, with all her powerful energies, she can repair her loss. The planter has not only lost his mansion, his crops, and his flocks, but he has to clear his lands anew, covered and entangled as they are with the trunks and branches of trees that are everywhere strewn. The bark, overtaken by the storm, is cast on the lee shore, and if any are left to witness the fatal results, they are "wreckers" alone, who, with inward delight, gaze upon the melancholy spectacle.

Our light bark shivered like a leaf the instant the blast reached her sides. We thought she had gone over; but the next instant she was on the shore. And now in contemplation of the sublime and awful storm, I gazed around me. The waters drifted like snow; the tough mangroves hid their tops amid their roots, and the loud roaring of the waves driven among them blended with the howl of the tempest. It was not rain that fell; the masses of water flew in a horizontal direction, and where a part of my body was exposed, I felt as if a smart blow had been given me on it. But enough—in half an hour it was over. The pure blue sky once more embellished the heavens,

and although it was not quite night, we considered our situation to be a good one.
The crew and some of the party spent the night in the boat. The pilot, myself, and one of my assistants took to the heart of the mangroves, and having found high land, we made a fire as well as we could, spread a tarpaulin, and fixing our insect bars over us, soon forgot in sleep the horrors that had surrounded us.

Ornithological Biography, Volume II

The Zenaida Dove (*Zenaida aurita*)

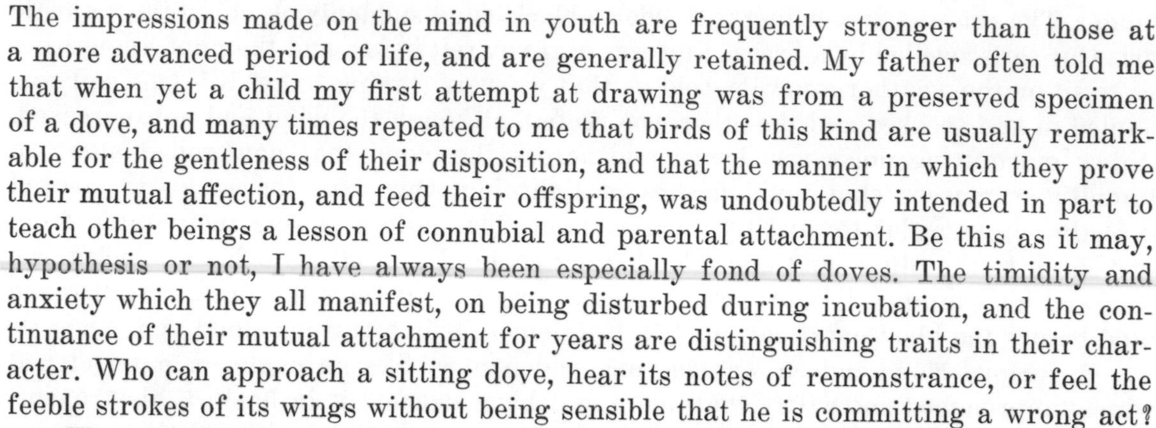

The impressions made on the mind in youth are frequently stronger than those at a more advanced period of life, and are generally retained. My father often told me that when yet a child my first attempt at drawing was from a preserved specimen of a dove, and many times repeated to me that birds of this kind are usually remarkable for the gentleness of their disposition, and that the manner in which they prove their mutual affection, and feed their offspring, was undoubtedly intended in part to teach other beings a lesson of connubial and parental attachment. Be this as it may, hypothesis or not, I have always been especially fond of doves. The timidity and anxiety which they all manifest, on being disturbed during incubation, and the continuance of their mutual attachment for years are distinguishing traits in their character. Who can approach a sitting dove, hear its notes of remonstrance, or feel the feeble strokes of its wings without being sensible that he is committing a wrong act?

The cooing of the zenaida dove is so peculiar that one who hears it for the first time naturally stops to ask, "What bird is that?" A man who was once a pirate assured me several times while at certain wells dug in the burning shelly sands of a well-known key, which must here be nameless, the soft and melancholy cry of the doves awoke in his breast feelings which had long slumbered, melted his heart to repentance, and caused him to linger at the spot in a state of mind which he only who compares the wretchedness of guilt within him with the happiness of former innocence can truly feel. He said he never left the place without increased fears of futurity, associated as he was, although I believe by force, with a band of the most desperate villains that ever annoyed the navigation of the Florida coasts.

So deeply moved was he by the notes of any bird, and especially by those of a dove, the only soothing sounds he ever heard during his life of horrors, that through these plaintive notes, and them alone, he was induced to escape from his vessel, abandon his turbulent companions, and return to a family deploring his absence. After paying a parting visit to those wells, and listening once more to the cooings of the zenaida dove, he poured out his soul in supplications for mercy, and once more became what one has said to be "the noblest work of God," an honest man. His escape was effected amidst difficulties and dangers, but no danger seemed to him to be compared with the danger of one living in the violation of human and divine laws, and now he lives in peace in the midst of his friends.

The zenaida dove is a transient visitor of the keys of East Florida. Some of the fishermen think that it may be met with there at all seasons, but my observations induce me to assert the contrary. It appears in the islands near Indian Key about the fifteenth of April, continues to increase in numbers until the month of October, and then returns to the West India Islands, whence it originally came. They begin to lay their eggs about the first of May. The males reach the keys on which they breed before the females, and are heard cooing as they ramble about in search of mates, more than a week before the latter make their appearance. In autumn, however, when they take their departure, males, females, and young set out in small parties together.

The flight of this bird resembles that of the little ground dove more than any other. It very seldom flies higher than the tops of the mangroves, or to any considerable distance at a time, after it has made choice of an island to breed on. Indeed, this species may be called a ground dove too; for, although it alights on trees with ease, and walks well on branches, it spends the greater portion of its time on the ground, walking and running in search of food with lightness and celerity, carrying its tail higher than even the ground dove, and invariably roosting there. The motions of its wings, although firm, produce none of the whistling sound, so distinctly heard in the flight of the Carolina dove; nor does the male sail over the female while she is sitting on her eggs, as is the habit of that species.

When crossing the sea, or going from one key to another, they fly near the surface of the water; and, when unexpectedly startled from the ground, they remove to a short distance, and alight amongst the thickest grasses or in the heart of the low bushes. So gentle are they in general that I have approached some so near that I could have touched them with my gun, while they stood intently gazing on me, as if I were an object not at all to be dreaded.

Those keys which have their interior covered with grass and low shrubs, and are girt by a hedge of mangroves, or other trees of inferior height, are selected by them for breeding; and as there are but few of this description, their places of resort are well known, and are called "Pigeon" or "Dove Keys." It would be useless to search for them elsewhere. They are by no means so abundant as the white-headed pigeons, which place their nests on any kind of tree, even on those whose roots are constantly submersed. Groups of such trees occur of considerable extent, and are called "Wet Keys."

The zenaida dove always places her nest on the ground, sometimes artlessly at the foot of a low bush, and so exposed that it is easily discovered by anyone searching for it. Sometimes, however, it uses great discrimination, placing it between two or more tufts of grass, the tops of which it manages to bend over, so as completely to conceal it. The sand is slightly scooped out, and the nest is composed of slender dried blades of grass, matted in a circular form, and imbedded amid dry leaves and twigs. The fabric is more compact than the nest of any other pigeon with which I am acquainted, it being sufficiently solid to enable a person to carry the eggs or young in it with security. The eggs are two, pure white and translucent. When sitting on them, or when her young are still small, this bird rarely removes from them, unless an attempt be made to catch her, which she however evades with great dexterity.

On several occasions of this kind, I have thought that the next moment would render me the possessor of one of these doves alive. Her beautiful eye was steadily bent on mine, in which she must have discovered my intention, her body was gently made to retire sidewise to the farther edge of her nest, as my hand drew nearer to her, and just as I thought I had hold of her, off she glided with the quickness of thought, taking to wing at once. She would then alight within a few yards of me, and watch my motions with so much sorrow that her wings drooped, and her whole frame trembled as if suffering from intense cold. Who could stand such a scene of despair? I left the mother to her eggs or offspring.

Ornithological Biography, Volume II

245. RICHARDSON'S GROUND SQUIRREL *(Citellus richardsonii)*. These "picket pins" of the western prairies usually keep to one small area, often within a radius of fifty feet of their burrows. Their call is a shrill, birdlike whistling note. The litters of these ground squirrels may vary from two to eleven.

246–247. MOURNING DOVE *(Zenaidura macroura)*. The low, repeated, mournful sound of this dove's cooing gives the bird its name. It is one of the characteristic sounds of the country. The mourning dove is found in all forty-nine continental states of the Union. Its nest, a makeshift platform of twigs, is one of the flimsiest of bird nests. All but a few northern doves fly south when winter comes. Some stay in southern states, others fly on to Mexico and Central America.

248–249. BLACK-BILLED CUCKOO *(Coccyzus erythropthalmus)*. Among American songbirds, the cuckoos are noted for their destruction of caterpillars. They consume vast numbers and flock to areas of special infestation. They even dine on hairy species such as the larvae of the gypsy moth. The range of the black-billed cuckoo extends from Manitoba south to Arkansas and the mountains of Georgia. Winters are spent in South America.

250. ROSEATE TERN *(Sterna dougallii)*. Audubon first saw this bird, one of the most beautiful and graceful of the world's terns, during his visit to the Florida keys. After his death, in the latter part of the nineteenth century, the species was almost exterminated along the Atlantic coast by the plume hunters of the millinery trade. Today, slowly recovering, it nests in widely separated localities that are scattered from Nova Scotia to Texas.

251. WHITE PELICAN *(Pelecanus erythrorhynchos)*. While the brown pelican is never found far from salt water, the larger white pelican, with a wingspread that often exceeds eight feet, nests as far inland as Manitoba and Mackenzie in Canada. Where the brown pelican dives for fish, the white resorts to a unique stratagem to obtain its food. A number of the birds move toward the shore, beating the water with their wings and driving a school of fish into the shallows where the birds easily fill their pouches.

Wildlife since Audubon

In the century and more since the death of John James Audubon, much, as we have seen, has happened to his woods and streams, his prairies and swamps and coasts. Even in the 1830s, as he looked back on the transformation of the wilderness along the Ohio, he reflected: "When I remember that these extraordinary changes have all taken place in the short period of twenty years, I pause, wonder, and, although I know all to be fact, can scarcely believe its reality." In the century since, "the ever whirling wheele of Change," as the poet Spenser termed it, has continually speeded up.

In many ways for Audubon's wildlife, the intervening years have formed a century of retreat. Age-old habitats have been wiped out, the pure water of ancient streams has been polluted, poisons from the laboratory have been broadcast over the land, whole species down to the last survivor have disappeared without hope of return. Others—the whooping crane, the California condor, the Everglade kite, the grizzly bear, the kit fox, the trumpeter swan—all, in critically reduced numbers, are fighting a similar fate. This is the dark side. Much has been lost but something has been gained during the century after Audubon.

Today laws unknown a hundred years ago protect many forms of wildlife. The hunting of endangered species has been halted. Songbirds, during their long migrations, enjoy the protection of international treaties. No longer are robins and meadow larks and tree swallows piled up for sale in the windows of American butcher shops. In virtually all parts of the nation sanctuaries have been established in which wild creatures can live their natural lives, protected and undisturbed. Hawks and owls and other predators, ruthlessly wiped out in former times, have been increasingly recognized as a valid and valuable part of nature's balance, deserving and receiving protection. Public awareness of the need for preserving wildlife and conserving what is left from an era of slaughter and destruction is continually growing.

Never before have so many Americans been interested in the study of birds, in the welfare of wildlife, in the efforts of conservation organizations. Millions now enjoy the pleasure of watching winter birds close at hand at window trays and backyard feeding stations. Hundreds of thousands, winter and summer, are going afield with binoculars and field guides to observe more intimately the lives of their wild neighbors. Each summer millions of visitors flock to the national parks of the West. And never before have so many volumes on nature been published and purchased in America. The old preponderance of sportsmen's accounts and hunting books, in which the only happy ending seemed monotonously to be the destruction of something living, no longer prevails. A higher, more intelligent interest in nature is taking its place.

The feeding tray by the kitchen window and the summer vacation in the national park enable a host of Americans, even in cities, to retain links with nature. What has been lost or destroyed is seen in a new perspective a century after Audubon. In pioneer times the wilderness was everywhere. It was close at hand. It was a surplus. Today, with cities spreading, mechanization growing, nature receding, wild areas and the wildlife they shelter have become more remote. As they have retreated, appreciation of them has increased, a determination to save some of them before it is too late has strengthened. This is the gain in the years since the death of Audubon.

When Zebulon Pike, the army explorer for whom Pike's Peak is named, first approached the Rockies in 1806, he encountered such vast herds of animals on the high plains that he declared that they alone could supply enough food to sustain every red man in America for a hundred years. This represented a viewpoint of his day. Wildlife was regarded predominantly as a source of food. Today our viewpoint has shifted. We realize that basic needs, other than the satisfaction of physical hunger alone, are met by an association with nature. It was Henry Thoreau's belief—a belief shared by more and more who live in a later generation—that: "In wildness is the preservation of the world"; that: "We need the tonic of wilderness—to wade sometimes in marshes where the bittern and the meadow-hen lurk, and hear the booming of the snipe; to smell the whispering sedge where only some wilder and more solitary fowl builds her nest, and the mink crawls with its belly close to the ground."

Marshes to wade in have become fewer. But something of their original freshness in days when they were virtually untouched has been caught by Audubon's work. All the wildness of another time has been arrested for the eyes of future generations to see and appreciate, amid surroundings increasingly diverse. The genius of the American Woodsman has increased the world's perception of our heritage of wildlife. And the more we appreciate this heritage, the greater will be our concern for its welfare, the greater will be our chances of preserving what remains for others coming later to enjoy, as we enjoy glimpses into the richness of a wilder past made possible by the brush and pen of Audubon.

Index to Illustrations